BRUNETTI'S VENICE

Toni Sepeda

BRUNETTI'S VENICE

Walks with the City's
Best-Loved Detective

With an Introduction by Donna Leon

Grove Press
New York

Contents

Introduction by Donna Leon

I first became aware of how little, and how badly, I knew Venice about thirty years ago, when I was invited to dinner at the home of friends of friends. I'd been there for dinner a number of times, but I'd always gone in the company of my friends Roberta and Franco, trailing along as the foreign guest. They, Venetian for generations, led the way, and I walked along with them, listening, learning Italian and a bit of Veneziano as we walked. I heard the names of their friends, picked up vocabulary, greeted the relatives and colleagues we passed on the street, stopped to have a coffee, was advised which shops to use and which to avoid.

Every trip with them had been a discovery as well as a bombardment of information. Because they led the way, I didn't have to be bothered with boring details like where to turn left or where to turn right: I merely followed the leader. They were the sharks, I the pilot fish following in their wake.

This time, however, and for reasons I no longer recall, I had to get there on my own. And couldn't. The host lived, I knew, over near San Giacomo dell'Orio, down on the right of that little *calle* that ran into the canal, almost at the end. Further, I knew that Franco's father, during World War II, had once fallen into the *laguna* when he went fishing with a man who lived on the second floor of the house opposite the apartment I was looking for.

Unfortunately for my purposes, the dinner began at 8:30, so it was dark when I walked through Rialto, on the way to what I was sure was the *campo*. Map? Me? I wasn't a tourist, was I, so why would I bother with a map? I was the friend of Venetians, on the way to dinner at the home of other Venetians, so why a map?

A half-hour later, I stumbled upon Campo San Giacomo dell'Orio and began to look for the little *calle* that ran down towards the canal, the one where lived the man who . . . etc.

etc. etc. They all looked alike. Even if I had had a map, I had no idea of the name of the *calle*, and I doubt that any map I might have carried would have marked the address of the man who was with Franco's father when he fell into the *laguna*.

Finally I went back to the *campo* and asked in a bar where Giuliano the jeweller lived. When I finally arrived, I lied – of course – about the delay and we got on with the serious business of drinking and eating.

Because I did not grow up in Venice, I lacked the imprinting of *calli, campielli e canali* that is part of the Venetian heritage. It comes of walking there and walking back home and walking to the other place, and walking back home; hundreds of times, every day for decades. That's how the city goes into the memory. Along with that comes the more personal and colourful part: the stories of people falling into the *laguna*, the story about the house where the butcher's wife went to live when she ran off with the shoemaker; the shop that used to sell the best stracchino in the city before it became a real estate office.

There is the majestic history of the city: the Doges and the Battle of Lepanto and Daniele Manin and Paolo Sarpi, a victim of the Inquisition. There is the memory of the Serenissima and its trading empire; there are the painters and the architects and the endless line of composers.

But there is also a different, more personal, history, and my experience of the city is that many people use this as the basis for their geography. Take, for example, Il Ponte dei Giocattoli, the bridge of the toys. It stands at the end of the street that leads from Rialto, past Coin, to Campo Santi Apostoli, and that is the name it has had for at least fifty years: Ponte dei Giocattoli. But the toy store, at the bottom of the bridge that still bears its name, is an ex-toy store now and sells shoes. Venetians, however, still call it Il Ponte dei Giocattoli, and probably will for many decades. As they still call it Calle dei Fabbri, though there are no more *fabbri*, and Calle del Cafetier might not any longer be a place where coffee beans are roasted.

How dull, a street with a number for a name.

As I imagine him, Brunetti is a man whose sense of the city was fashioned in this way. He grew up here, speaking Veneziano at home, listening to his parents and relatives and their friends tell stories about the way the city was when they were younger. He went to school here, walking home for lunch and returning to class until he finished university; walking across the city to visit or study with his friends and walking to meet his first girlfriends to walk again to a cinema or a party or to a boat that would take them to Lido or to one of the islands.

This instinctive sense of the city is acquired only by those who grew up here or who have lived here for decades and, by force of repetition, have had the city program itself into their feet. Those who come to Venice as visitors must hope to find a Venetian friend who will guide them through the narrow streets, explaining a bit of history here, a story from his youth there, perhaps grumbling about the tourists, occasionally pausing for *un' ombra*.

Brunetti's Venice does those things, for it allows the reader to move through the city in the company of a Venetian who has, over the course of years, become a friend. Because he is Venetian, Brunetti does not have to give conscious thought to taking the correct left turn or finding the proper *calle*. His memory is filled with the legends and lies that have accumulated around places and events for the last thousand years, and it is those things which often fill his mind as he walks through the city, not the need to check the map to see that the second turn on the left is the one to take. Much as he might be distracted, he never gets lost.

The book accompanies Brunetti through the various *sestieri* and records his emotional, as well as his visual, response to the places he has known all his life. Loyal to San Polo, where he now lives, he still cannot remove Castello from his heart, for it was there he spent much of his youth. Whenever he has to go to San Marco, his awareness of the presence of so much well-hidden wealth causes him a vague uneasiness, no matter how much he might try to dismiss it, though this uneasiness never succeeds in dulling his powerful response to the lavish beauty on offer. Giudecca is Patagonia: after all, his parents and their friends called it '*l'isola delle foche*', and he's been there often enough in the winter to have felt the wind's assault and the slow penetration of cold and damp. But Brunetti is a man who is always warmed and comforted by beauty, and so his spirit can still be lifted by a glance across the canal. Solid, bourgeois Cannaregio comforts him with its busy propriety and the sound of Veneziano in the shops and bars. Dorsoduro, now virtually stripped of food stores, has only one restaurant that interests him; sometimes, though, on a Sunday afternoon, the memory of the views available from the Zattere proves too strong for him, and he'll promise Paola a drink and the kids an ice-cream to lure them into coming along for a walk. Santa Croce, just beyond the door of his home, is the neighbourhood in which he feels most comfortable, though its proximity to Piazzale Roma, and thus to automobiles and buses, sometimes makes him uneasy.

During the lifetime of Brunetti's parents, it was not uncommon for people to pass their entire lives in their own *sestieri*, sometimes without ever leaving the city, and this choice was hardly worthy of comment. I've spoken to people whose grandparents saw no reason ever to leave Venice: everything they wanted was here: work, family, friends. Though this must sound strange in the age of grand tourism, I can only assert that many of the old people who live in the villages near my mountain house, an hour and a half from Venice by train, have never been to the city. They too have everything they want where they are: family, work, friends. My next door neighbour there – may she rest in peace – went to Torino to visit relatives once, sixty years ago, and was sick for a week while there. Other than that, she was never farther from home than Belluno, fifteen kilometres away, and certainly had no desire to go to see Venice. 'What for?' she asked, and I confess I had no answer to give her.

Brunetti grew up among people like this: one can hardly imagine his mother getting on the train to go and have a look at the Arena of Verona or the Cappella degli Scrovegni in Padova. 'What for?' one can almost hear her asking. I cannot count the number of Venetian friends who still speak of the Giudecca as though it were a suburb of Buenos Aires.

Brunetti has to traverse the city daily and is often confronted with the decision of how best to do it: walk or take a vaporetto. His choice, as with all of us, is generally based on time: calculate where you have to go and how much time you have to get there, and then decide. As often as not, it is faster to walk. Unless the city is crowded and the walk will pass through a part of the city with heavy tourist traffic. Unless there is *acqua alta* and the street will be impassable. Unless it is raining and everyone will have umbrellas.

Sometimes, therefore, the vaporetto is faster. Unless the boat isn't running because of *acqua alta* and it can't get under the bridges. Unless there is low water and the boat can't pass through the canal. Unless there's a strike.

These calculations are automatic and are often made without conscious thought, just as we adjust our walking pace always to take the first step up a bridge with the left or the right foot, not in the least conscious of the calculation that leads to that choice.

Brunetti has walked everywhere in the city, and he's done it so often that he doesn't really pay much attention to what his feet decide to do. They take him where he has to go and get him home. They take over for him and leave him free to think about his job or his family, work towards the solution of some problem or puzzle, or think about dinner.

Occasionally he gets to travel by police boat, and it must be remarked that the experience, even after all these years, can still thrill him and make his heart pound with delight. Like most Venetians, he finds the automobile an alien thing. He can drive, yes, though he is the one man on the planet who admits he does it badly. Traffic always confuses him and the ugliness of most highways appals him. It's always with relief that he gets back to Piazzale Roma and safely on to a boat.

San Polo, near which *campo* he lives, is the second largest in the city. His apartment, added to the top of a building some time in the fifties, is *abusivo* and serves as a perfect symbol of what could be, and was, done in and to the city until some order in the building code was introduced. Like

Brunetti's, the real apartment is not visible from the pavement below the house. Perhaps the people doing the building believed that, if no one could see it, then the apartment would, in a sense, not be there. But it is, and I've spent many hours inside or out on the terrace, from which can be seen those things Brunetti sees, ponders, and enjoys.

A careful look at façades and rooflines shows how much illegal restoration and addition was done over the years, before the city administration decided that a private citizen did not have the right, and could not be trusted, to remove a window or add a few extra floors to his house. Friends of mine once discovered, when they were putting an elevator into their sixteenth-century *palazzo*, that someone had removed – some time during the last four hundred years – an entire weight-bearing wall.

It was not uncommon, as well, for people to steal rooms, simply to open a door and take over a room in the apartment next door, should it happen to have remained uninhabited for a long time. An even closer look at some of the buildings will show a window where there makes no sense for one to be or windows bricked up and plastered over when someone decided they would prefer a solid wall. Over the course of a millennium, things happen and people forget.

Much of Brunetti's work takes him to Castello, the *sestiere* which remains the least discovered and fashionable. The Ospedale is there, as is the Questura where he and his colleagues work. The real Questura, the one where those other police work, is at Piazzale Roma, but the building is not attractive, and it's on a road with – horrors – cars, and so Brunetti remains faithful to the Platonic ideal of the Questura, in the same place it was when he began his career. From his office, he still can look out at the Casa di Cura of San Lorenzo, long since restored, and at the Chiesa di San Lorenzo, as untouched by restoration as it was when he began his investigation into the death of a famous conductor, almost twenty years ago.

The bar is still down there at the bottom of the bridge, and if he crosses the bridge, he travels even deeper into Castello and farther away from the hordes of tourists whose ever-increasing numbers wear away at his patience. If he turns right at the bar, he will quickly end up on the *riva*, with glory off to his right.

I forget the exact year when it became a status symbol to have a second home in Venice. 1652? It certainly complicates life to have an apartment in Venice – ask a Venetian. While you're at it, ask him what it's like to try to restore an apartment: it's always such a revelation to see a grown man burst into tears. These difficulties, however, seem to have no effect upon the growing desire to have a second home in Venice, one of the great curses of the city, for it leads non-Venetians to buy up apartments they will use a few times a year, leaving native Venetians to struggle on as best they can to find a place to rent or can afford to buy, just as it leaves merchants who sell anything other than tourist tat with an ever-declining client base.

Brunetti sees this, watches as various *sestieri* become fashionable among prospective buyers and are then replaced by another. He sees the toy store go out of business, regrets the closing of Domus, where pots and pans and coffee-makers had been on sale since he was a boy, and dreads the day when a shop like Mascari will close, and then where will they buy figs and *mostarda*?

Brunetti, a thoughtful man, a man whose reading of history has given him a longer perspective on events, does not lament the tourist invasion because of the people who block his passage through the streets or who squeeze themselves into narrow spots, hoping to be able, from there, to take the photograph of the city that no one has ever taken before. He minds it in a historical sense, because of the damage it does to the fabric of the city he loves. Tourism has driven out of business the shop where Paola could once buy buttons, just as it has made it necessary for him now to cross the city to get new heels put on his shoes. His is no unconsidered, mindless opposition to foreigners or to progress and change so much as it is a considered lament for a city which once existed – as real cities do – to serve the convenience and needs of permanent residents, not to cater to the desires of an entirely transient, artificial population.

Brunetti, however, does feel affection and affinity for the non-arriving tourist, and, like them, has travelled to places he's never been: to Byzantium and Esfahan, to the Pompei Pliny saw being destroyed and – because of Paola – to the London of Dickens. Because Brunetti is a reader, he knows what it is to seep into a different personality and to feel entirely at home in places which ceased to exist centuries before he was born; he can find his way about in cities he has never seen. He views these tourists as spiritual neighbours.

But, like most historians, Brunetti has a long view: he knows that fashions, and economies, change; thus he knows there exists the possibility, however slim, that the city will come back into the hands of people like him, who learned its language by listening to their parents speak it and learned its geography by following along with them as they went about the business of their lives.

Brunetti's Venice follows him, his thoughts and reflections, as he moves instinctively through the maze of *calli* and *rughe*, along the many *rive*. It pauses with him to reflect and observe, and it attempts to show the reader why his attachment to this wondrous city – regardless of the disappointments and grumbling it provokes in him – is as passionate and total as is his love for his family.

Practical Guideline

Venice is a complicated place, physically and spiritually, and it is extraordinarily difficult to establish Venetian facts. Nothing is ever quite certain.

Jan Morris, *Venice* [ch. 4 p. 51]

In the long line of foreign writers on Venice, Morris best describes the quite simple dilemma faced by anyone attempting to understand, much less navigate, this endlessly fascinating city – nothing is as it seems. Guidebooks abound, memoirs proliferate, fictional accounts line the shelves – and nearly all written by earnest, helpful foreigners. La Serenissima's unique geography is detailed, her history recorded, her peculiarities attended to; still she remains an enigma to her legions of visitors. Caught in *acqua alta*, bewildered by the sinuous *calli*, stumped by a dialect that makes spellings differ, defeated in attempts to make the maps fit the reality – the visitor tends to feel unsettled by Venice's peculiar geography and dreams of a likeable, reliable native guide.

Fortunately, Donna Leon has created Commissario Guido Brunetti, the perfect companion for any walk through his Venice. The series of mystery novels, beginning in 1992 with *Death at La Fenice*, reveals a world, fictional in its plots and characters, engagingly accurate in its portrayal of his native city. Even the few invented businesses and palaces exist in actual locations, each recognizable from Leon's description of precise physical details, all enhanced when seen through Brunetti's sensitive vision.

Designed both for Donna Leon readers at home and for actual walkers in Venice, this guide offers a comprehensive exploration of the city Brunetti adores and laments. Whether he is investigating a poisoning at the opera, sex tourism, clerical corruption, familial homicide, the waste of youthful death, the closed world of the lagoon, or the exalted world of his aristocratic in-laws, his job makes him traverse the city, alert to its many faces. His acute eye for both beauty and change, his fascination with the past, ear for language and the talk of the streets, passion for food and drink, musings on morality and corruption . . . all combine to make any journey across Venice in his company far more than a mere stroll.

Through a series of twelve walks, encompassing all six regions of Venice (the *sestieri*), and using the first sixteen of the novels, *Brunetti's Venice* examines the people, the themes, the weather, the settings, the churches, the markets, the food and wine, to explore the Commissario's native city. The final chapter, not an actual walk, offers an overview of the lagoon world and its islands, focusing on the settings for *Sea of Troubles* and *Through a Glass, Darkly*.

Unlike most walking guides of Venice, this book is not organized solely by *sestieri* since Brunetti spends far more time in some regions than others. Instead, the aim is to trace certain themes that embody Brunetti's engagement with specific areas: Home and Neighbourhood; the Questura, etc. Designed to last from one to two hours and ordered in sequential form, the routes allow the user to stop or continue with ease after any chosen walk: for example, Walk 1 begins with *Death at La Fenice* in front of the opera house to introduce Brunetti's first late night stroll across the city, and ends at the foot of the Rialto Bridge. Walk 2 begins with his climb over the white marble arch of the Rialto, includes a journey through the markets and ends with his first arrival at the family apartment and the appearance of Paola. The only exception to this convenient pattern occurs at the end of Walk 8 near Piazza San Marco. The text offers a choice of continuing east into Castello for Walks 9 and 10, or moving west into Cannaregio for Walks 11 and 12.

Each walk traces passages through an average of nine different novels to offer a complete picture of Brunetti's vision of that particular part of the city. To appeal to the book's dual audience – both those in and those away from Venice – a map of the route with numbered stops begins each chapter; all specific walking directions for users in the city are confined to side-bars and numbered at the appropriate locations. To further aid the traveller, Venetian spellings have been used in the side-bars whenever appropriate. The reader at home need not be distracted by the directions in side boxes: only the main stops (marked with bold numbers) are included in the actual text, making it obvious where Brunetti is on the map. Sites of interest are marked with letters, also in bold type.

Since this is not a conventional guidebook to Venice, the focus remains on Brunetti's city presented in the novels. While there are no specific recommendations for hotels, bars, or restaurants, the places Brunetti frequents are indicated with an * in the text; details of these are contained in a box at the end of each walk.

This is Venice, however, so nothing is ever as clear as it sounds. The maps and the street signs might have slightly different spellings: 'Calle alla Madonna' in Italian on the map looks familiar, 'al la Madona' in Venetian on the street sign less so, making the map a safer guide. Numbers and addresses are, for the most part, pointless, as are north–south attempts at orientation. Landmarks are few and hard to see in the narrow streets. Canals and bridges meander. But these small incongruities never seriously confuse, and often add to the unique charm of the city. In native Brunetti's company all becomes understandable and enjoyable – even the chance of getting lost in what he calls 'the world's most beautiful city'.

Numbers **(1)**, **(2)**, etc indicate major stops. Other directions for walkers appear in the boxes: these do not have numbers.

Letters **(A)**, **(B)**, etc. mark additional sites at various stops.

* An asterisk indicates that additional details are given at the end of each walk.

→ indicates time to move for walkers.

References to Donna Leon's books are to the UK editions. In the United States, two of the books are published with different titles. *The Anonymous Venetian* in Britain is *Dressed for Death* in the US; and *A Venetian Reckoning* is *Death and Judgment*.

WALK 1 : *Meeting Brunetti*

San Fantin—Sant'Angelo—Manin—San Luca—
San Bartolomeo

1.5 hours

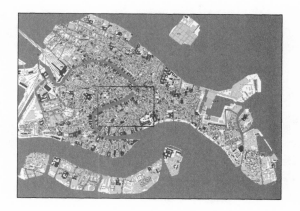

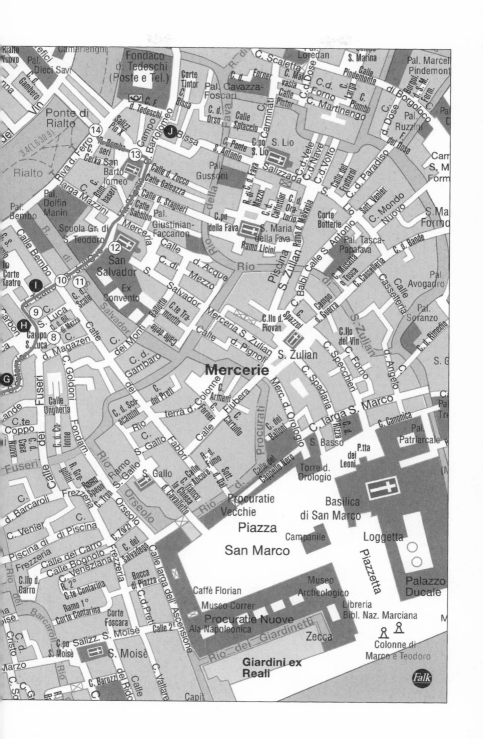

Walk 1 accompanies Guido Brunetti across Venice, beginning at La Fenice opera house and ending at the foot of the Rialto Bridge. Throughout this introductory walk, the many faces of Venice surface as Brunetti crosses some of the *campi*, which still serve as the major social meeting places for the city's strollers. Once dominated by churches, functioning wells, and even grassy fields for cows, they now offer cafés and ample room to lounge – lures for both residents and foreigners. For Brunetti, the delight in their architectural glory and their social ambience is often countered by dismay at the increasingly intrusive crowds. Whatever the Commissario encounters, he reveals himself to be a true Venetian, bewitched by the city's beauty though aware of her corruption – never more so than in the initial book that introduces this walk and places Brunetti in the footsteps of history's pageant of lovers of Venice.

* * *

Risen again from the ashes like its namesake the phoenix, Venice's La Fenice opera house **(A)** and its elegant *campo* offer a perfect midnight setting to introduce a solitary Commissario Guido Brunetti in Donna Leon's first novel, *Death at La Fenice*. With one of Venice's finest restaurants, a renowned centre for Classical studies, a Renaissance church, and an eighteenth-century musical theatre, Campo San Fantin mirrors many of the Commissario's interests: his passion for food and drink, music and art, Greek and Roman classics – and, when the conductor is found dead in the opera house, crime.

Campo San Fantin **(1)**

Earlier in the evening Brunetti would have approached this scene through a lively *campo* filled with well-dressed opera-goers and seen diners sipping prosecco at Ristorante Antico Martini* **(B)**. He would have overheard the waiting audience in elegant groups chatting in front of the Church of San Fantin (C), its white stone Renaissance façade facing the Fenice's own row of columns. The façades enclosing the *campo* would offer an excellent background to the spectacle outside as the one on stage inside is about to begin. And this outdoor theatre would have seemed no rarity to Brunetti, but a familiar part of the city's ever-vain attempt to resuscitate its fading grandeur. The nearby institute of the Ateneo Veneto (D) with its Greek heritage would remind him of the city's heritage, contributing to his lifelong passion for the classics and finely tuned ear for the subtleties of language. That it was once an institution whose members accompanied criminals to the scaffold is an irony not likely to be lost on the history-minded Commissario.

By the time Brunetti escapes the opera house after the death of Wellauer, the earlier crowds in the *campo* are gone, leaving him in rare solitude to reflect on his native city. He begins by remembering her glory – Venice is always a female, if not always a lady – for the contrast between her regal past and her faded present is never far from his mind. Pausing at the opera house's steps, exhausted from the late night back-stage encounters with singers and musicians reluctant to discuss Maestro Wellauer's violent death, Commissario Guido Brunetti delays the night's last unrevealing interview with opera director Santore to linger over his city's history and beauty.

Once the capital of the dissipations of a continent, Venice had become a sleepy provincial town that virtually ceased to exist after nine or ten at night. During the summer months, she could remember her courtesan past and sparkle, as long as the tourists paid and the good weather held, but in the winter, she became a tired old crone, eager to crawl early to bed, leaving her deserted streets to cats and memories of the past.

But these were the hours when, for Brunetti, the city became most beautiful, just as they were the same hours when he, Venetian to the bone, could sense some of her past glory. The darkness of the night hid the moss that crept up the steps of the *palazzi* lining the Grand Canal, obscured the cracks in the walls of churches, and covered the patches of plaster missing from the façades of public buildings. Like many women of a certain age, the city needed the help of deceptive light to recapture her vanished beauty. (. . .)

He glanced up at the stars, seen clearly above the darkness of the unlighted street, and noticed their beauty. Holding their image in mind, he continued towards the hotel. (*Death at La Fenice*, ch. 4)

$\longrightarrow$

At these late hours of the night, after the Opera, the Hotel La Fenice (E) offers another glimpse backstage in Venice's eternal play between truth and illusion. In any other city, the scene might appear incongruous for discussing a gruesome poisoning: a plush hotel lobby, amiable banter over brandies, tragedies in Greek, and accents bringing to mind an exalted past. But everything contributes to Brunetti's exploration of a witness, no matter how cultured.

Calle della Fenice into Campiello della Fenice (2)

In a city that even in recent times published four different Italian–Venetian dictionaries to help the natives preserve their isolated character, the way someone speaks remains crucial to identity. Whether Brunetti hears the accents of Florence or the South, or Venetian dialect, the pronunciation of words often counts as much as the information they convey.

Brunetti walked up towards the hotel, still lighted, even at this hour when the rest of the city was darkened and sleeping. (. . .)

The lobby was empty and had the abandoned look common to public places at night. Behind the reception desk, the night porter sat, chair tilted back against the wall, that day's pink sporting newspaper open before him. An old man in a green-and-black-striped apron was busy spreading sawdust on the marble floor of the lobby and sweeping it clean. When Brunetti saw that he had trailed his way through the fine wooden chips and couldn't traverse the lobby without tracking a path across the already swept floor, he looked at the old man and said, '*Scusi*.' (. . .)

Brunetti continued on into the lobby of the hotel. Six or seven clusters of large stuffed chairs were pulled up around low tables. Brunetti threaded his way through them and went to join the only person in the room. If the press was to be believed, the man sitting there was the best stage director currently working in Italy. (. . .)

Santore rose to his feet as Brunetti approached. (. . .) He asked Brunetti if he would like a drink, and from that mouth came words spoken in the purest of Florentine accents, pronounced with the clarity and grace of an actor. Brunetti thought Dante must have sounded like this. (*La Fenice*, ch. 4)

In literature, Brunetti often finds parallels to the contemporary world he inspects, giving his observations a depth and historical resonance appropriate for a native of a thousand-year-old city. Hearing Santore's Florentine-accented Italian brings Dante to his mind. By book fifteen, *Through a Glass, Darkly*, Brunetti's readings of the *Inferno* become essential to unravelling a fiery murder. In all the novels, whether his beloved Tacitus, the cranky Gibbon, or the well-thumbed stack of Greek and Roman writers that is always near to hand, Brunetti discovers constant reference to former worlds, forcing him to ponder how little humane nature – or crime – has changed. It is this background that allows him to approach police work in a very humane and cultivated way. His late night conversation with Santore has the grace of civil company, allowing all questions of violent death to wait till after the brandy.

'Thanks,' Brunetti said, accepting the glass and taking a large swallow. He pointed at the book and decided to begin with that, rather than the usual obvious questions about where he had been, what he had done. 'Aeschylus?'

Santore smiled at the question, hiding any surprise he might have felt that a policeman could read the title in Greek.

'Are you reading it for pleasure, or for work?'

'I suppose you could call it work,' Santore answered, and sipped at his brandy. 'I'm supposed to begin work on a new production of the Agamemnon in Rome in three weeks.' (*La Fenice*, ch. 4)

When Brunetti leaves the interview to walk home, Donna Leon marks her entry into a long and prestigious line of expatriate writers describing Venice – by providing Brunetti a rare emptiness for his first walk across the city. No place has been recorded so faithfully and affectionately by its foreign writers as La Serenissima. And no place has evoked such detailed descriptions of first sights as has Venice: Thomas Mann in *Death in Venice* insists the traveller arrive by sea – anything less is like entering a palace by the back door; Jan Morris in *Venice* sails into the lagoon from the sea, spotting the palaces like 'so many invalid aristocrats jostling for air'; Goethe called her a 'beaver-republic'; Hemingway in *Across the River and into the Trees* makes the dying Colonel Cantwell leave the back seat of his military sedan and climb a high hill for a sight of the city he loves more than any other.

Brunetti, however, is not an expatriate but a native with a unique way of registering the city, the people, the *calli* and canals, the boats and buildings. And he inhabits a city almost inconceivable in the twenty-first century: an urban space where people still move at a pace not much swifter than the oar. He is not rich, does not own a boat. There will be no exhausted late night calls for a private, costly water taxi. Instead, his struggles with the criminal world are mirrored throughout the novels by his walks along the sinuous *calli* and his daily attempts to navigate the city by the transport available; vaporetti, *traghetti*, police launch; on foot he steadily battles the tourist throngs and the narrow and clogged passageways, some too small to open an umbrella.

In this first walk, however, blessed by solitude and silence, Commissario Brunetti, after glancing up at the stars and noticing their beauty, heads towards home, cherishing the rare empty pathways and the peace of the deepening night. Again, he shares his vision of Venice influenced by mood, the time of day and the surrounding atmosphere with literary ancestors. He is preceded by a long line of writers, all paying their tribute to the city: John Ruskin, Jan Morris, Henry James, Ernest Hemingway, Heinrich Heine, Rainer Maria Rilke, Goethe, Nietzsche and Proust.

Brunetti decided to walk home, to take advantage of the star-studded sky and the deserted streets. He paused in front of the hotel, measuring distances. The map of the city that lay imprinted in the minds of all Venetians showed him that the shortest way was across the Rialto Bridge. (. . .) No one passed him as he walked, and he had the strange sensation of having the sleeping city entirely to himself. (. . .)

Across the bridge, he walked through the now abandoned market. It was usually a cross to bear, shoving and pushing through the crowded street, through herds of tourists jammed together between vegetable stalls on one side and shops filled with the worst sort of tourist junk on the other, but tonight he had it to himself and could stride freely. Ahead of him, in the middle of the street, a pair of lovers stood, glued hip to hip, blind to the beauty about them but perhaps, after all, somehow inspired by it.

At the clock, he turned left, glad to be almost home. Five minutes brought him to his favourite shop, Biancat, the florist, whose windows offered the city a daily explosion of beauty. Tonight, through the clinging humidity of the glass, tubs of yellow roses preened themselves, while behind them lurked a cloud of pale jasmine. He walked quickly past the second window, crowded with lurid orchids, which always looked faintly cannibalistic to him. (*La Fenice*, ch. 5)

$\longrightarrow$

Over Ponte Storto **(3)** to Calle Caotorta **(4)** into Campo Sant'Angelo **(5)**

Brunetti's walks are rarely so serene or peaceful as this first journey across from the opera house to his apartment in *Death at La Fenice*. Whenever police business takes him into the far reaches of the city, the urgency of crime at his heels forces him to calculate how to get from one place to the next in the shortest time and over the fewest bridges. Since the physical geography of Venice is so confusing, further complicated by an erratic address system arranged not by *calli* but by the six existing regions (*sestieri*), locations remain a central preoccupation for its residents, with everyone measuring distances.

In Donna Leon's sixteenth novel, *Suffer the Little Children*, Brunetti tries to explain to Paola the tragedy that has enveloped Dr Pedrolli and his family. But first he must establish the location of the (invented) pharmacy so different from the one his friend Danilo manages in nearby San Luca. For Venetians *what* and *why* follow the all-important *where:*

'The pharmacist in Campo Sant'Angelo? **(5)**' she asked. (. . .)
   'You know him?'
   'No. It's out of the way for me. Besides, it's one of those *campi* where you don't think of stopping, isn't it? You just walk across it on your way to Accademia or Rialto: I've never even bought one of those cotton shirts from the place by the bridge.' (*Suffer the Little Children*, ch. 24)

Brunetti's inner map focused on the *campo*, viewed first from the entrance from the bridge and then from Calle della Mandola. A restaurant where he had never eaten, an art gallery, the inevitable real estate agency, the *edicola* with the chocolate Labrador.

→

Location is a prime consideration not only for residents. Since Venice has the reputation of being a notoriously difficult city in which to find a decent restaurant, visitors fret that they will be condemned to tourist fare. The pair of American doctors who witnessed the shooting of the young African street seller in *Blood from a Stone* have the sense to depend on a native and call on Brunetti for help. He directs them across Campo Sant'Angelo and on to Calle della Mandola **(6)**, and wisely recommends a place where he is known, thus ensuring their kind treatment.

Calle della Mandola **(6)** into Campo Manin **(7)**

Outside, in the *campo*, he pointed to the right and told them to walk along Calle della Mandola to the Rosa Rossa **(F)*** and to tell the owner that Commissario Brunetti had sent them. (*Blood from a Stone*, ch. 3)

On Brunetti's way to see the lawyer Santomauro, supposed head of the Lega della Moralità, he too must pass through Calle della Mandola. But *The Anonymous Venetian* (US: *Dressed for Death*) is set during sweltering *ferragosto*, increasing his need to struggle through the crowds to get into Campo Manin **(7)**.

It was like wading through a heavy surf, pushing his way through the late-morning crowds of people who gawked in front of shop windows, paused to talk to one another, or stood in the momentary relief of a cool breeze escaping from an air-conditioned shop. Down through the narrow confines of Calle della Mandola he raced, using his elbows and his voice, careless of the angry stares and sarcastic remarks created by his passing.

In the open space of Campo Manin, he broke into a trot, although every step brought sweat pouring out on to his body. He cut around the bank and into Campo San Luca, crowded now with people meeting for a drink before lunch. *(The Anonymous Venetian*, ch. 27)

In his hurry Brunetti has no time to linger over the historic importance of Campo Manin to his own life as someone who loves books. The dedicated Roman humanist Aldus Manutius (1450–1515) chose this spot to print over a hundred editions of Classical texts in a readable typeface for people who had never before been able to afford books. Today, the former site of the Aldine Press, the Renaissance world's cultural centre for the humanities, is reduced to a marble plaque enshrining this spot's contribution to knowledge **(G)** – ironically, now on the right side of what Brunetti refers to as 'the broad horror of the Cassa di Risparmio', arguably Venice's most hideous bank.

(. . .) once, years ago, he had noticed on a wall he must have passed five times a week since he was a child a lapidary stone that commemorated the site of the Aldine Publishing House, the oldest in Italy. He had gone right around the corner and into a bar in Campo San Luca and ordered himself a Brandy Alexander, though it was ten in the morning. (*Death in a Strange Country*, ch. 12)

In the empty pre-dawn hours, however, in *Fatal Remedies*, a vastly different Campo Manin faces Paola Brunetti: trapped between her own sense of honour and her shame at the modern world's corruption, she stands in the centre of the *campo* dedicated to the revolutionary patriot Daniele Manin and looks up at his marble statue. As she remembers Manin's struggles to regain the Republic's independence from the Austrians, she aligns herself with the long train of Venetians committed to liberty above all else – in her case the freedom to act, even illegally. Feeling morally compelled to violate the very laws so determinedly upheld by her Commissario husband, she prepares to fling a grapefruit-sized stone through the glass windows of a (fictional) travel agency she suspects of offering sex-tourism trips.

The woman walked quietly into the empty *campo*. To her left stood the grill-covered windows of a bank, empty and sleeping the well-protected sleep that comes in the early hours of the morning. She crossed to the centre of the *campo* and stood beside the low-hung iron chains enclosing the monument to Daniele Manin, who had sacrificed himself for the freedom of the city. How fitting, she thought. (*Fatal Remedies*, ch. 1)

Suffused with neither regret nor remorse, suffering merely exhaustion after finally committing her criminal act of throwing the stone, Paola awaits the arresting officers to take her to the Questura. This scene offers a perfect example of Donna Leon's accuracy of Venetian detail. Even when she invents a business or a building, the surroundings are described with absolute fidelity.

Silently she pushed herself away from the pillar and started towards the entrance to a narrow *calle* to the left of the destroyed window. Neither policeman made note of the fact that she knew the way to begin the shortest route to the Questura. (ch. 1)

→

Campo Manin serves the city's residents, like Brunetti, primarily as an artery to more lively *campi*, especially nearby Campo San Luca **(8)** where the Commissario frequently enjoys what was once his favourite bar.

Campo Manin to Campo San Luca **(8)**

Rosa Salva, it was generally agreed, was one of the best bars in the city; Brunetti especially liked their small ricotta cakes. So he stopped there for coffee and a pastry, exchanged pleasantries with a few people he knew, nods with some he only recognized. (*Fatal Remedies*, ch. 6)

The former Rosa Salva (**H**) that has figured so prominently throughout the novels from the second book *Death in a Strange Country*, where Paola insists it serves 'the best coffee in the city' has changed hands in 2006 and been updated; like so many altered establishments in Venice, it is now beyond recognition, and Brunetti will need to find another place for a *caffè* and gossip. At least the Tarantola bookstore, another favourite stop, still remains. With its nearly impassable aisles and myopic owners, the shop makes as little concession to the modern 'chain' epidemic that has hit other cities as Brunetti makes to reading modern history.

Just as Paola laments the corruption of the modern world while in Campo Manin, Brunetti surveys Campo San Luca in *The Anonymous Venetian* and ruminates on the moral decline behind so many respectable façades. Suspecting Avvocato Santomauro to be a member of the dubious Lega della Moralità, he recognizes the irony of the office's location, musing how closely the everyday life and the criminal cohabit with nothing more than a piece of glass in between.

The *avvocato*'s office was in Campo San Luca, on the second floor of a building that was within twenty metres of three different banks. How fitting that proximity was, Brunetti thought, as Santomauro's secretary showed him into the lawyer's office only a few minutes after his arrival.

Santomauro sat at his desk, behind him a large window that looked out on the *campo*. The window, however, was tightly sealed, and the office cooled to an almost uncomfortable degree, especially in view of what could be seen below: naked shoulders, legs, backs, arms all passed across the *campo*, yet here it was cool enough for a jacket and tie. (*The Anonymous Venetian*, ch. 24)

Years later in *Friends in High Places*, Brunetti returns to Campo San Luca in search of information. San Luca is one of the main squares in the city where Venetians gather – before work to exchange gossip over a *caffè*, before lunch for a chat, before dinner for more gossip and an aperitif. Brunetti is here for less cheerful reasons: he has come in the hope of finding a money-lending couple or, if all else fails, to appeal to his old friend Danilo the pharmacist for gossip and clues. Rosa Salva, with its packed stand-up counter and only one window, would normally be Brunetti's choice, but for strategic reasons he chooses Bar Torino, its tables convenient for a long wait and its broad expanse of glass allowing him to see anyone entering the open space of Campo San Luca.

→

He went into Bar Torino and ordered a *spritz*, then took it and stood at the window, studying the figures who still congregated in the *campo*.

Straight ahead to Farmacia **(9)**

There was no sign of either Signora Volpato or her husband.

(. . .) Outside, Brunetti turned left, and left again, and went into the pharmacy **(9)**, just closing now.

'*Ciao*, Guido,' his friend Danilo the pharmacist said, locking the door behind them. 'Let me finish and we'll go have a drink.' (*Friends in High Places*, ch. 20)

Danilo represents just one example of the recurring characters Donna Leon has provided as a supporting cast for the Commissario. His exchanges with Brunetti reveal how acutely attentive the city's residents are to everything around them, from the cost of spring artichokes to overheard details of local crimes. In a walking city everyone talks to one another, to the bartender, to the newspaper seller – and certainly to the pharmacist who hears about everyone's illnesses and everyone's neighbours. Brunetti admits that over the years Danilo has supplied him with 'an Eldorado of gossip and innuendo'.

Just as language and accent alert Brunetti to the origins and possible criminality of the people he encounters, they also serve as mockery and revelation of character. Over coffee,

Danilo offers a monologue parody of the odious moneylenders and their fake piety; their very language drips with hypocrisy:

'Don't tell me they've finally made a mistake, and someone's filed a complaint against them?' Danilo said with the beginnings of a smile. 'Ah, what joy.'

'You know them that well?' Brunetti asked.

'I've known them for years,' he said, almost spitting out his disgust. 'Especially her. She's in here once a week, with her little pictures of her saints, and her rosary in her hands' (. . .) Turning his usual Trentino dialect into purest Veneziano and pitching his voice into a high squeal, he said, 'Oh, Dottor Danilo, you don't know how much good I've done to the people in this city. You don't know how many people are grateful to me for what I've done for them (. . .)' Though Brunetti had never heard Signora Volpato speak, he heard in Danilo's savage parody the echo of every hypocrite he'd ever known. (*Friends*, ch. 20)

When Venice has gone to bed, and even sociable Campo San Luca is empty, Danilo's pharmacy, with its occasional lonely all-night hours, reminds Brunetti of a less hospitable Venice. Despite the beauty of the starry night which begins that first walk in *Death at La Fenice*, despite the exalted surroundings in a city of marble majesty, the underside of Venice continues to haunt his thoughts, as he passes the pharmacy, 'one of the few places that were open all night, except for the train station, where slept the homeless and the mad'.

→

Right on Calle del Teatro (**10**) Throughout the novels Brunetti is inescapably confronted by the contrasts between the two faces of the city he journeys through, repeatedly reminded of the way crimes and violence connect the rich and the poor. And in a walking city where proximity matters, it comes as no surprise to find lawyers and notaries often validating illegal dealings conveniently close to the banks in San Luca, easily allowing a secretary to walk secretly a mere three minutes to the banks to check any client's financial reliability: 'The studio of Notaio Sanpaolo was on a small *calle* near the Teatro Goldoni' (*Wilful Behaviour*, ch. 24).

But the city also offers its residents and visitors ample entertainment that allows them to escape the seemingly relentless world of murder and deceit that hounds the Commissario. For many foreign visitors to Venice, too often denied any views of local life in the *palazzi*, the theatre is their finest chance to see Venetians at ease. Teatro Goldoni **(I),** named after one of the few authors native to Venice, the comic playwright Carlo Goldoni, offers just such an opportunity for people to mix. On his first trip to Italy, recorded in *Italian Journey*, Goethe shows his delight in finally turning Venice into a real place instead of just a haunting name. Part of his new-found pleasure comes from an evening at this theatre in 1786, where he seems more drawn to the raucous scene of the native spectators than the events on the stage: 'I have never in my life witnessed such an ecstasy of joy as that shown by the audience,' he wrote. The Goldoni theatre continues to play an important role in the cultural life of the city, as do his plays. Over two hundred years after Goethe's visit, Brunetti recalls evenings spent laughing at the comedies.

(. . .) Goldoni, perhaps not his favourite playwright but certainly the one who could make him laugh the hardest, especially when the plays were presented in their original Veneziano dialect, as they always were here, in the city that swarmed to his plays and loved him. (*The Anonymous Venetian*, ch. 13)

But the comic relief is brief and the physical condition of the city perilous. Just as no audience was spared Goldoni's acid political remarks, no walk around Venice is spared Brunetti's often merciless but sensitive observations. Of the many changes he registers during the sequence of novels, the physical condition of the city herself and her fragile foundations receive his most serious attention. From her very first novel, Donna Leon creates in Brunetti an eloquent and sustained voice with which to observe the fearful devastation the Serene Republic faces from tourist affluence and

Foot of Ponte dell'Ovo (del Teatro) **(11)**

environmental problems. The July Feast of the Redeemer, first held in 1576 to celebrate yet another of Venice's escapes from the plague, forces Brunetti to consider what sort of salvation can be had in modern times, what can stop the onslaught now coming from polluting Porto Marghera with its

clouds of smoke that would gradually sneak across the *laguna* to dine on Venice's white Istrian marble. He wondered what divine intercession could save the city from the oil slick, this modern plague that covered the waters of the *laguna* and had already destroyed millions of the crabs that had crawled through the nightmares of his childhood. What Redeemer could come and save the city from the pall of greenish smoke that was slowly turning marble to meringue? A man of limited faith, he could imagine no salvation, either divine or human. (*Death at La Fenice*, ch. 14)

Even less overwhelming ecological fears attract his withering attention. As he stares down into the canals and recalls his privileged childhood in this rare environment, he laments the ruinous changes that continue to beset Venice.

He paused for a moment on Ponte del Teatro [Ponte dell'Ovo] **(11)** and studied the rebuilt foundations of the buildings that lined the canal on either side. When he was a boy, the canals had undergone a perpetual process of cleaning, and the waters were kept so clear that people could swim in them. Now, the cleaning of a canal was a major event, so rare that it was greeted with headlines and talk of good city management. And contact with their waters was an experience many people might choose not to survive. (*A Noble Radiance*, ch. 12)

$\longrightarrow$

Over Ponte dell' Ovo to Chiesa San Salvador **(12)**

The Church of San Salvador **(12)** holds the remains of Caterina Cornaro, daughter of a doge who sacrificed her youth and her reign over Cyprus to aid the Venetian republic; a grateful state provided her with an exalted funeral and eventually a fine tomb. In *A Noble Radiance*, Brunetti must attend the funeral of a less noble young Venetian aristocrat whose decomposed corpse has been found buried in the foothills of the Dolomites – and whose end will be commemorated by few. Even in such desolate circumstances – a grieving family, a mysterious death, increasing suspicions – Brunetti is yet again forced to endure the inescapable presence of tourists bent on photos that the church's Titian demands.

Because the following day was Sunday, Brunetti left the Lorenzonis to themselves and returned his attention to the family only the next morning, when he attended Roberto's funeral, a rite as solemn as it was grim. The mass was cele-brated in the Church of San Salvador, which stood beyond one end of Campo San Bartolomeo and which, because of its proximity to Rialto, received a constant flux of tourists during the day and hence during the mass. Brunetti, seated at the back of the church, was conscious of their invasive arrival, overheard the buzz of their exchanged whispers as they discussed how to photograph the Titian *Annunciation* and the tomb of Caterina Cornaro. But during a funeral? Perhaps, if they were very, very quiet and didn't use the flash. (*A Noble Radiance*, ch. 18)

The hushed setting appears at first to have tamed his irrita-tion; the sarcasm of 'very, very' reveals it has not.

The anonymous, uninterested tourists remind Brunetti of the importance of family to Italians, all the more saddening as he ponders the absence of close relatives and friends to wish the Lorenzoni boy farewell.

Brunetti stepped suddenly into the aisle and joined the trickle of people making towards the door of the church. On the steps, he was surprised to see the sunlight pouring down on the *campo*, the people trailing past on their way to Campo San Luca or Rialto, utterly unmoved by thoughts of Roberto Lorenzoni or his death. (ch. 18)

$\longrightarrow$

Almost daily Brunetti takes the narrow, congested *calle* from
San Luca, past the church and into Campo San Bartolomeo
(13). A recurring location in most of Donna Leon's novels,
the *campo* serves as a mirror for his wavering moods. Like
San Luca, this crowded spot is nearly impassable in the early
evening hours when Venetians gather for a last chat or drink
before heading home to dinner. It has also proven a lure for
many of history's famous foreigners in Venice. In 1862 the
American novelist and honorary consul to Venice, W. D.
Howells, lived on the *campo*, and the English poet Robert
Browning, dying in the eighteenth-century Ca' Rezzonico
across the Grand Canal, wrote a poetic tribute to this picturesque spot. In the centre of all the chaos stands the smiling
bronze statue of Goldoni erected in 1883, a figure Brunetti
rarely fails to acknowledge on his trips through the *campo*:

he walked (. . .) into Campo San Bartolomeo. His eyes went
up to the bronze statue of Goldoni, (. . .) in full stride, which
made this *campo* the perfect place for him to be, for here,
everyone rushed, always on their way somewhere: across the
Rialto Bridge to go to the vegetable market; from Rialto to
either the San Marco or the Cannaregio district. If people
lived anywhere near the heart of the city, its geography would
pull them through San Bartolomeo at least once a day. (*The
Anonymous Venetian*, ch. 13)

This path often draws Brunetti when he walks from the
Questura to his apartment and back. As a Venetian and a
policeman, he will be only too aware of the area's long and
disreputable history. In the Middle Ages, nearby Calle della
Bissa **(J)** and its surrounding streets became so dangerous
that laws were enacted to prohibit any disguise that might
camouflage criminals. Even today, this highly public *campo*
is more than a busy meeting place or crossing path: the underside of the city also surfaces – at least after midnight when
it may serve as a spot to deal drugs.

The instant Brunetti saw him there, cowering full length on
the ground, his arms wrapped around his thin body to protect

it from the expected kicks or blows and his neck pulled down into his shoulders, he recognized the young man. He was one of a trio of drug addicts, all in their early twenties, who had for years spent their days near or in Campo San Bortolo, going from bar to bar, growing more out of touch with reality as day passed into night and year into year. (*Friends in High Places*, ch.19)

No surprise that this Janus-like *campo* features as a central place in the majority of the Donna Leon novels, and also serves to remind Brunetti of the potential dangers he fears for his own son. Whether the calamity of addiction, as he observes in *Friends in High Places*, or the smug arrogance of the privileged young, both are perils to beware. In *Uniform Justice* Campo San Bartolomeo makes his fear palpable:

Just as he was approaching the underpass leading into Campo San Bartolomeo, his mind on this unsettling parallel, he registered a sudden darkness in front of him. He looked up, still not fully attentive to his surroundings, and saw four San Martino cadets wheeling, arms linked, as straight across as if on parade, into the *calle* from the *campo*. The long dark capes of their winter uniforms swirled out on either flank and effectively filled the entire width of the *calle*. Two women, one old and one young, instinctively backed up against the plate glass windows of the bank, and a pair of map-embracing tourists did the same against the windows of the bar on the other side. Leaving the four shipwrecked pedestrians in their wake, the unbroken wave of boys swept towards him.
Brunetti raised his eyes to theirs – boys no older than his own son – and the glances that came back to him were as blank and pitiless as the sun. His right foot might have faltered for an instant, but by an act of will he shoved it forward and continued towards them, stride unbroken, his face implacable, as though he were alone (. . .) the entire city his. (*Uniform Justice*, ch. 16)

Certainly the majority of Brunetti's family life is devoid of fret and fear, and this offers one of the many pleasures of entering his world. The sanity and comfort of home life punctuates the novels with scenes of everyday problems, meals, work, school, and all the familiar things that differ little simply because they occur in historic Venice.

Yet in *Fatal Remedies*, after Brunetti is awakened to an empty bed at his side by a call from the Questura and goes to retrieve his wife, the conflict between Brunetti the husband and Brunetti the policeman is too deep for him to be cheered up by Goldoni:

They entered the underpass and were quickly out into Campo San Bartolomeo, where the cheerful smile on the statue of Goldoni seemed wildly out of place. Brunetti glanced up at the clock. Venetian, he knew to add an hour: almost five, not early enough to bother to go back to bed, yet how to fill the hours between now and the time when he could legitimately leave for work? He looked to his left, but none of the bars was open. He wanted coffee; far more desperately, he needed the diversion it would provide. (*Fatal Remedies*, ch. 3)

Years later, in *Blood from a Stone*, their former dispute long healed, the couple arrange to meet for an evening out. Brunetti's good mood is reflected as he affectionately uses the *campo*'s shortened Venetian name San Bortolo while preparing himself for Christmas shopping in the world's most beautiful city.

(. . .) he continued down Calle della Mandola, through Campo San Luca, and into San Bortolo.

Paola was, as she had promised, waiting for him, right where she had waited for him for decades: beneath the statue of a perpetually dapper Goldoni. He kissed her and wrapped his right arm around her shoulder. 'Tell me you ate badly and I'll get you any Christmas present you want,' he said. (*Blood from a Stone*, ch.17)

→

To left side of Ponte di Rialto
(14)

As the Brunettis do in so many of the novels, they head from San Bortolo to the Grand Canal and the foot of the Rialto

Bridge **(14)**. It is a spot with a once exalted past: for centuries the financial exchange for most of the known world, Rialto Bridge and the Venetian *zecchino* determined the price of most of the globe's exchanges. When Shakespeare's Shylock in *The Merchant of Venice* asks, 'What news on the Rialto?' he signals the importance of Venice as money-broker to the world, but also the importance of intrigue in this deceptively lovely city.

Four hundred years later, in *Death at La Fenice,* Brunetti describes his ambivalent feelings for this white marble span over water that will slow down his movements in so many of the novels. Unlike Shylock, tortured by his uncertain existence in Venice, Brunetti wonders not about pirates and ducats, carnage and Christians, but the centuries-long paradox of Venice's two faces – that inescapable union of fair and foul. Having shared his company from the opera house to the famous bridge, it seems only just to leave him to his watery reflections before he crosses the Grand Canal and heads for the sanctity of home.

And then he was at the water's edge, the bridge to his right. How typically Venetian it was, looking, from a distance, lofty and ethereal but revealing itself, upon closer reflection, to be firmly grounded in the mud of the city. (*Death at La Fenice,* ch. 5)

---

*Antico Martini was initially the location of a coffee-house in the early 1700s. Now one of Venice's finest restaurants, it offers both traditional and sophisticated dishes, plus an exceptional wine list.

*Ristorante Rosa Rossa is a surprisingly unspoiled *trattoria* situated on a busy tourist artery.

WALK 2 : *Rialto and the Senses*

Rialto—Do Mori—Canal Grande—Brunetti apartment

1 hour

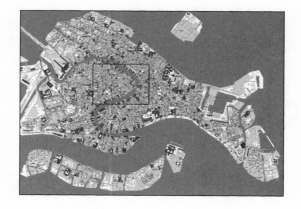

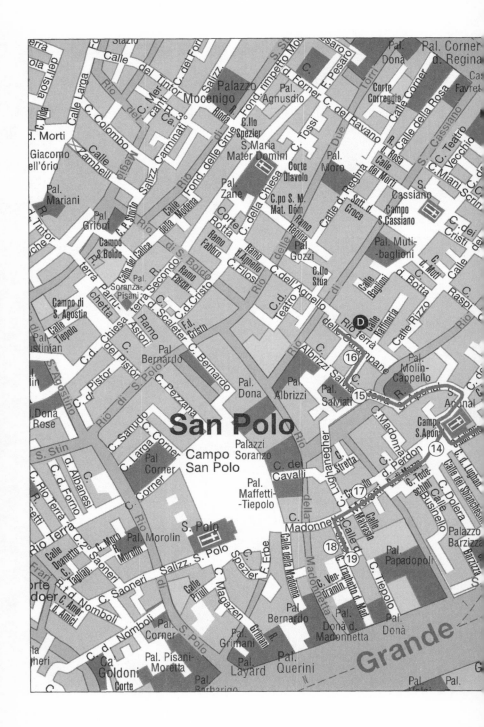

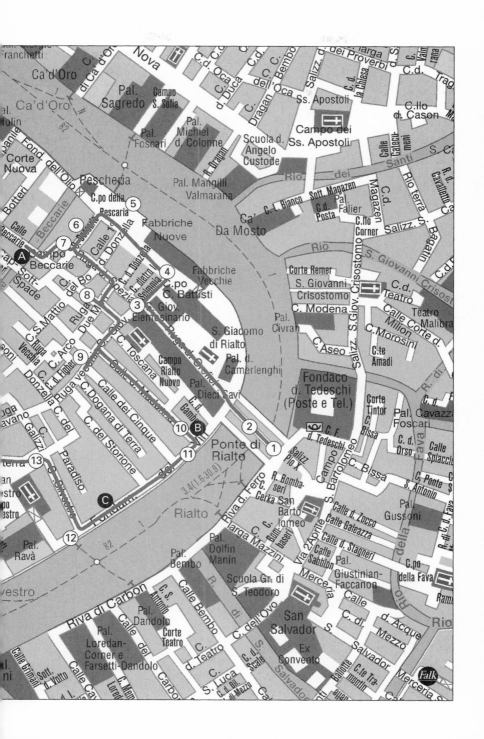

Walk 2 accompanies Brunetti on his usual walk home from the Questura as he climbs the steep Rialto Bridge, wanders through the busy food market, stops at favourite wine bars, dines at nearby waterside restaurants, feeds his senses with the fragrance and beauty from Biancat's banked windows of flowers. His journey ends as Donna Leon provides the initial view of Brunetti arriving at the family apartment and the reader's first meeting with his wife Paola.

Ponte di Rialto (1)

As Leon develops the Brunetti books, she offers a rich and humorous portrait of his family: wife Paola, son Raffi, daughter Chiara. She also creates a second family for him at the Questura. Just as Brunetti and Paola unite to protect their growing children, their illegally constructed apartment, and their sanity where they work – the university and the Questura – his community of comrades eases Commissario Brunetti's battles with crime, with his boss Vice-Questore Patta, and with the ever-creeping plague of bureaucratic nonsense.

* * *

Work often fills Brunetti's mind, even as he crosses the Rialto Bridge. Although Officer Vianello has been with him from the beginning, in *The Death of Faith*, he begins to take on a larger role, demonstrating his ability with witnesses, computer finesse, environmental fears, and his new commitment to exercising and fitness. After a surprised Brunetti first inquires into Vianello's new slender form, the Commissario sets off for home and lunch with renewed vigour, eager to assure himself that he certainly needs no gym to stay in shape:

→

He felt trapped in his woollen suit, and then the traitorous thought came to him that both slacks and jacket were tighter

Top of Ponte di Rialto (2)

than they had been in early winter when he had first worn the suit. When he got to the Rialto Bridge, he pushed ahead in a sudden surge of buoyant energy and started to trot up the steps. After a dozen steps, he found himself winded and had to slow down to a walk. At the top, he paused and gazed off to the left and up toward the curve that took the Grand Canal off toward San Marco and the Doge's Palace. The sun glared up from the surface of the water on which bobbed the first black-headed gulls of the season.

His breath caught, he started down the other side, so pleased with the softness of the day that he felt none of his usual irritation with the crowded streets and milling tourists. (*The Death of Faith*, ch. 2)

Difficult as Brunetti often finds it to cross the Rialto, battling the chaotic midday crowds, the occasion can also offer him a view so exalting that his pride in being a Venetian counters his dismay at the changes in his city.

Brunetti found himself on the top of the Rialto, gazing south toward Ca' Farsetti and the scaffolding that still covered the façade of the university down at the bend, the buildings softened by the evening light. Look at those *palazzi*, he told some silent audience of non-Venetians. Look at them and tell me who could build them today. Who could come and stack those blocks of marble one on top of the other and have the finished products display such effortless grace?

Look at them, he went on, look at the homes of the Manins, the Bembos, the Dandolos, or look farther down to what the Grimanis and the Contarinis and the Trons built in their names. Look on those things and tell me we did not once know greatness. (*Through a Glass, Darkly*, ch. 5)

→

Straight to Piero's
(3) Tribunale (4)
The uniqueness of his native city is never far from Brunetti's thoughts; yet he reflects, in the first book how rare is the solitude encountered on his initial walk home.

Across the bridge, he walked through the now abandoned market. It was usually a cross to bear, shoving and pushing through the crowded street, through herds of tourists jammed together between vegetable stalls on one side and shops filled with the worst sort of tourist junk on the other, but tonight he had it to himself and could stride freely. (*Death at La Fenice*, ch. 5)

The Rialto area also serves as a convenient place for Brunetti to meet judges and officials from the courthouse **(4)** nearby with its expansive views of the Grand Canal – another example of how in Venice the criminal and the everyday world are closely intertwined. A simple stroll to gauge the seasons and the produce or a stop to buy cheese from Piero's tiny shop, La Baita **(3)**,* are often punctuated by uniformed guards armed with machine-guns and business-suited officials armed with dubious authority.

The main criminal courthouse of the city lies at the foot of the Rialto Bridge, not the San Marco side but the side that holds the fruit and vegetable market. In fact, those who go early to the market can sometimes see men and women in handcuffs and shackles being led into and out of the various entrances to the courthouse, and infrequently machine-gun-carrying carabinieri stand amidst the crates of cabbages and grapes, guarding the people who are taken inside. Brunetti showed his warrant card to the armed guards at the door and climbed the two flights of broad marble stairs to Judge Beniamin's chambers. Each landing had a large window that looked across to the Fondazione dei Tedeschi, under the Republic the commercial centre for all German traders in the city, now the Central Post Office. At the top of the stairs, two carabinieri wearing flak jackets and carrying assault rifles stopped him and asked to see his identification.

'Are you wearing a weapon, Commissario?' one of them asked after a close examination of his warrant card.

Brunetti regretted having forgotten to leave the gun in his office; it had been open season on judges in Italy for so long that everyone was nervous and, too late, very cautious. (*A Venetian Reckoning*, ch. 17)

→

Through Mercato, to Campo della Pescaría **(5)**

Regardless of the crowds and the chaos, nowhere in Venice affords Brunetti so vital a scene of the city's ceaseless variety as the Rialto market area. And nowhere so challenges his ingenuity to accomplish his goals than the artery from the foot of the bridge to his favourite wine bars. He'll pass through corridors of both imported and Venetian-made junk, separating him on the one side from home and peace, on the other from the Grand Canal, its *riva* recently refurbished with trendy restaurants and wine bars dotted along the water. Next he must brave the temptations of flanks of fruit and vegetable dealers, artichokes trimmed like rosebuds: *20 per 5 Euro!* Then, he'll pass the strings of fishmongers **(5)** calling out *Tonno! Rombo! Calamari! Vongole veraci!* Brunetti often succumbs to the temptation of the abundant produce in the markets, but he resists the flower sellers at the Tuesday and Saturday markets, preferring to wait for his favourite florist Biancat. Through it all, the hordes may lessen and his mood lighten, but this continual see-saw that Brunetti encounters daily both animates and plagues his every crossing of the city.

Given the hour and the crowds of tourists who flooded the boats, he decided to walk, sure that he could avoid the worst gaggles of them until he neared Rialto and equally certain that their numbers would decrease again once he got past the *pescheria*. So it proved, but the brief period he spent pushing and evading his way through the streets (. . .) and the fish market soured his humour and brought his ever-simmering dislike of tourists to the boil. (*Wilful Behaviour*, ch. 19)

After Paola has vandalized a tourist agency in *Fatal Remedies*, Brunetti is distraught by his wife's arrest and the intrusive press outside the Questura. He is granted a much-needed diversion at the Rialto market, offering him reminders of his passion for food.

When he arrived at the Grand Canal, the wind made him decide not to take the *traghetto* and, instead, he crossed the Rialto. As he walked, he ignored the glory that surrounded him on all sides and, instead, thought about what he wanted to ask Avvocato Zambino. He was distracted from this only once when he saw what he was sure were porcini mushrooms on one of the vegetable stalls and was filled with a momentary hope that Paola would see them too and serve them with polenta for lunch. (*Fatal Remedies*, ch. 17)

The Rialto area also illustrates the seasons so crucial to Brunetti's moods and travails: his keen sensitivity to both the despair of winter and the coming of spring. Nature rewards him with a sense of renewal in a universe filled with human crime. Unlike much of the twenty-first century West, Venice remains strongly tied to the seasonal world. Whether they observe the strange curly chicory known as *puntarelle* or the delicate green asparagus appearing in early spring, all Venetian residents can be heard chattering about the first sighting in the markets – and the appalling costs.

'Is that *puntarelle*?' he asked, surprised to find it in the market this early.

'Yes, and the best in Rialto,' the vendor assured him, his face flushed with years of wine drinking. 'Six thousand a kilo and cheap at the price.'

Brunetti refused to respond to this absurdity. When he was a boy, *puntarelle* cost a few hundred lire a kilo, and few people ate it. (. . .) (*The Death of Faith*, ch. 2)

→

Whatever his journeys through the market entail, even if it's courthouses or body searches, Brunetti will be surrounded by food and wine. A string of fancy fish restaurants line the Grand Canal along the Riva del Vin, simple *trattorie* dot the smaller *calli*, and Venice's unique *bacari* are nowhere more prevalent than in the Rialto area. For hundreds of years they have provided a pedestrian population with frequent stops for *un cicheto e un' ombra* – a little bite and a 'shadow' of

Calle Beccaríe **(6)** to Campo Beccaríe **(7)**

wine. Originally, whichever side of Piazza San Marco was in shade was where the wine sellers moved to dispense their small glasses to customers, and names in Venice often come from history and legend. Certainly, as so often in the city, the versions of a story are as numerous as the tellers. Similar to Spanish *tapas*, *cicheti* range from toothpicks of seafood, vegetables, cheeses, *salumi* to small bites to be picked up from the bar; native only to Venice, they are a favourite snack among residents, including Brunetti. Stuck in a swamp of confusing clues in *Doctored Evidence*, Brunetti turns, for once, to the forces of law in the hope of finding aid. But even the officers of justice in Venice are suspicious of being overheard; the judge prefers to leave the courthouse to meet, instead, at one of the nearby *bacari*, Osteria Sora al Ponte **(A)**:*

'It's almost six,' Galvani said. 'I'll leave here in about half an hour. Shall we meet at that place on the Ponte delle Becarie?' he asked, describing an *enoteca* not far from the fish market. 'At six-thirty?' (. . .)

Galvani's grip was firm, warm and brisk. 'Shall we try to find a place to sit?' he asked, turning towards the tables at the back of the room, most of them occupied at this hour. Just as he turned, three men got up from a table on the left, and Galvani headed for it quickly, Brunetti staying behind to order a glass of Chardonnay. (*Doctored Evidence*, ch. 13)

→

Ruga degli Speziali, right on to Ruga Do Mori to Cantina Do Mori **(8)**

Cantina Do Mori **(8)*** is another place where Brunetti likes to stop on his way home, often to stave off hunger, equally often to delay climbing the ninety-four steps to his nearby apartment.

(. . .) he stopped in at Do Mori, his favourite bar, just a few steps from Rialto, and said hello to Roberto, the grey-haired proprietor. They exchanged a few words, and Brunetti asked for a glass of Cabernet, the only thing he felt like drinking. With it, he ate a few of the fried shrimp that were always available at the bar, then decided to have a *tramezzino*, thick with ham and artichoke. He had another glass of wine and, after it, he began to feel human, for the first time that day. Paola always accused him of becoming foul-tempered when he didn't eat for a long time, and he was beginning to believe she might be right. (*Death in a Strange Country*, ch. 9)

Do Mori's atmosphere of ceilings hung with old copper pots and wooden walls browned with age still remains, but even in historic Venice old institutions give way and traditions either die or are replaced by more modern versions. Several years after the first scene of Brunetti sipping *un' ombra* in Do Mori, his discussion with the architect, Signora Gismondi, in *Doctored Evidence*, reminds them both how resistant the Venetians are to change, no matter how minor.

'I think I know you,' she said.

'Yes,' he answered. 'And I think I know you, too. Do you work near Rialto?'

She smiled and relaxed. 'No, I work at home, over by the Misericordia, but I come to the market at least three times a week. I think that's where we've seen one another.'

'At Piero's?' Brunetti asked, naming the postage-stamp-sized shop where she bought *parmigiano*.

'Of course. And I think I've seen you in Do Mori,' she added.

'Less and less, though.'

'Since Roberto and Franco sold it?'

'Yes,' he said. 'I know the new guys are perfectly nice, but it's not the same, somehow.'

How maddening it must be to take over a successful business in this city, she thought. No matter how good you are and no matter how many improvements you might make, ten, twenty years after you take over, people will still be whining about how much better it was when Franco or Roberto or Pinco Pallino, for that matter, ran the place. These two new owners – she had never learned their names – were just as nice as the former ones, had the same wine, even had better sandwiches, but no matter how good anything they sold could be, they were doomed to spend their professional lives being held up to a long-forgotten standard, held up and found wanting, at least until all the old customers died or moved away, when they would become the new standard against whom the inadequacy of whoever replaced them would be measured. (*Doctored Evidence*, ch. 4)

→

To Ruga Vecchia, to Antico Dolo **(9)**

Like the seasons and the weather, Brunetti's responses to food are a clear indication of his mental or spiritual state. Bewildered over a case, or despondent over a victim, he eats with inattention, sometimes with sorrow and a dry taste in his mouth. Police preoccupations can lead him to choose a less familial wine bar, avoiding the camaraderie of Do Mori for the more neutral Antico Dolo **(9)*** nearby, especially in *Fatal Remedies*, when life at home with the recently arrested Paola is, at best, strained.

He looked down at his watch and saw that it was after six; certainly a full commissario, particularly one who was still officially on something called administrative leave, could go home.

On the way, he continued to mull it over, once even stopping to pull out the list of countries and study it again. He went into Antico Dolo and had a glass of white wine and two cuttlefish, but he was so preoccupied that he barely tasted them. (*Fatal Remedies*, ch. 21)

→

Calle della Madonna **(10)** to Canal Grande **(11)**

Brunetti's daily walks and searches through the city for an appropriate lunch mirror an Italian and Venetian preoccupation with the right food in the right season, and, importantly, in the right restaurant. Where, when, what, and with whom one eats is a never-ending matter for discussion: overheard on trains, on boats, and in bars, the subject never fails to engage conversation and dispute. That Italy remains a country where friends and family often sit down to traditional meals twice every day gives Donna Leon the opportunity to dramatize a social occasion fast disappearing from twenty-first-century life.

Even though Brunetti dines all over the city, he prefers his own neighbourhood restaurants, which provide him with the most glamorous setting to probe a friend for information. The varied selection along the Grand Canal **(11)*** on the Riva del Vin creates a theatrical atmosphere appropriate to meals of consequence. Whether dining at the Cafè Saraceno **(B)** or the Ristorante Canal Grande **(C)**, Brunetti uses the occasion to observe the crowds, to register with comical bewilderment the excesses of foreign visitors' orders, and, ultimately, to validate the excellence of Venetian cuisine:

The restaurant was full, tables covered with things, marvellous things: one couple sat with lobsters the size of dachshunds in front of them, while to the left a group of businessmen were eating their way through a platter of seafood that would have fed a Sri Lankan village for a week.

Brunetti went straight into the kitchen, where he found Marco talking to Signora Maria, the cook. Marco came over to Brunetti. 'Do you want to eat?' he asked.

This was one of the best restaurants in the city, and Signora Maria was a woman whose genius had provided Brunetti with endless pleasure. 'Thanks, Marco, but I had lunch at home,' he said. He took Marco by the arm and pulled him away from the disappointment in Maria's eyes and out of the way of a waiter who scrambled past, a loaded tray held at shoulder height. They stood just inside the door to the storeroom that held clean linens and cans of tomatoes. (*Wilful Behaviour*, ch. 18)

Meals are not only occasions for work, but also serve Brunetti as an escape from the criminal world. In *Uniform Justice*, the Moro boy has been found hanged at the military academy, and Brunetti's particular despair at the harm or death of children has resurfaced. His mind turns to the *riva* and its wealth of restaurants that can offer him solace, a treat of gorgeous food and fine champagne to escape his fears and steep him in love with the woman who provides him with another kind of solace – the comma after 'bed' no accident.

On an impulse, he called Paola and asked her if she felt like going out to dinner. She hesitated not an instant, said only that she'd have to prepare something for the kids and would meet him wherever he chose. (. . .)

'Oh my,' she answered. 'What brings this on?'

'I need a treat,' he said.

'Maria's cooking?' she asked.

'Your company,' he answered. 'I'll meet you there at eight.'

Almost three hours later, a lobster-filled Brunetti and his champagne-filled consort climbed the stairs to their apartment, his steps slowed by satisfying fullness, hers by the grappa she'd drunk after dinner. Their arms linked, they were looking forward to bed, and then to sleep. (*Uniform Justice*, ch. 19)

In *Through a Glass, Darkly*, to flee the social demands of a Murano art gallery opening, Brunetti even uses his local restaurant as the ultimate salvation. Putting down his flute of prosecco and, like Paola, hesitating not an instant, he resorts to the one option he knows always works – the artful lie:

He put his arm around Paola's shoulder and said, 'I'm afraid I've got to drag us away, though.' He looked at his watch. 'We've got to meet people for dinner, and we're already late.'

Paola, no slouch as a liar, looked at her watch and gasped, 'Oh my God, Guido. We *are* late. And we've got to get to Saraceno.' She reached into her bag, searching for something, finally abandoned the search, and asked Brunetti, 'I forgot my *telefonino*. Can you call Silvio and Veronica and tell them we'll be late?'

'Of course,' Brunetti said smoothly, though Paola had never had a *telefonino*, and none of their friends were called Silvio. 'I'll do it from outside. The reception will be better.' (*Through a Glass, Darkly*, ch. 4)

Sometimes even Brunetti's neighbourhood, vulnerable to the economic predations steadily altering Venice, can unexpectedly fail him. Stuck with a mysterious case in *Doctored*

Evidence that seems further than ever from any sane solution, he's spent a sleepless night fretting over a corpse beaten to death, a Romanian maid fleeing the scene, and no clues. Not far from his apartment he stops randomly at one of his local bars, desperate for a second coffee and a much-needed brioche in hopes of revival. But things have changed.

As he walked towards Rialto, he decided to have another coffee at the bar on the next corner. (. . .) He went to the counter and asked for a coffee and a brioche. He paid no real attention to the familiar sound of the coffee machine, the thud and the hiss, nor to the sound of the cup being set in front of him. But when he looked up, he saw that the woman who had been serving him coffee for decades was gone; that, or she had been transformed into a Chinese woman half her age. He looked at the cash register, and there was another Chinese, this one a man, standing behind it.

He had seen this happening for months, this gradual taking over of the bars of the city by Chinese owners and workers, but this was the first time it had occurred in one of the places he frequented. (. . .) He walked over to the plastic case but saw that the brioche were different from the fresh ones with *mirtillo* he had eaten for years; the tag on the case explained that they were manufactured and frozen in Milano. He finished his coffee, paid, and left. (*Doctored Evidence*, ch. 19)

$$\longrightarrow$$

Brunetti is not the only one who futilely seeks respite after visiting a depressing crime scene. He and Vianello, already sickened by the Lorenzoni boy's gruesome death in *Noble Radiance*, find another family member in the *palazzo* murdered by a shotgun blast. Their departure from one of the many bars that punctuate the novels leaves them with little taste for food, or even for conversation.

*Traghetto &
gondola landing
(12)*

Together they left the bar, neither of them bothering to answer the barman's farewell. (. . .) The *traghetto* had stopped running at seven, thus leaving Brunetti no choice but to cross the bridge and then walk back up the other side of the Grand Canal towards his home.

The sight of Maurizio's body and the terrible evidence of the manner of his death that spread out on the wall behind him followed Brunetti down the *calle*. *(A Noble Radiance*, ch. 23)

In nearly every novel Brunetti battles the city's diffuse forms of transportation, each one with its own quirks and problems. Ever alert to the petty crimes of his fellow citizens, he observes the unsuspecting boat passengers and the traps laid for them by the clever masters of the canals.

How he wished there were some other way he could get to work, some means to avoid being trapped in the narrow zigs and zags of Ruga Rialto. He (. . .) walked down to the Canal Grande. As he emerged from the underpass, a *traghetto* pulled up to the *Riva.* (. . .)

When there were thirteen people, one of them with a sodden German Shepherd, standing in the gondola, all trying to huddle under the umbrellas spread above their heads in an almost unbroken shield, the *gondolieri* shoved off and took them quickly to the other side. (. . .)

It occurred to Brunetti that he had just witnessed a series of crimes. The number of people in the boat had exceeded the legal limit. There was probably a law stating that umbrellas had to be furled while they crossed the canal, but he wasn't sure and so let that one go. The dog had worn no muzzle and wasn't on a leash. Two people speaking German had been given change only when they asked for it. (*Uniform Justice*, ch. 20)

→

Rio terrà San Silvestro **(13)** to Campo Sant'Aponal **(14)**

One of the welcome markers on Brunetti's walk to his apartment is the small Campo San Aponal with its plain brick Gothic church (now deconsecrated). Had the Correr Museum not removed the sculpture from the base of the campanile, Brunetti might have delighted in a daily vision of Venice's earliest example of the symbol of Saint Mark, surely the world's only literate lion, paw firmly planted on his book. In *The Death of Faith*, after a restorative stop at Do Mori's for 'a piece of prosciutto wrapped around a thin breadstick and a glass of Chardonnay', he heads 'up toward San Aponal and home'.

But the *campo*, with its café and restaurant, is also a familiar place he can use for meetings in the pursuit of crime. In *Acqua Alta* the urgency of finding the young American archaeologist in time allows no confusion about where or how to meet.

He looked out of the window; it was fully dark and the rain continued as before. 'I'll meet you at Campo San Aponal. As soon as you can get there. And, Vianello,' he added, 'don't wear your uniform coat.' The only response to this was a deep laugh, and then Vianello was gone. (*Acqua Alta*, ch. 23)

→

The imperiousness of the Venetians has never been in doubt, nor their sense of always knowing the best way to do anything and the only place to do it. To buy *fritelle* during Carnival season at the 'wrong' bakery is to court immediate comment – one should have known better. The initial haughtiness with which the Doges and citizens of Venice met the Crusaders in 1202, who came in vain to beg for passage to the Holy Land, has been transmitted down the ages to the taxi drivers, gondoliers, and especially waiters today. The esteemed Ristorante Antiche Carampane (**D**),* (despite its name derived from the former red light district), where Brunetti indulges in a rare costly expense account lunch, sometimes posts a hand-scribbled sign outside their door, warning the unwary that only serious eaters need enter: 'No Lasagne – No Pizza – No Menu Turistico!'

Through Sottoportego and Calle Albrizzi Salviati **(15)**, right to Rio terrà Carampane **(16)**

Paola had given him Padovani's number that morning and told him that the journalist was planning to go back to Rome the following day. Knowing that the lunch could go on his expense account as 'interviewing a witness', Brunetti called Padovani and invited him to lunch at Galleggiante

[Carampane], a restaurant Brunetti liked but could seldom afford. (. . .)

Padovani was waiting inside the restaurant when Brunetti got there. The journalist stood between the bar and the glass case filled with various antipasti: periwinkles, cuttlefish, shrimp. They shook hands briefly and were shown to their table by Signora Antonia, the Junoesque waitress who reigned supreme here. Once seated, they delayed the discussion of crime and gossip while they consulted with Signora Antonia about lunch. Though a written menu did exist, few regular clients ever bothered with it; most had never seen it. The day's selections and specialties were listed in Antonia's head. She quickly ran through the list, though Brunetti knew that this was the merest of formalities. She quickly decided that what they wanted to eat was the antipasto di mare, the risotto with shrimp, and the grilled branzino, which she assured them had come fresh that morning from the fish market. (. . .) and said they wanted a bottle of the house white wine, which she went to get. (*Death at La Fenice*, chs 19 & 20)

→

Back to Campo Sant'Aponal to Biancat on right **(17)**
In a city of stone on an island surrounded by water like Venice, the sight of greenery, trees and flowers is a much rarer delight than in towns surrounded by landscape. So it is not only the bloom of seasons in window boxes and court-yards that Brunetti appreciates, but also the exotic flowers he faces on every walk home past the florist Biancat **(17)**.

Spring advanced, and Brunetti continued to measure it florally. The first lilacs appeared in the flower shops, and he took an enormous bouquet home to Paola; the little pink and yellow flowers made their full appearance in the garden across the canal, were succeeded by random daffodils, and then by ordered rows of tulips at the side of the path bordering the garden. (. . .)

Then there was Palm Sunday, which he was aware of only when he saw people walking around with olive branches in their hands. And then Easter and explosions of flowers in the windows of Biancat, displays so excessive that Brunetti was forced to stop every evening on the way home from work to consider them. *(Through A Glass, Darkly*, ch. 4)

Any journey far from the city centre increases the joy Brunetti feels when he sees Biancat as he nears home: to leave Venice makes his homecoming even more poignant. In *Death in a Strange Country*, Brunetti must leave his native city to travel to Vicenza's American military base, so radically different from anything he knows in Italy.

Stunned by the foreignness of this alien world, Brunetti pauses on his walk home to view Biancat's latest offerings, which are a welcome reminder of his good fortune to live surrounded by such elegant beauty. The pause also serves as a chance for Brunetti to chat with his neighbour, the orchid specialist, and ponder the strangeness of his own profession. If the flowers function as further indicators of his mood, so do the stairs he must climb to deliver his bounty of irises.

In front of Biancat, he stopped to study the flowers in the window. Signor Biancat saw him through the immense glass window, smiled and nodded, so Brunetti went inside and asked for ten blue irises. As he wrapped them, Biancat talked about Thailand, from which he had just returned after a week-long conference of orchid breeders and growers. It seemed to Brunetti a strange way to spend a week, but then he reflected that he had, in the past, gone to both Dallas and Los Angeles for police seminars. Who was he to say that it was stranger to spend a week talking about orchids than about the incidence of sodomy among serial killers or the various objects used in rapes? *(Death in a Strange Country*, ch. 9)

→

The first arrival of Brunetti at his apartment **(19)** in *Death at La Fenice* sets the pattern of the books to follow. His arduous climb, the remembered illegality of the place, the scent that meets him at the opening of his door, followed by the smells from the kitchen – all embrace him in a welcome escape from a life spent with the criminal world. But nothing sets the tone to be explored in Donna Leon's later novels like

Biancat left on Calle del Forno **(18)** to end **(19)**

this very first appearance of Paola, followed by Brunetti's ironic and loving though mute response. But now it is apt that they be left to their private meeting.

He let himself into the *palazzo* in which he lived, bracing himself, as he always had to do when he was tired, for the task of climbing the ninety-four steps to their fourth-floor apartment. The previous owner had built the apartment illegally more than thirty years before, simply added another floor to the existing building without bothering with official permission of any sort. This situation had somehow been obscured when Brunetti bought the apartment ten years ago, and ever since, he had lived in recurrent fear of being confronted with a summons to legalize the obvious. He trembled at the prospect of the Herculean task of getting the permits that would authenticate both that the apartment existed and that he had a right to live there. The mere fact that the walls were there and he lived within them would hardly be thought relevant. The bribes would be ruinous.

He opened the door, glad of the warmth and smell he associated with the apartment: lavender, wax, the scent of something cooking in the kitchen at the back; it was a mixture that represented to him, in a way he couldn't explain, the existence of sanity in the daily madness that was his work.

'Is that you, Guido?' Paolo called from the living room. He wondered who else she might be expecting at two in the morning, but he didn't ask. (*Death at La Fenice*, ch. 5)

*La Baita, Piero's cheese shop, is the perfect example of the Venetians' insistence on patronizing select places. Even with no sign, the locals know where to go.

*Osteria Sora al Ponte wine bar sits on a small bridge facing the end of Rialto market, making it a convenient and local place for *cicheti* and *un' ombra*.

*Do Mori, one of the oldest *bacari* still operating in Venice, draws large crowds to its stand-up bar. Abundant *cicheti* and large selection of wines by the glass – no sit-down area.

*Antico Dolo, another old city establishment, offers a small but select range of *cicheti*, and then offers dinner to follow.

*Grand Canal restaurants on the Riva del Vin offer extensive selections of fresh seafood from the Rialto fish market. Most recently, Brunetti has been patronizing Canal Grande and Caffè Saraceno, despite its name, a full-scale restaurant.

*Ristotante Antiche Carampane's exacting standards means it stays close to traditional Venetian food.

WALK 3 : *Brunetti's Neighbourhood*

Brunetti Apartment—Canal Grande—San Polo—Santa Croce

1 hour

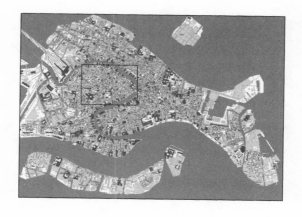

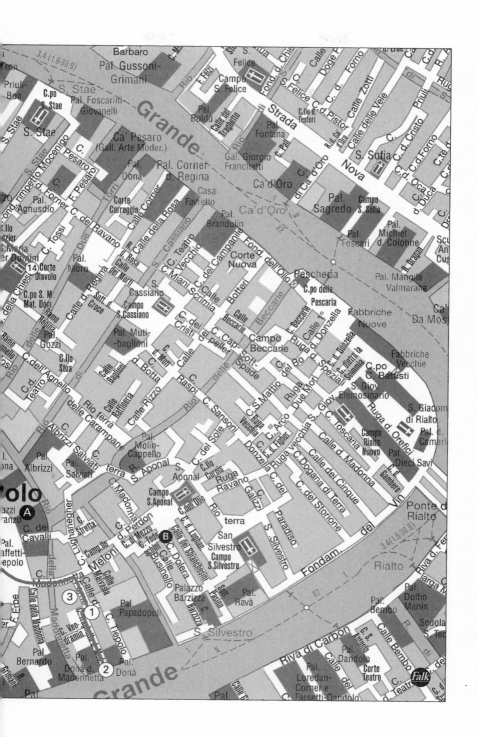

W alk 3 focuses on only a very small section of the
well-trod *sestiere* of San Polo before venturing west
into less familiar Santa Croce. San Polo's eastern side was
once the ancient centre of the city; its commercial throb is
still felt at the nearby Rialto stalls, while the quieter western
section, on the opposite side of the *rio* that bisects the
region, is dominated by the great Franciscan church of the
Frari. The area immediately around Campo San Polo, its
church bells giving Brunetti's days a rhythm, serves as the
centre of his world – his family home and neighbourhood.
From his apartment, with the entrancing views visible only
to the Brunettis, a short walk down Calle Traghetto della
Madonnetta offers a fair vantage point to stop and muse as
Brunetti does so often, facing the Grand Canal while waiting
for a boat and to get a glimpse of his top-floor apartment.

Brunetti apart-
ment **(1)**

As in so much of low-lying Venice bordered by canals,
weather takes on menacing dimensions in San Polo, especially in *Acqua Alta*, when Brunetti is reunited with the
two women he first met in *Death at La Fenice*: archaeologist Brett Lynch and soprano Flavia Petrelli. Certainly the
importance of property occupies Brunetti, as he fears for
his own apartment's legality, and wanders into isolated areas
to find both unkempt, squalid buildings and unexpected
beauties.

* * *

In Brunetti's initial approach to his family apartment in *Death
at La Fenice*, he already alludes to the alarming lack of docu-
ments for his home **(1)**. Nearly ten years later in *Friends in
High Places*, the worst happens! He becomes a victim of a
governmental office's attempt to regularize all the illegal struc-
tures in the city, hopeless though that attempt is sure to
prove. When a building inspector arrives to tell Brunetti his

apartment doesn't exist, the Commissario departs from his usual calm control:

'What?' Brunetti cried before he could stop himself. He could hear the outrage in his voice but made no attempt to modify it. 'What do you mean, it doesn't exist?'

Rossi leaned back in his chair as if to remove himself from the immediate orbit of Brunetti's anger. He looked as if he found it puzzling to have someone react strongly to his having called into question the very existence of a perceived reality. When he saw that Brunetti had no violent intention, he relaxed minimally, adjusted the papers on his lap, and said, 'I mean that it doesn't exist for us, Signor Brunetti.'

'And what does that mean, not for you?' Brunetti asked.

'It means there are no records of it in our office. No requests for building permits, no plans, no final approval of the work that was done. In short, there exists no documentary evidence that this apartment was ever built.' Before Brunetti could speak, Rossi added, placing his hand upon the file Brunetti had given him, 'And, unfortunately, you can't provide us with any.' (*Friends in High Places*, ch. 2)

→

Left on to Calle Traghetto della Madonnetta **(2)** to Canal Grande

Conspiring with Paola provides no solution. Frustrated, they stand on their terrace and survey the captivating beauty of their imperilled view out over the Grand Canal and ponder how many of the city's buildings have been condoned long after their illegal alterations. The brief walk down Calle Traghetto d. Madonnetta and out on to the end of the wooden platform perhaps makes understandable their seduction by all that lay before them!

When they were standing side by side, the city lying stretched out before them, she waved at rooftops, terraces, gardens, skylights. 'I'd like to know how much of that is legal,' she said. 'And I'd like to know how much of it has the right permits and has received the *condono*.' . . .

'We should have made sure he [the owner] had them before we bought it,' Brunetti attempted to reason. 'But we didn't. All we had to do was see that –' he said, sweeping his hand in an arc that encompassed all that lay before them – 'and we were lost.' (*Friends in High Places*, ch. 3)

The Donna Leon novels penetrate deeply into the immediate orbit of Brunetti's family life: problems with growing children, domestic tensions, stress at work, the joys of meals, games, conversation, kisses. In all these scenes the apartment serves as a litmus test of the family members' states of mind – who goes where, when, alone or in company, signals the tenor of their relationships. Paola's political harangues at the table, Brunetti's lectures in the kitchen, are staples of family exchange, but the terrace, at least, seems to offer neutral territory.

This was the best time of day for Brunetti, for he could see, from their terrace, the sunset off in the West. On the clearest of days, he could see the Dolomites from the small window in the kitchen, but it was so late in the day now that they would be hazed over and invisible. He stayed where he was, forearms propped on the railing, studying the rooftops and towers that never ceased to please him. He heard Paola move down the hall, back into the kitchen, heard the clang of shifted pots, but he stayed where he was, listening to the eight o'clock bells ring out from San Polo, then to the answering resonance of San Marco, a few seconds late, as always, come booming across the city. When all the bells were silent, he went back into the house, closing the door against the growing evening chill. (*Death in a Strange Country*, ch. 12)

The tranquillity of his terrace and the comfort of his home are rarely needed more than after Brunetti's trip to the US Army base at Vicenza, a mere one-hour journey that creates little besides bewildering cultural confusion. Backed by the Dolomite mountains, its city squares dominated by Palladian architectural magnificence, Vicenza is also home to a community of Americans who have transported their own world to this unlikely spot. Burger Kings, Taco Bells and bowling alleys rest beside commissaries full of white sliced Wonder bread and frozen American pizza, all flown into Italy. The Army BX offers giant coffee urns for the office and smaller twelve-cup pots for home, so the drink need be made only once a day to be heated up in the ubiquitous microwaves.

Returned to Venice, the sound of the ever-present church bells may have soothed his mood, but Brunetti still struggles to make sense of the foreign place he has just visited to investigate why a young sergeant's body was found floating face down in a canal:

'How was Vicenza?' she asked.

'Better to ask me how was America.'

'Yes, I know,' she said. 'It's incredible, isn't it?' (. . .)

'It was very clean, and everyone smiled a great deal.'

'Good,' she said, stirring again. 'Then it hasn't changed.'

'I wonder why it is, that they always smile so much.' He had noticed the same thing, each time he was in America.

She turned away from the risotto and stared at him. 'Why shouldn't they smile, Guido? Think about it. They're the richest people in the world. Everyone has to defer to them in politics, and they have convinced themselves, somehow, that everything they have ever done in their very brief history has been done for no purpose other than to further the general good of mankind. Why shouldn't they smile? (*Strange Country*, ch. 12)

The apartment's sunny views and the peace of the early morning quiet usually help to stave off the two things Brunetti must face when getting up: Paola's complaints over the early newspapers and the memories of what awaits him at the Questura. Yet in *Uniform Justice* even a welcome solitude in wonderful weather can do little but remind him of the loss of young life:

The next morning, he woke to ignorance. The rays of the sun, reflected off the same mirror and on to his face, pulled him from sleep, and in the first moments of waking, he had no memory of the events of the previous day. (. . .) he turned his head to the left and saw the bell tower of San Polo, the sunlight so clear upon it that he could make out the grey blobs of cement that held the bricks together. A pigeon glided towards the eaves under the tower roof, spread its wings to reduce speed, and then set itself down in a soft-footed landing. It turned around twice, bobbed about a bit, and then tucked its head under one wing.

Nothing the bird did was reminiscent of the events of the previous day, but as its head disappeared under its wing, Brunetti had a sharp vision of Ernesto Moro's face at the moment that Vianello pulled the hem of his cape across it. (*Uniform Justice*, ch. 10)

Just as his usual walks back from the Questura across the Rialto to reach his home fill Brunetti's mind with thoughts far from the violence he leaves behind, the varied boat trips to and from his apartment offer him opportunities for reflections on history, tourists, language, the frustration of travel, and the rewards of living in a city floating on water. Throughout the series of novels, Brunetti repeatedly finds himself standing on the small, empty landing parallel to Calle Traghetto della Madonnetta that extends from Calle Tiepolo out into the Grand Canal, surrounded by beauty. Either at dawn, awaiting an early launch from the Questura to arrive, or a late night arrival after too much blood and too much crime, he traverses this lonely alleyway that connects him with home and safety, his head filled with images. No passage in the novels surpasses the one in *Death in a Strange Country* when he is reminded of, not just the city's glorious past, but his own unique place in it.

'Would you mind taking me up to San Silvestro?' he asked.

'I'll take you right to the end of the *calle* if you'd like, sir.'

'Thanks, Monetti. I would.' (. . .)

It would have been easy for Brunetti to grow indifferent to the beauty of the city, to walk in the midst of it, looking and not really seeing. But then it always happened: a window he had never noticed before would swim into his ken, or the sun would gleam in an archway, and he would actually feel his heart tighten in response to something infinitely more complex than beauty. He supposed, when he bothered to think about it, that it had something to do with language, with the fact that there were fewer than eighty thousand people who lived in the city, and perhaps with the fact that he had gone to kindergarten in a fifteenth-century *palazzo*. He missed this city when he was away from it, much in the same way he missed Paola, and he felt complete and whole only while he was here. One glance around him, as they sped up the canal, was proof of the wisdom of all of this. He had never spoken of this to anyone. No foreigner would understand; any Venetian would find it redundant. *(Death in a Strange Country*, ch. 5)

Once off the boat, he must walk down this tiny, silent *calle* to reach home, his legs resisting the long climb upstairs, leaving him far too exhausted from confronting violence and death to muse on beauty.

Brunetti walked up the *calle*, legs tired with all the jumping on and off boats that he seemed to have been doing all day, since the first boat had picked him up here more than twelve hours ago. He opened the enormous door into the building and closed it quietly behind him. The narrow stairway that hairpinned its way up to the top of the building served as a perfect trumpet of sound, and they could, even four floors above, hear it whenever it slammed. Four floors. The thought burdened him. (ch. 5)

Medieval Venice's unique preservation – palaces wrapped in marble, churches stuffed with artistic masterpieces that the charitable *scuole* painted on every surface – leaves even natives marvelling at her longevity. Unlike anywhere else on the planet, Venice offers an occasion to wander in still living history: never more so than in the quiet dawn hours before modern footsteps and boats alter the peace and change the views:

When he turned into the *calle* that led to the canal, the silence told him that the boat had not arrived. (. . .) Occupied with these thoughts, he reached the edge of the canal and looked to the right. And saw what he had seen only in photos taken in the early part of the last century: the mirror-smooth waters of the Grand Canal. Not a ripple stirred the surface, no boats passed, not a puff of wind, no gulls paddled around. He stood transfixed and looked on what his ancestors had seen: the same light, the same façades, the same windows and plants, and the same vital silence. And, as far as he could distinguish the reflections, it all existed in double. (*Through a Glass, Darkly*, ch. 14)

After dawn and until midnight, the peace is broken all over the city by the noisy intrusion of the modern world. Brunetti, too much of a realist to deny the sweeping changes, admits that Venice's legendary greed has remained safely intact.

Brunetti often wondered what it must have been like to live in the days of the Most Serene Republic, to have made this grand passage by means of the power of oars alone, to move in silence without motors or horns, a silence broken by nothing more than the shouted '*Ouie*' of boatmen and the slip of oars. So much had changed: today's merchants kept in touch with one another with the odious '*telefonini*', not by means of slant-rigged galleons. (. . .) The one thing that the ages had left unchanged was the city's thousand-year-old heritage of venality, and Brunetti always felt uncomfortable at his inability to decide whether he thought this good or bad. (*The Death of Faith*, ch. 3)

Just as Brunetti makes a game out of discovering a new statue or marble piece in his daily wanderings, he tries to reward himself whenever he is forced into taking the most crowded vaporetti in the city. From the crown of the Rialto Bridge, he can easily see the number 82 stop across the canal and can gauge the number of people he must face, although he can do little about the buzz of noise and the bags of belongings. Still, even a slight glimpse from the boat of the terrace of his apartment he has just left will brighten his spirits.

(. . .) he saw a number eighty-two pulling up to the *embarcadero* on his right and, without thinking, ran to get it, which he managed to do just as it was starting to pull away from the dock and out into the centre of the Grand Canal. He moved to the right side of the boat but stayed outside on the deck, glad of the breeze and the light that danced up from the water. He watched Calle Tiepolo approaching on the right side and peered up the narrow *calle*, searching for the railing of his terrace, but they were past it too quickly for him to see it, and so he turned his attention back to the canal. (*The Death of Faith*, ch. 3)

→

Back to apartment **(1)** Calle del Forno **(3)**, left into Campo San Polo **(4)**

Given the incomprehensible layout of Venice, when at home, residents rely on the *Calli, Campielli, e Canali* guide to navigate the centuries-old address scheme that attempts to bring some clarity – if not order – to the various *sestieri* and their labyrinthine streets. Brunetti is no exception.

While location is never inconsequential for Venetians, in *Blood from a Stone* it is crucial. Searching for evidence of the hidden residences of the African bag sellers, hoping for clues to solve the seemingly pointless murder of one of them on the city streets, Brunetti begins with landlords. One is his San Polo neighbour who owns a second property in distant Castello – contract unregistered, thus rent untaxed.

Cuzzoni, then. He lived in San Polo, at an address only a few numbers distant from Brunetti's, owned the apartment where he lived and a house in Castello, though no contract was on file at the Ufficio delle Entrate to indicate that the house was being rented.

How convenient, that the city offices never bothered with even the most simple cross-check. If no rental contract was on file, then there was no reason to believe that the owner was being paid rent, and who could be expected to pay tax if an apartment was empty? (. . .)

He pulled down his copy of *Calli, Campielli, e Canali* and looked for Cuzzoni's address: he found it on the other side of Rio dei Meloni, literally the building next but one to his own (. . .) Using the same book, he checked the address of the house Cuzzoni owned. It was a high number in Castello, a location that was, for many Venetians, as far away as Milano. (*Blood from a Stone*, ch. 10)

Brunetti's search for the suspicious landlord reveals to him again how deceptive are properties in Venice and how vulnerable the residents to all forms of water.

'Brunetti, Guido,' he said and followed Cuzzoni into the apartment. The first thing he noticed was a tremendous water stain on the back wall of the entrance hall and an equally dark circle on the ceiling above it. His eyes followed it down to the floor, where he saw strips of parquet lying about in concave ruin.

'My God. What happened?' he couldn't stop himself from asking.

Cuzzoni looked at the wreckage of ceiling, wall, and floor and quickly away, as if to spare himself a painful experience. He raised a finger to the centre of the ravished ceiling. 'It happened four days ago. The woman upstairs put a wash in her washing machine and went out to Rialto. The tube that's supposed to drain the water came loose, so the entire cycle ended up coming down my wall. I had already gone to work, and she was out all morning.'

'Oh, I'm sorry,' Brunetti said. 'Water. Nothing's worse.'

Cuzzoni shrugged and tried to smile, but it was obvious that his heart was not in it. 'Luckily – for her, at least – the building's all lopsided, so the water ran towards the wall and came down here. She didn't have much damage at all.'

As the other man spoke, Brunetti studied the far wall, where he thought he saw rectangles of darker paint. The other walls held paintings and, ominously, prints and drawings, one of which might have been a Marieschi. 'What was on the wall?' he finally asked.

Cuzzoni took a deep sigh. 'The title page of the *Carceri*.

The first impression, and with a signature added that was probably his. And a small Holbein drawing.' (*Blood*, ch. 10)

Brunetti's walks from his modest *calle* into the largest square in Venice after Piazza San Marco, Campo San Polo **(4)**, steep him in a richer, more historic atmosphere. Had the Commissario lived in earlier centuries he might have been implored to quell the violence surrounding the frequent bull and bear baitings. Today, Campo San Polo is filled with trees and locals sunning in cafés while their children exhaust themselves in a space large enough for serious games and bicycle races. Only during film festivals, when the *campo* hosts an outdoor cinema, does the scene again become frenetic.

Since the exalted and wealthy also commit crimes, Commissario Brunetti conducts much of his investigative work in stunning *palazzi*, though the interiors are sometimes different from the façades, a difference often evident in the people he must interview. In *Fatal Remedies*, when Brunetti tries to locate a lawyer's office, nothing prepares him for the contrast between glamorous exterior and the barren room he finally enters – further evidence that things are rarely as they appear in Venice. Facing the largest wellhead in the city, the late Gothic Palazzo Soranzo **(A)** still boasts Byzantine adornments from the 1300s, and, in Brunetti's Venice, the offices of Avvocato Zambino.

He walked quickly along Rughetta [die Meloni], past his own *calle*, through the underpass, and out into the *campo*. The leaves had long since fallen from the trees, so the broad expanse seemed curiously naked and exposed.

The lawyer's office was on the first floor of Palazzo Soranzo, and when he arrived Brunetti was surprised to have the door opened by Zambino himself. (*Fatal Remedies*, ch. 17)

Besides the air of superiority of those born in Venice, there is a belief still in evidence that other areas of Italy, other accents, are somehow suspect – and usually inferior. Socializing with their Venetian neighbours on the *piano nobile* of a *palazzo* like Soranzo with grand views seems perfectly normal for the Brunettis, despite Paola's recent arrest by the Questura staff in *Fatal Remedies*. They are Venetians, after all, so dinner comes before criminal investigation.

Together, they left the apartment and headed down towards San Polo. They crossed the *campo*, went over a bridge, and turned into a narrow *calle* on the right. Just beyond it, they walked right and rang the Morosinis' bell. The door snapped open almost instantly and they ascended to the *piano nobile*, where Giovanni Morosini stood at the open door to their apartment, the sound of voices flowing out and down the steps from behind him.

A large man, Morosini still wore the beard he'd first grown as a student caught up in the violent protests of sixty-eight. It had turned grey and grizzled with the passing of the years, and he often joked that the same thing had happened to his ideals and principles.

(. . .)

Clara's voice called out from behind them, '*A tavola, a tavola, ragazzi*' and Giovanni led them into the next room, where a long oval table stood parallel to a bank of tall windows that looked across at the buildings on the other side of the *campo*. (*Fatal Remedies*, ch. 18)

This sort of social harmony and acceptance does not, however, extend to new neighbours from the South – like Signor La Capra in *Acqua Alta*. Nor does his prestigious address on the Grand Canal, near Campo San Polo, impress Brunetti, who suspects him, first of the theft of antiquities, and second of murdering director Semenzato of the Palazzo Ducale.

For a moment, he had to stop himself and accept the fact that Signor La Capra might well be no more than what he appeared to be: a man of wealth who had bought and restored a *palazzo* on the Grand Canal. (. . .)

The *palazzo* stood at the end of Calle Dolera, a small street that dead-ended into the Grand Canal. As he approached, Brunetti could see the sure signs of newness. The exterior layer of *intonaco* plastered over the bricks from which the walls were contructed was still virgin and free of graffiti. Only near the bottom did it show the first signs of wear: the recent *acqua alta* had left its mark at about the height of Brunetti's knee, lightening the dull orange of the plaster, some of which had already begun to crumble away and now lay kicked or swept to the side of the narrow calle. (. . .)

The nameplate by the single bell was taste itself: a simple italic script with only the name, 'La Capra'. (. . .)

He found himself in a large courtyard with a circular well in the centre. Off to the left, marble pillars supported a flight of steps that led up to the first floor of the building that enclosed the courtyard on all sides. At the top, the stairs turned back upon themselves, still hugging the exterior wall of the building, and climbed to the second and then the third floor. The carved heads of stone lions stood at equal distances on the marble banister that ran along the stairs. Tucked below the stairs were the signs of recent work: a wheelbarrow filled with paper bags of cement, a roll of heavy-duty plastic sheeting and large tins dripping colours of paint down their sides. (*Acqua Alta*, ch. 19)

Weather plays an important role in all the Brunetti novels, as it does in pedestrian Venice, where a boat is rarely available at the front door. But it is during *acqua alta* that the city's unique geography becomes most evident and most challenging. The full moon, the warm winds of the *scirocco* up from North Africa, the freezing *bora* down from Trieste, all conspire to create the high waters that make so much of the city nearly impassable. Certainly no accommodation is made to the urgencies of crime. In Donna Leon's fifth novel *Acqua Alta*, the struggle to save Brett Lynch, abducted to San Polo by two of La Capra's thugs, is made maddeningly difficult by high waters. Even the *passarelle*, the high platforms placed in the lowest parts of Venice to aid passage, seem in scarce supply.

On the other side, the two men tried to turn left, but the water had risen too high alongside the Grand Canal, so they had to continue down through the market, empty now of all except the most hardy. They turned left, climbed up on to the wooden boards that had been set on their metal risers, and continued down towards San Polo. (. . .) The one in front of her turned left, stepping off the boards into the water below, and down towards the Grand Canal. She recognized it, Calle Dolera **(B)** (. . .). In water that was now well above their ankles, they stopped in front of a large wooden door. (*Acqua Alta*, ch. 21)

Struggling in boots and against lashing winds, Brunetti and Flavia try to reach the La Capra *palazzo*, with, they fear, too little time to save Brett. The agonizing slowing of their pace by the numbing necessity to drag their feet underwater as they try to run only increases the tension.

When Brunetti and Flavia reached the bottom of the steps, they saw that the water had risen even higher, and from beyond the door came the roar of the rain as it bucketed down.

They picked up the umbrellas and stepped out under the rain, water reaching up towards the tops of their boots. Few people were out, so they got quickly to Rialto, where the water was even deeper. Had it not been for the wooden walkways on their iron stanchions, the water would have flooded into their boots and made progress impossible. On the other side of the bridge, they descended again into the water and turned down towards San Polo, both of them now soaked and exhausted with forcing their way through the rising floods. (ch. 23)

→

None of the pleasures of his San Polo neighbourhood will be available as Commissario Brunetti enters the most western of the *sestieri* of Venice, Santa Croce. Instead of romantic musings over the view from his terrace or dinners in *palazzi*, Brunetti will find himself, in *Wilful Behaviour*, trapped in a tiny, fetid apartment reeking of stale cigarettes, surrounded by a priceless art collection. Reluctantly entangled in a familial

Calle Bernardo **(5)** to Campo San Boldo **(6)**

nightmare where none of the usual relationships apply, he must investigate the inexplicable stabbing of a young woman.

Brunetti knew that the address in Santa Croce had to be somewhere near San Giacomo dell'Orio. (. . .) From there, instinct took over and he soon entered Campo San Boldo. In the *campo* he saw that the numbers were close to the one he was looking for, so he stopped in a *tabacchaio* and asked for directions. (. . .)

He did as he was told and saw, beside the second door on the left, the name 'Jacobs'. (. . .)

The door snapped open and he went in. The floor of the entrance hall was green with mould, lit only by a dim bulb in a filthy glass case. He started up the stairs, the green of the mould growing lighter as he rose. At the first landing there was another bulb, no brighter, which dimly illuminated the octagonal marble medallions that patterned the floor. A single door, a thick metal *porta blindata*, stood open to his left and just inside it was a tall, painfully stooped woman (. . .) Brunetti closed the door and followed her. (. . .) Looking around him, he stopped dead, assaulted by the beauty he saw spread around him as if by a profligate hand.

The walls on either side of the corridor were crowded with rows of paintings and drawings, lined up shoulder to shoulder like people waiting for a bus. *(Wilful Behaviour,* ch. 11)

Signora Jacobs' apartment sits appropriately in hidden away Campo San Boldo. Cramped by high-walled buildings with only a tiny canal for relief, it turns its back on the expansiveness of nearby Campo San Giacomo dell'Orio **(8)** in studied isolation.

$$\rightarrow$$

Calle del Tintor **(7)** to Campo San Giacomo dell'Orio **(8)**

Some legends claim Campo San Giacomo dell'Orio got its name from the laurel tree, and today's leafy space with a dozen sheltering trees and ample benches makes this sound true. Ringed with cafés, and one of the city's rare good pizzerias, the square offers a welcome escape from Campo San

Boldo's silent austerity. Even the church with its unpainted and irregular shape seems modest from the outside, denying the wealth of artwork housed inside. Although this *campo* punctuates a main passage through Santa Croce, whenever business sends Brunetti to Campo San Giacomo dell'Orio, he effortlessly resists the temptation either to enter the church or to linger.

$$\longrightarrow$$

As Brunetti and Vianello go in search of the former priest Don Alvise, their route from the Grand Canal passes through two streets that seem to mirror the old man's vision: narrow *calli* that demand a neighbourly closeness; cramped private houses encouraging contact; working-class cafés filled with easygoing mixed populations. Brunetti and Vianello comment on how aptly titled the streets are to surround the house of a man with such universal sympathies.

Calle Larga **(9)** left on Ramo Megio **(10)** on to Fondaco dei Turchi **(11)**

'Calle dei Preti,' the ever-observant Vianello read. 'Seems the right place for him to live.'

Brunetti, turning left at the end of the street and heading back towards the Grand Canal, said, 'Well, almost, except that we're on the Fontego dei Turchi **(11)**.'

'He probably helps them, too,' Vianello began, 'so it's probably just as good a name.'

Brunetti remembered the door, a heavy green *portone* with twin brass handles in the shape of lions' heads. He rang the bell and waited. When a voice from the answerphone asked who it was, he gave his name, and the door snapped open, allowing them to enter a long narrow courtyard with a capped well at one end, wooden doors lining both sides. Without hesitating, Brunetti went to the second door on the left, which was open. At the top of the first flight of steps was another open door, where a short, stooped figure stood waiting for them as they climbed to the top. (*Blood from a Stone*, ch. 8)

Since the former priest's surprisingly earthly and ecumenical attitude gives him easy and reliable access to the closed world of the *clandestini*, the two hope for help from the man driven out of his church because of his worldly political ideas.

Alvise Perale had for years been a parish priest in Oderzo, a small, torpid town north of Venice. In his time as *parroco* of the local church, he had dedicated his considerable energies not only to the spiritual well-being of his parishioners but also to the material well-being of the many people whom the currents of war, revolution, and poverty had washed up on the banks of the Livenza river. Among these people were Albanian prostitutes, Bosnian mechanics, Romanian gypsies, Kurdish shepherds, and African shopkeepers. To Don Alvise, regardless of their nationality or religion, they were all children of the god he worshipped and thus worthy of his care. (. . .)

As the boat made its way slowly up the Grand Canal, Brunetti explained to Vianello why he wanted to see the former priest. 'They trust him,' he said, 'and I know he helps find houses for a lot of *clandestini.*' (*Blood*, ch. 8)

→

Calle dei Preti into Campo San Zan Degolà (12)

One of the many convincing features of Brunetti's walks across Venice is the determined secularity in his attitudes to churches, saints, and relics. Although the lovely Church of San Zan Degolà (12) with its eleventh-century interior and ship's keel ceiling was closed for twenty years, its restoration and reopening shortly before Brunetti arrives in the *campo* in *Noble Radiance* fails to stimulate his interest. Instead, it offers him the unwelcome chance to consider his life spent surrounded by so many saints and their often bizarre legends, as he goes in search of a former girlfriend of the dead Lorenzoni boy. In a city so filled with relics and reminders of a medieval urge to an almost visceral piety, it is hard to escape their ghostly presence. San Giovanni Decollato is no exception, whether you call him by his biblical name or by the abbreviated Venetian version Degolà:

Soon he came out in Campo San Zan Degolà. To the best of Brunetti's knowledge, no one knew whether it was the decapitated body of San Giovanni or his missing head which was venerated in the church. It seemed to him to make little difference. (*A Noble Radiance*, ch. 7)

→

In fact, this portion of Santa Croce is a world distant enough for Signorina Elettra to check the city's official street guide for the address of a wealthy lawyer who rents to *vu cumprà*. His office sits in a strange neighbourhood, far from the city's commercial centre, in the remote Campo Santa Maria Mater Domini (14). However, being surrounded by houses from the fourteenth and fifteenth centuries and a rebuilt church first founded in 960 makes the lure of location understandable.

Campo San Zan Degolà to Calle del Tintor (13) to Campo Santa Maria Mater Domini (14)

'Is this his office?' Brunetti asked, looking at the address listed for Renato Bertolli and trying to calculate where it might be.

'Yes. I checked it in *Calli, Campielli e Canali*, and I think he's got to be just before the *fabbro*, the one who makes keys.' This was enough for Brunetti. He had been over there a few times, about five years ago, to have a metal banister made for the final flight of stairs leading to their apartment. He knew the area, though it seemed a strangely out of the way location for a lawyer's office. (*Blood from a Stone*, ch. 9)

With location ever on the minds of Venetians, and the social importance they attach to favoured *sestieri* undiminished, it is time to leave the Commissario as he ponders Signorina Elettra's admission that the whole idea of residential status in Venice is absurd: 'Pathetic, isn't it? Famous for living here? As if the city were contagious.'

Echoed by Brunetti's thoughts:

Brunetti had often reflected on this, finding it especially strange in foreigners, this belief that some cachet adhered to their address, as if living in Dorsoduro or having a *palazzo* on the Grand Canal could elevate the tone of their discourse or the quality of their minds, render the tedium of their lives interesting or transmute the dross of their amusements into purest gold.

If he thought about it, he felt happiness in being Venetian, not pride. He had not chosen where to be born or what dialect his parents spoke: what pride to be taken in those things? Not for the first time, he felt saddened by the vanity of human wishes. (*Blood from a Stone*, ch. 9)

WALK 4 : *Food and Faliers*

Santa Maria Mater Domini—San Polo—Santa
Margherita—Ca' Rezzonico—San Barnaba

1 hour

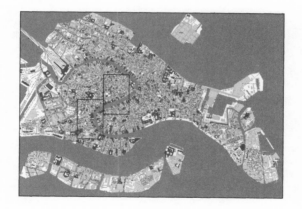

The walk from San Polo to San Barnaba is a favourite with the Brunettis in their, typically Venetian, quest for perfect food and wine, a quest made more difficult in a city not known for the excellence of its places to eat. Whether searching for cream-filled swan pastries, or the city's unarguably best bread, the Commissario counters the demands of crime with the pleasures of the palate. In all the books the necessity for public justice is balanced by the need for private joy. With less enthusiasm and only on special occasions, Brunetti also leaves his cosy home in San Polo to enter the grander world of his in-laws, the Faliers. Nevertheless, the Count and Countess continue throughout the series to play a key role in contributing to the happiness of their grandchildren, and in making available the rarefied world of the aristocratic rich, both through their social gatherings, as seen in the party they host in *Death at La Fenice*, and their access to the city's hidden stories.

Santa Maria Mater Domini **(1)** Calle del Cristo **(2)** left on Calle Bernardo **(3)** to Campo San Polo **(4)**.

* * *

Whatever Brunetti's mission from his apartment to Campo San Barnaba, he passes many of the city's lesser-known delights, including the birthplace of the Venetian playwright Goldoni. The author of the eighteenth-century comedies that so delighted audiences speaking local Veneziano and which Brunetti admits made him 'laugh the hardest', is now commemorated in the small but exquisite Palazzo Centanni **(7)**. Its marble wellhead and stunning exterior staircase ornamenting the courtyard entrance into the only literary museum of Venice create a theatrical setting appropriate for the dramatist who brought the city so much joy.

To Salizzada San Polo **(5)**, to Rio terrà dei Nomboli to Calle dei Nomboli **(6)** to Ca' Goldoni **(7)**

$\rightarrow$

The area around Campo San Pantalon contains some of Venice's finest pastries, an excellent cheese and fresh pasta

Through Campo San Tomà **(8)** left to Calle Gozzi **(9)** across bridge, right to Tonolo **(10)**

shop, plus a spate of new slick cafés – it is a region the Brunettis know well. Although the last people to encourage or endure wine snobs, they seek out some of the city's wine stores that dot this walk, willing to go to the trouble of hauling heavy bottles, not just up the dreaded ninety-four steps to their apartment, but over bridges as well. For Brunetti, in *Through a Glass, Darkly*, spending his free hours to find a 'Nebbiolo, a Sangiovese, and a very young Barbera' makes the journey worth the effort.

A favourite haunt of Venetians in search of good pastries is the corner bakery Tonolo **(10)** near Campo San Pantalon **(11).** Brunetti often calls in here on Sunday mornings to pick up brioche for the family and it is a stop he and Paola regularly make on their strolls to get special bread. When alone, he indulges in more excessive treats, always justifying himself: '[he] went down to Tonolo for a coffee and a pastry. Because he had had no lunch to speak of, he had two: a cream-filled swan and a tiny chocolate éclair as light as silk' (*Through a Glass, Darkly*, ch. 18)

In *Doctored Evidence*, Donna Leon has transformed well-known Tonolo with its fine array of sweets to create a fictional bakery, Romolo:

They went into the pastry shop together. Vianello ordered a coffee and a glass of mineral water, and Brunetti nodded his request for the same. The glass cabinet was filled with the pastries Brunetti knew so well: the cream-filled puffs of pastry, the chocolate bigne, and Chiara's favourite, the whipped-cream-filled swans. The heat rendered them all equally un-appetising. (*Doctored Evidence*, ch. 18)

One of the bakers in Caffè Romolo is the only living relative and heir of a murdered old woman loathed by everyone. This niece may also have poisoned the Golden Labrador belonging to her lawyer in a particularly horrible fashion as an act of revenge. Hoping to interrogate the niece at work in the bakery, Brunetti braves the crowds and the heat to cross the sweltering city. Yet the owner refuses to allow an interview with the niece, seeing it as a waste of time. A hot and weary Brunetti resorts to the only certainty he knows will work to lead him backstage, behind the sweet façade – a barely veiled threat:

'So perhaps it would be better if I were to return later and place uniformed officers at the door while I talk to her. Or perhaps I could have a word with the people at the Department of Health and ask them how it is you know about next week's inspection.' Before she could say a word, he concluded, 'Or perhaps we could just go into the kitchen and have a word with Signorina Simionato.' (. . .)

Vianello led the way into the kitchen, which was lit by a bank of windows set into the far wall. Empty metal racks stood against three walls, and the windowed doors of the vast ovens gleamed. A man and a woman, both wearing immaculate white coats and hats, stood in front of a deep sink from which rose the steam of soapy water. Emerging from the suds were the handles of implements and the tops of the broad wooden boards on which the dough was set to rise before baking.

Running water drowned all other sound, so Brunetti and Vianello were within a metre of the two before the man became aware of their presence and turned. When he saw them standing there, he turned back and shut off the water and, into the silence, said, 'Yes?' He was shorter than average, stocky, but had a handsome face in which only inquisitive-ness was evident.

(. . .)

It was Vianello who addressed himself to the man, 'Perhaps there's a place where we might talk to Signorina Simionato in private?'

The man shook his head. 'There's nothing like that here,' he said. 'But I can go outside and have a cigarette while you talk.' When Brunetti nodded, the man removed his cap and wiped the sweat from his face with the inside of his elbow. Hitching up his jacket, he pulled a blue packet of Nazionali from the pocket of his trousers and walked away. Brunetti noticed that there was a back door into the *calle*. (*Doctored Evidence*, ch. 18)

→

Venice might once have been the 'capital of dissipations', with Carnevale lasting six riotous months, and twice the number of courtesans as ladies of more chaste repute, but its modern reputation has been one of early silence and little late night fun. By the twenty-first century, however, at least two major areas have expanded into the early morning hours: Campo Santa Margherita **(12)** and across town in western Cannaregio the Fondamenta Misericordia: live music, belly dancing, ethnic restaurants, most open till late at night.

Although the Brunettis seem unlikely to remain into the early hours, leaving Tonolo's and heading just over the bridge from fairly tranquil San Pantalon they must enter Venice's longest – and one of its liveliest – *campi*, Santa Margherita. Vast and elongated, it is part of the artery between Campo San Polo and Campo San Barnaba, offering local residents and strolling shoppers a nearly self-contained and charming village. Past the Chiesa di Santa Margherita, with its stumpy tower, now part of the University of Venice, the *campo* opens up into a scene filled with *pizzerie, trattorie,* cafés and bars – all with tables outside to lure the sociable in every season. Giant plane trees for shade, ample benches for lounging, two lovely Renaissance wellheads for posing, outdoor food stalls, the largest coffee emporium in the city, a wine shop, and at the far end, a florist, butcher, hardware store, and two small supermarkets, all combine to create a place both convenient and companionable. Varied enough to satisfy the daily needs of the neighbourhood, the shops of Campo Santa Margherita are further graced by historical atmosphere: a free-standing square building, the Renaissance Tanners Guild Hall **(A)** has a plaque on the outside regulating the minimum size of fish to be sold in order to preserve the species, and morning fish stalls still line up along the façade. Across the *campo* sits the long front of an attractive deep brown Gothic building, one part ornamented with a rose marble entrance, the other now housing a bank. It is an inviting area and the Brunettis on their way to find *pane Pugliese* might easily be tempted to stop for a pre-lunch *aperitivo*, ordering the local favourite, an ice-filled *spritz con Aperol*.

Eventually, when the daily shopping is over, the pigeons

settled in for the night, the dinners finished, the late hours encourage more than simple revelry, invite less innocent activities than the drunk in a canal or local complaints about noise – neither of which would involve the Commissario. But the criminals of Donna Leon's Venice have also found a new, convenient late night niche here, as Brunetti discovers in *Blood from a Stone*.

Struggling to uncover the mysterious world of the African street sellers – where they live, where they gather – forces Brunetti to face local prejudice in unsuspecting places. Out of frustration with his Sisyphean work, once he discovers in officer Moretti a penchant for ethnic slurs, he decides to switch topics:

'Was it about that black man? Did you remember where you saw him?'

'No, I didn't, but Cattanei did.' (. . .) 'We were out on a call one night about two months ago. Late, maybe two in the morning, and some guy came out of a bar and came running after us. He said he wanted us to come back with him because there was going to be a fight. It was over near Campo Santa Margherita. But by the time we got there, there wasn't much left of the argument.' (. . .)

'This was at two in the morning?' Brunetti asked, making no attempt to disguise his astonishment.

'Times have changed, Commissario,' Moretti said, but then qualified that by adding, 'or maybe it's only the area around Campo Santa Margherita that's changed. All those bars, the pizzerias, the music places. It's never quiet there at night any more. Some of them are open until two or three in the morning. (. . .)

'I don't think it was much of anything, really. As I said, it looked like things had quieted down before we got there: no chairs turned over, nothing broken. Just this atmosphere in the air and three other men – might have been four of them – standing between them and sort of holding them apart.' (*Blood from a Stone*, ch. 20)

Mixed feelings in those who live with the contradictions of the legal and the illegal in their daily work is one thing, but Brunetti encounters worse prejudice at home in Chiara's heartless response that the man murdered 'was only a *vu cumprà*'. This sudden moral quandary in the family home propels the parents to seek relief by buying fine food and wines in nearby Campo San Barnaba.

→

Campo Santa Margherita left to Rio di San Barnaba (13)

The short route from Santa Margherita to San Barnaba has always been a delight for visitors. The fanciful windows of the Mondo Nuovo mask shop **(B)**, which created the interior plasterwork for the rebuilding of the Fenice opera house, sits on the right. The Ponte dei Pugni, Bridge of Punches **(C)**, lies straight ahead, with its two inlaid footprints to mark the spot where in earlier centuries combatants stood to compete in hurling each other off the then parapet-less bridge.

→

To Ca' Rezzonico (14)

A brief detour introduces the neighbourhood of Brunetti's aristocratic in-laws, who live in a (fictional) palace on the Grand Canal. Although the Palazzo Falier is an invented building, Leon creates a setting commensurate with the other palaces in this area. Despite its glamorous surroundings, Brunetti resists all but holidays and family events.

Brunetti had never counted the rooms in the *palazzo* and had always been embarrassed to ask how many there were. Its four floors were surrounded on three sides by canals, its back propped up by a deconsecrated church. He entered it only on formal occasions: the vigil of Christmas, when they went to eat fish and exchange gifts; the name day of Count Orazio, when, for some reason, they ate pheasant and again gave gifts; and the Feast of the Redeemer, when they went to eat *pasta fagioli* and watch the fireworks soaring above Piazza San Marco. (*Death at La Fenice*, ch. 10)

The invented Palazzo Falier is much older than its eight-teenth-century neighbour, but the Ca' Rezzonico **(14)** can serve as a delightful substitute. Now a museum with frescoed ceilings by Tiepolo, walls covered with Longhi's painted scenes of Venetian interiors, and *vedute* (view) paintings depicting the city's sites, Ca' Rezzonico offers a unique opportunity to get a feel for aristocratic Venetian life – no matter which century. Inside the Rezzonico's courtyard is the perfect place to enjoy Brunetti's first description of his wealthy in-laws, the Faliers, in *Death at La Fenice*.

It would be an exaggeration to say that Brunetti disliked Paola's parents, the Count and Countess Falier, but it would be an equal exaggeration to say that he liked them. They puzzled him in much the same way that a pair of whooping cranes would puzzle someone accustomed to tossing peanuts to the pigeons in the park. They belonged to a rare and elegant species, and Brunetti, after knowing them for almost two decades, had to admit that he had mixed feelings about the inevitability of their extinction.

Count Falier, who numbered two doges on his mother's side, could, and did, trace his family back to the tenth century. There were crusaders perched on the limbs of his family tree, a cardinal or two, a composer of secondary importance, and the former Italian ambassador to the court of King Zog of Albania. Paola's mother was Florentine by birth, though her family had transferred itself to the northern city shortly after that event. They claimed descent from the Medici, and in a kind of genealogical chess that had a strange fascination for people of their circle, she matched her husband's doges with a pope and a textile millionaire, the cardinal with a cousin of Petrarch, the composer with a famous castrato (from whom, sadly, no issue), and the ambassador with Garibaldi's banker. (*La Fenice*, ch. 10)

The Ca' Rezzonico's courtyard with its long marble-floored colonnade leading out to the Grand Canal evokes another world; on the right sits a black nineteenth-century gondola, replete with its *felze*, the little covered house that discreetly protected lovers from prying eyes, and also recreates the sense of mystery and romance reproduced in the paintings upstairs, and reminds modern-day visitors how elegant had been the aristocrats' arrival for a social event. The wooden platform on the canal offers the opportunity to see the same sublime views the guests upstairs at the Falier party in *Death at La Fenice* would have seen from the windows of the family palace to the right near the vaporetto stop. Music lovers might have climbed to the top floor to gaze at the Palazzo Giustinian **(D)** to the left, where Wagner composed portions of *Tristan and Isolde* in 1859. The eighteenth-century Palazzo Grassi, now an art exhibition space, dominates the view straight across the water beside its little *campo* and a small deconsecrated church with a charming white bell tower, also now a gallery. To the left the Grand Canal bends at Gothic Ca' Foscari, the main centre for the university of Venice where Paola teaches, to head towards the Rialto Bridge. To the right, the views end with the high arc of the wooden Accademia Bridge framing the Salute church and the *bacino* beyond.

They lived in a *palazzo* that had belonged to the Falieri for at least three centuries, a vast rambling vault on the Grand Canal that was virtually impossible to heat in the winter and that was kept from imminent collapse only by the constant ministrations of an ever-present horde of masons, builders, plumbers, and electricians, all of whom joined Count Falier willingly in the perpetual Venetian battle against the inexorable forces of time, tide, and industrial pollution. (*La Fenice*, ch. 10)

Despite the spectacular views and lavish life inside a palace on the Grand Canal, Brunetti avoids unrequired visits to the Falier family home for a variety of reasons. His democratic soul finds ludicrous the aristocracy's laments that they are all in 'fallen times' because there are no more private gondoliers. And after nearly twenty years, relations with his in-laws remain ambiguous; he is still undecided how to address Paola's father – Count is too formal; Orazio impossible; Papà unthinkable.

Like most of the *palazzi* on the Grand Canal, Palazzo Falier was originally meant to be approached by boat, and guests were meant to enter by means of the four shallow steps leading down to the landing on the canal. But this entrance had long since been closed off by a heavy metal grating that was opened only when large objects were delivered by boat. In these fallen times, guests arrived by foot, walking from Ca' Rezzonico, the nearest vaporetto stop, or from other parts of the city. (*La Fenice*, ch. 12)

Besides the first eccentric view of Paola's family, Donna Leon uses her first novel to stage a party at the Palazzo Falier. The guests arriving at the palace in *Death at la Fenice*, would have avoided the usually dank and dark ground floor and headed for the balconies upstairs to admire the views. Modern visitors to the Ca' Rezzonico, however, have several choices for the best spot to imagine sharing the Count's champagne: whether wandering out on to the canal deck for some air and the view, lounging on the ample stone benches on the ground floor, or exploring the endless rooms upstairs, filled with paintings of Venice in her earlier grandeur. The whole party setting seems like the staging of a play about power, art, and luxury – things designed to arouse Brunetti's conflicting feelings about the world of privilege:

They rang the bell and then were ushered into the courtyard by a young man Paola had never seen before. Probably hired for the night.

'At least he's not wearing knee breeches and a wig,' Brunetti remarked as they climbed the exterior staircase. The young man had not bothered to ask who they were or whether they had been invited. Either he had a guest list committed to memory and could recognize everyone who arrived or, more likely, he simply did not care whom he let into the *palazzo*.

At the top of the stairs, they heard music coming from the left, where the three enormous reception rooms were located. Following the sound, they went down a mirror-lined hallway, accompanied by their own dim reflections. The huge oaken doors to the first room stood open. Light, music, and the scent of expensive perfume and flowers spilled from beyond them.

The light that filled the room came from two immense Murano glass chandeliers, covered with playful angels and

Cupids, which hung from the frescoed ceiling, and from candle-filled stanchions that lined the walls. The music came from a discreet trio in the corner, who played Vivaldi in one of his more repetitive moods. And the scent emanated from the flock of brightly coloured and even more brightly chattering women who decorated the room. (*La Fenice*, ch. 12)

The Falier party also introduces a host of new characters, most destined to reappear in the books. Much of the social glue that binds the people in Venice is the currency of gossip – they trade it like the legendary barterers history claims them to have been. No class seems able to resist its attractions, from the highly cultured and the well-connected social figures, to the woman who sells the papers and the man who serves the *cappuccini*.

He knew many of those in the room but, as it were, at second hand. Though he had never been introduced to most of them, he knew their scandals, their histories, their affairs, both legal and romantic. Part of this came from his being a policeman, but most of it came from living in what was really a provincial town where gossip was the real cult and where, had it not been at least a nominally Christian city, the reigning deity would surely have been Rumour. (*La Fenice*, ch. 12)

Although Brunetti relies on the powerful connections of Count Falier, he realizes that behind the scenes the Countess is no less powerful:

The countess, for her part, was 'in society', which meant that she attended the opening nights of Italy's four major opera houses, arranged benefit concerts for the Italian Red Cross, and gave a masked ball for four hundred people each year during Carnevale . . . (*La Fenice*, ch. 10)

And the Countess, despite her easy grace, appears in her own kind of armour, equipped with a female's weapons.

The count saw his wife come across the room and smiled, beckoning her to join them. She manoeuvred her way through the crowd with a combination of grace and social skill that Brunetti envied, stopping to kiss a cheek here, lightly touch an arm there. He quite enjoyed the countess, stiff and formal in her chains of pearls and layers of black chiffon. As usual, her feet were encased in dagger-pointed shoes with heels as high as kerbstones, which still failed to bring her level with her husband's shoulder. (*La Fenice*, ch. 12)

In fact, the countess might be better placed to supply him with gossip known only to her female friends. Sitting in her private room, surrounded by the same views the Ca' Rezzonico affords, in *The Death of Faith* she is surprised by the unannounced visit of her son-in-law:

The contessa looked away from him, toward the row of quatrefoil windows that gave an unimpeded view to the *palazzi* on the other side of the Grand Canal. 'What use is going to be made of this, Guido? Can you tell me that?' (. . .)

Behind the contessa, boats moved up and down the canal, and light spilled from the windows of the buildings on the other side. He wanted to say something to her, but before he could speak, she said, 'Please give Paola and the children our love.' She patted his arm and moved past him. Before he could say anything, she was gone, leaving him to study the view from the *palazzo* which would someday be his. (*The Death of Faith*, ch. 6)

Whether he likes it or not, Brunetti will escape neither his fascination with nor his ambiguous feelings towards his in-laws and the power they represent.

Brunetti, for his part, earned slightly more than three million lire a month as a commissario of police, a sum he calculated to be only a bit more than what his father-in-law paid each month for the right to dock his boat in front of the *palazzo*.

A decade ago, the count had attempted to persuade Brunetti to leave the police and join him in a career in banking. He continually pointed out that Brunetti ought not to spend his life in the company of tax evaders, wife beaters, pimps, thieves, and perverts. The offers had come to a sudden halt one Christmas when, goaded beyond patience, Brunetti had pointed out that although he and the count seemed to work among the same people, he at least had the consolation of being able to arrest them, whereas the count was constrained to invite them to dinner. (*Death at La Fenice*, ch. 10)

$\longrightarrow$

Into Campo San Barnaba **(15)**

On his way from the Faliers' *palazzo* to Campo San Barnaba **(15)**, still today one of the busiest locations in the city, the Commissario might have reflected on the Barnabotti, indigent Venetian aristocrats who, fallen on hard times, chose cheap lodgings in the *campo*. Certainly he'd recognize a familiar irony in the meagre pensions they received from the Republic.

With numerous cafés and restaurants in the *campo* and on nearby Lunga San Barnaba, plus a fine food store selling Venice's best bread **(E)**,* the area draws people from every *sestiere*. Even though both the restaurant and the bookstore featured in *The Anonymous Venetian* have disappeared, fruit and vegetable boats still float in the water of canal-sided San Barnaba – the only ones remaining from the hundreds that dotted the canals in centuries past **(F)**. These rocking boats are frequented by local shoppers as well as tourists eager for a picturesque photo of housewives buying glossy purple aubergines and fresh green and rose artichokes.

But Venetians and tourists alike are only a hindrance for the police when they struggle to capture the probable murderer of the banker found in drag in the mud around Marghera.

The building they sought was at the far right corner of the *campo,* its door just in front of one of the two enormous boats that sold fruit and vegetables from the embankment of the canal which ran alongside the *campo*. To the right of the door was a restaurant, not yet open for the day, and beyond it a bookstore. 'All of you,' Brunetti said, conscious of the stares and comments the police and their machine-guns were causing among the people around them, 'get into the bookstore. Vianello, you wait outside.' (*The Anonymous Venetian*, ch. 26)

A far different occasion will bring Brunetti back to San Barnaba in *Blood from a Stone*. Arriving at his apartment armed, not with a weapon, but with flowers for both his wife and daughter, Brunetti finds himself trapped in a bewildering discussion with Paola about their young daughter Chiara's eco-politics and muddled ethics. Vainly, he attempts to make some sense out of the girl's priorities: 'She worries about the flowers, but she can still dismiss the death of a *vu cumprà*.' But the ease, good humour, and patience of the parents triumph, as they opt for a stroll across the city in place of family strife. After the purchases, it is time to leave them to retrace their steps home, armed now with the treasures of the table.

'Shall we go and have a coffee?'
She slid the vase of irises to one side of the counter and stepped back to admire them. 'Yes, if we can go to Tonolo and have *un cigno*. And while we're over there, we could go to San Barnaba and see if they have any of that good bread.'
It would take, he calculated, more than an hour. First a cream-filled swan and a coffee at Tonolo, then the walk to Campo San Barnaba and the store that sold the good cheese and the bread from Puglia. He had fled his office in search of peace and quiet, seeking some evidence that sanity still existed in a world of violence and crime, and his wife suggested they spend an hour eating pastry and buying a loaf of bread. He leaped at the chance. (. . .)
Brunetti stopped at the first of the two produce-filled boats moored to the *riva*, then moved on to the second. Ignoring Patta for the moment, they discussed dinner and bought a dozen artichokes and a kilo of Fuji apples. (. . .)
Ten minutes later, they emerged with an entire loaf of the

Pugliese bread, a wedge of pecorino, and a jar of the pesto sauce the owner swore was the best in the city. (*Blood from a Stone*, ch. 15)

*Pantagruelica gourmet store, so popular that bread is gone on Saturdays before lunchtime closing, also has excellent white truffles for the holidays.

WALK 5: *Weather and Houses*

San Barnaba—San Sebastiano—Angelo Raffaele—
San Basegio—Fondamenta Zattere

1 hour

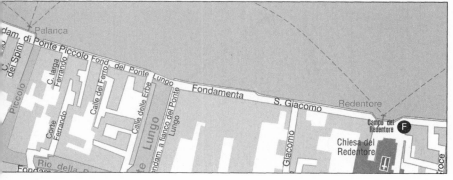

To cross from the San Barnaba **(1)** area into the rarefied region of Dorsoduro is to move from local colour to eccentricity and style. Establishing one of the oldest areas in the city, the original settlers were drawn to this region for its durable soil, crucial in a lagoon full of swampy islands. In more recent centuries, foreign artists and local oddities have made this *sestiere* their centre, bringing with them their sexual mores, fashion flair, and exotic tastes. But the Dorsoduro area possesses a peculiar divide: its remote and less familiar west houses the abandoned, both people and buildings; the fashionable and well-travelled east commands some of the highest prices for property in the entire city. The two areas are linked by the long Fondamenta Zattere, a former working-class region, now a popular meeting place lined with cafés. Yet it is property that dominates the following two walks through Brunetti's Dorsoduro – as a Venetian obsession, as an occasion for greed.

Campo San Barnaba **(1)**

Whatever the area's liabilities and charms, its geographical exposure – formerly to pirate attacks, now to weather – is a clear disadvantage. Unless crime calls or the day is fine, Commissario Brunetti shows little interest in either enjoying the desirable properties with commanding views, or enduring the wide Giudecca Canal's choppy waters and winds, that leave the area especially vulnerable to *acqua alta*, fog, and rain.

* * *

More than any other Donna Leon novel, *Friends in High Places* reveals the Venetian fixation with real estate. For the most part residents are forbidden to expand either up or out, the city's uniquely static nature making property in Venice of absorbing interest: it is not uncommon to meet people who have lived in the family home for generations with no

Calle lunga San Barnaba **(2)** to Campo San Sebastiano **(3)**

intention of moving or buying, carefully inspecting houses newly on the market.

In *Friends in High Places*, the young building inspector who first shocked Brunetti and Paola by pointing out the illegal state of their apartment has been found on the street at an abandoned building site, in western Dorsoduro. Having known the victim, Brunetti is highly suspicious that a man so terrified of heights would have carelessly fallen from the top of a four-floor scaffolding.

To the left was a photo; he recognized the face but couldn't place it until he read the name in the caption: 'Francesco Rossi, city surveyor, in a coma after falling from scaffolding.'

Brunetti's hands tightened on the pages of the newspaper. He glanced away and then back to the story below the photo.

> Francesco Rossi, a surveyor in the employ of the Ufficio Catasto, fell on Saturday afternoon from the scaffolding in front of a building in Santa Croce, where he was conducting the inspection of a restoration project. Rossi was taken to the emergency room at the Ospedale Civile, where his condition is given as 'riservata'. (*Friends in High Places*, ch. 5)

In few areas of the city is Brunetti less at home than in western Dorsoduro. And Vianello's strengths are rarely more evident than when the pair venture into these more remote neighbourhoods. Vianello, with his Castello background and with relatives in other parts of the city, has a network of familiarity different from Brunetti's. During the years they have worked together, Brunetti has come to rely more heavily on Vianello's sound instincts and spontaneous access to witnesses, especially where Brunetti is on unfamiliar ground.

Together, they turned from the boat and walked back toward the *campo*, a part of the city Brunetti seldom visited. He and Paola used to eat in a small fish restaurant over here, but it had changed hands a few years ago, and the quality of the food had rapidly deteriorated, so they'd stopped coming.

Brunetti had had a girlfriend who lived over here, but that had been when he was still a student, and she had died some years ago. (*Friends*, ch. 8)

Brunetti begins an investigation, both into the suspicious fall and into a part of the city where he feels a stranger. With Vianello in the lead, they will head into the squalor of the drug world and a neighbourhood whose dereliction reminds them of the underside of Venice's famed beauty. The Church of San Sebastiano **(A)** contains the burial site of the great colourist Veronese, its walls layered with his paintings and works by other important Venetian artists, yet it draws few of the city's art fans to this remote area. Uncomfortably crowded against a bridge, the church is bypassed by most strollers on their way to the *trattorie* which spangle the area.

→

Campo Angelo Raffaele **(4)** seems equally forlorn and in need of attention, and any Venetian would notice new scaffolding on a long-abandoned building, presaging a possible change in the neighbourhood. The *campo*'s most recent change is the addition of an *enoteca* with chairs and tables, drawing a crowd that enlivens the scene.

Into Campo Angelo Raffaele **(4)**

They crossed the bridge and walked through Campo San Sebastiano, toward the large area of Campo Angelo Raffaele. Vianello, leading the way, turned immediately into a *calle* on the left, and up ahead they saw the scaffolding attached to the façade of the last building in the row, a four-storey house that looked as if it had been abandoned for years. (. . .) There was, at least for people born in Venice – which means born with an interest in the buying and selling of houses – an emptiness about the house which would have registered on them even if they had not been paying particular attention. (*Friends*, ch. 8)

→

San Basilio is the region where an increasing number of tour boats dock with exotic names – *Pasiphae, Ikarus, Aphrodite* – and their far from exotic passengers: a new and

Calle Nuova, left to Salizzada San Basegio **(5)** to San Basilio boat stop **(6)**

an increasingly large invasion of tourists arrives to clog the city streets. The unsettling dockside scene greets Brunetti on his trips to western Dorsoduro; whether from police launch or vaporetto, the recent view from the San Basilio stop is, for Venetians, still a shock.

The boat took them toward the end of the Zattere, in the waters beyond which loomed an enormous ship, moored to the embankment and dwarfing the area beside it.

'My God, what's that?' Vianello asked as their boat approached.

'It's that cruise ship that was built here. It's said to be the biggest in the world.'

'It's horrible,' Vianello said, head back and staring at its upper decks, which loomed almost twenty metres above them. 'What's it doing here?'

'Bringing money to the city, Sergeant,' Brunetti observed drily.

Vianello looked down at the water and then up to the rooftops of the city. 'What whores we are,' he said. Brunetti did not see fit to demur.

The pilot pulled to a stop not far from the enormous ship, stepped off the boat, and began tying it to the mushroom-shaped metal stanchion on the embankment, so thick it must have been intended for larger boats. (*Friends*, ch. 8)

$$\longrightarrow$$

Left on Calle Cartellotti, right on to Fondamenta Ognissanti **(7)** to Ospedale Giustiniani **(8)**

Just as the map of Venice is imprinted in the mind of every resident – *calli* memorized for distance, *ponti* avoided for ease – which parts of the city rest on high or low ground is another preoccupation, and familiarity a salvation. In *Acqua Alta*, Brunetti continues to assess the weather in this area remote from his usual paths. Like any sane Venetian far across the city from home, he calculates the chances of high water: full moon, northern rains, the siren to warn the shopkeepers to raise their merchandise and start their pumps.

It was fully dark now, and Brunetti found himself eager to be at home, out of this cold, and away from the wind that still sliced across the open space along the waterside. He crossed in front of the French consulate, then cut back alongside the Giustiniani Hospital **(8)**, a dumping ground for the old, and headed towards home. (. . .) The sirens for *acqua alta* had sounded at three that morning, waking them all, but the tide had turned before the waters had seeped up through the chinks in the pavement. The full moon was only a few days away, and it had been raining heavily up north in Friuli, so there was a chance that the night would bring the first real flooding of the year. (*Acqua Alta*, ch. 6)

The Ospedale Giustiniani area is, appropriately, the setting chosen by Leon for an invented nursing home far more horrible than just 'a dumping ground for the old'. In *The Death of Faith*, otherwise healthy elderly patients are dying mysteriously. Although doubtful that the causes of death are unnatural, Brunetti owes a debt to the pretty ex-nun who has been so crucial over the years in calming his mother's frequent bouts of madness. Reluctantly, he returns to this remote section of the city in the hope of alleviating the young woman's suspicions, only to find himself trapped in the web of a secret society.

The nursing home stood behind yet another high wall. A bronze plaque announced its name and stated that visiting hours were from nine until eleven in the morning, every day of the week. After he rang the bell, Brunetti stepped back a few paces, but he could see no glass embedded into the top of the wall. It wasn't likely that anyone in a nursing home would have the strength to climb that wall, glass or not, Brunetti admonished himself, and the old and infirm had nothing but their lives that could any longer be stolen from them. (*The Death of Faith*, ch. 11)

→

Donna Leon's long residence in Venice makes her an acute recorder of the unique perils created by weather. *Acqua alta* not only hinders foot traffic in Venice, requiring rubber boots or climbing the high *passarelle*, it can also thwart boat travel,

Left on to Calle dei Cartellotti to Fondamenta Zattere **(9)**

preventing the *motoscafi* from moving under the lower bridges. But the unpredictable fogs are the most troublesome for residents and the most dangerous for unwary tourists. The otherwise lovely Fondamenta Zattere **(9)** along the Giudecca Canal is particularly dangerous: cold, inescapable moisture clings, vision diminishes, and just a few of the boats can travel, and then only with radar. The city halts.

The next morning was as dismal as his mood. A thick fog had appeared during the night, seeping up from the waters on which the city was built, not drifting in from the sea. When he stepped out of his front door, cold, misty tendrils wrapped themselves around his face, slipped beneath his collar. He could see clearly for only a few metres, and then vision grew cloudy; buildings slipped into and out of sight, as though they, and not the fog, shifted and moved. Phantoms, clothed in a nimbus of shimmering grey, passed him on the street, floating by as though disembodied. If he turned to follow them with his eyes, he saw them disappear, swallowed up by the dense film that filled the narrow streets and lay upon the waters like a curse. Instinct and long experience told him there would be no boat service on the Grand Canal; the fog was far too thick for that. He walked blindly, telling his feet to lead, allowing decades of familiarity with bridges, streets, and turns to take him over to the Zattere and the landing where both the number 8 and the number 5 stopped on their way to the Giudecca. (*Death at La Fenice*, ch. 23)

When Brunetti leaves the extreme west of Dorsoduro and begins to enter the eastern area more desirable for residence, he also enters a neighbourhood steeped in pretence and myth, an area that reminds him of his youthful credulity, a trait not useful for an adult policeman.

(. . .) It was an area of the city with which he was not very familiar, no doubt because it did not stand between his home and any of the parts of the city where he would ordinarily have cause to go. (. . .)

What he knew of the area was as much legend as fact,

as was so much of the information he and his fellow Venetians tended to have about their city. Behind that wall was the garden of the former movie star, married now to the industrialist from Torino. Behind that one was the home of the last of the Contarini family, rumoured not to have left the house in twenty years. And that was the door to the house of the last of the Donna Salva, who used to be seen only at the opening night of the opera, always in the royal box, and then always dressed in red. He knew these walls and doors as other children could recognize the heroes of cartoons and television, and like those figures, these houses and *palazzi* spoke to him of youth and a different vision of the world.

Just as children outgrew the antics of Topolino or Braccio di Ferro and came to realize the illusion behind them, Brunetti had, over the course of his years as a police officer, come to learn the often dark realities that lurked behind the walls of his youth. The actress drank, and the industrialist from Torino had twice been arrested for beating her. (*The Death of Faith*, ch. 11)

$$\longrightarrow$$

In *The Anonymous Venetian*, the Commissario has been chasing the wrong sin. The male banker battered to death in women's clothing leads the police to suspect sex as the motive for the grisly crime. But, once again, property and the sin of greed rear their ugly heads in Venice. Brunetti discovers a series of apartments ostensibly rented at low rates to the poor, but some are in Dorsoduro, and with canal views – and that would flag any Venetian's suspicions.

To Ponte Lungo
(10)

'Where is the professor's apartment?'

'On the Zattere, with a view across to the Giudecca,' Vianello said, naming one of the most desirable areas in the city. Then he added, 'I'd say it's six rooms, the apartment, though I saw only the entrance hall.'

'Two hundred twenty thousand lire?' Brunetti asked, thinking that this was what Raffi had paid for a pair of Timberlands a month ago.

'Yes, sir,' Vianello said.

'Why don't you ask the professor and his wife to come in, then, Sergeant? By the way, what is the professor a professor of?'

'I don't think of anything, sir.' (*The Anonymous Venetian*, ch. 23)

Desirable as the Dorsoduro area is, the Giudecca island **(B)** facing it across the wide canal suffers an unfortunate reputation – especially among the native Venetians. Far from the centre, or even the main islands linked by bridges that allow a late night walk home, the *giudecchini* can be spotted in the late hours at the nearby vaporetti stops, frantically checking their watches in desperate hope of getting the last regularly scheduled boat over to the island. Even the peripatetic Brunetti avoids the place.

The island of the Giudecca was a part of Venice Brunetti seldom visited. Visible from Piazza San Marco, visible, in fact, from the entire back flank of the island, in places no more than a hundred metres away, it nevertheless lived in strange isolation from the rest of the city. The grisly stories that appeared in the paper with embarrassing frequency, of children being bitten by rats or people found dead of overdoses, always seemed to take place on the Giudecca. Even the presence of a dethroned monarch and a fading movie star of the fifties couldn't redeem it in the popular consciousness as a sinister, backward place where nasty things happened. (*Death at La Fenice*, ch. 14)

In *Uniform Justice* Donna Leon selects the perfect spot to locate the fictional Academy of San Martino in the distant wastes of the Giudecca, far from any scrutiny. Brunetti and Officer Pucetti head out to the island to investigate the death of a young cadet found hanging in the academy's shower, an apparent suicide. Moving up the Giudecca Canal accompanied by fine weather before inspecting the boy's corpse, they realize that, although both are native Venetians, neither of them knows where the academy is. As they near the island, the old prejudices, myths, and animosities about the Giudecca surface.

Brunetti's reflections were cut off as the boat pulled into a canal just after the Church of Sant' Eufemia **(C)** and then drew up at a landing spot. (. . .)

'It's up here, isn't it?' Brunetti asked, pointing towards the back of the island and the lagoon, just visible in the distance.

'I don't know, sir,' Pucetti confessed. 'I have to admit I come over here only for the Redentore **(D).** I don't think I even know where the place is.' (. . .)

As if sensing his commander's disappointment, Pucetti added, 'It's always seemed like a foreign country to me, sir. Must be my mother: she always talks about it like it's not part of Venice. If they gave her the key to a house on the Giudecca, I'm sure she'd give it back.' (*Uniform Justice*, ch. 2)

By the end of the novel, Brunetti finally gets some relief from a crime he has been unable to treat with detached professionalism. A too-young boy, a sobbing and grieving father, a damaged and distant mother, all conspire to remind him of the fears for his own children that permeate the books. But nature offers respite, while the joy of a speeding boat – in Venice only manageable on the wide Giudecca Canal – seduces him into pleasure – no matter what awaits at the journey's destination.

Full throttle, the launch sped out into the *Bacino*, straight across, then turned into the open mouth of the Canale della Giudecca. The pilot, warned by Pucetti, used the flashing blue light but not the siren.

The first thrill of excitement was followed almost immediately by Brunetti's embarrassment that, in the midst of death and deceit, he could still revel in the simple joy of speed. He knew this was no schoolboy holiday, no cops and robbers chase, but still his heart soared with delight at the rush of wind and the rhythmic thump of the prow against the waves.

He glanced at Pucetti and was relieved to see his own feelings reflected on the younger man's face. They seemed to flash by other boats. Brunetti saw heads turn and follow their swift passage up the canal. Too soon, however, the pilot pulled into the Rio di Sant' Eufemia, slipped the motor into reverse, and glided silently to the left-hand side of the canal. (*Uniform Justice*, ch. 25)

During his various trips to the remote Academy San Martino, Brunetti has ample opportunity, looking back at the Zattere from a distance, to muse on the fate of his beloved Venice.

He went down to the edge of the Canale della Giudecca. Turning right, he started to walk along the *riva*, intending to catch a vaporetto. As he walked, he kept his attention on the buildings on the other side of the canal: Nico's Bar **(D)** and, above it, an apartment he had spent a lot of time in before he met Paola; the Church of the Gesuati, **(E)** (. . .) the former Swiss Consulate, the flag gone now. Have even the Swiss abandoned us? he wondered. (. . .) He saw a boat coming from Redentore **(F)** and hurried on to the *imbarcadero* at Palanca to cross back to the Zattere. When he got off, he looked at his watch and realized that it really did take less than five minutes to make the trip from the Giudecca. Even so, the other island still seemed, as it had ever seemed, as far distant as the Galapagos. (*Uniform Justice*, ch. 5)

As the widest of Venice's three major waterways, the Giudecca Canal in good weather offers a sweeping view and bracing air not so easily found in the city's more closed-in areas. It also seems exhilaratingly spacious in *The Death of Faith* when, finally after having been attacked, Brunetti leaves the hospital.

(. . .) they arrived at the door of the hospital. Paola stood just outside, holding it open for him, and as he stepped outside, she said, 'Welcome to springtime, Guido.'

And so it was. During the ten days he had been inside, spring had advanced magically and conquered the city. The air smelled of softness and growth, the mating calls of small birds filled the air above their heads, and a spray of forsythia thrust its way out of a metal grating in the brick wall across the canal. As Brunetti had known he would, the police launch was waiting for him, drawn up to the steps leading down to the canal. The pilot greeted them with a nod and with what Brunetti suspected was a smile.

Muttering, '*Buon giorno*,' the pilot helped Paola aboard, then assisted Brunetti, who almost stumbled, so blinded was he by the explosion of sunlight. Vianello flipped the mooring rope free and stepped aboard, and the pilot took them out into the Canal of the Giudecca. (*The Death of Faith*, ch. 23)

→

Già Schiavi wine bar **(11)** is a favourite haunt of the Sunday crowds. Whether for a prosecco and one of their *cicheti* or crostini before Nonna's Sunday lunch, or just to pick up bottles of wine for a late night dinner, it is a comforting place to end this walk and for Brunetti to end an unusually difficult day – a day when even spring cannot console him.

Over Ponte Lungo **(10)** to Fondamenta Nani to Già Schiavi **(11)**

Leaving Zecchino in front of the house, Brunetti started towards home, but he found no consolation in the soft spring evening, nor in the long walk along the water he permitted himself. His route would take him far out of his way, but he wanted the long views, the smell of the water, and the comfort of a glass of wine at a small place he knew near the Accademia. (*Friends in High Places*, ch. 20)

WALK 6: Expatriate Venice

San Trovaso—Fondamenta Zattere—Incurabili—Salute

1 hour

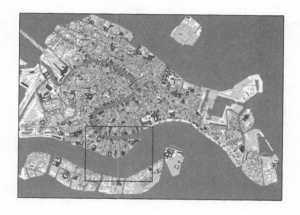

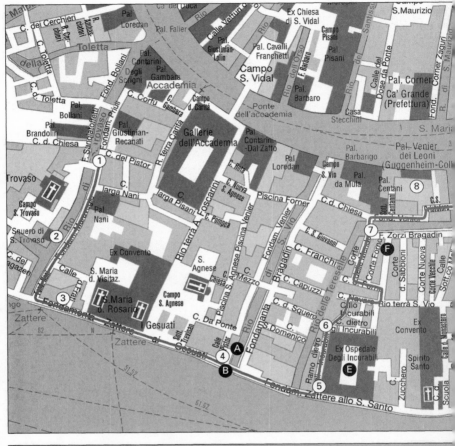

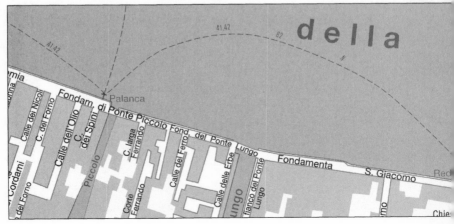

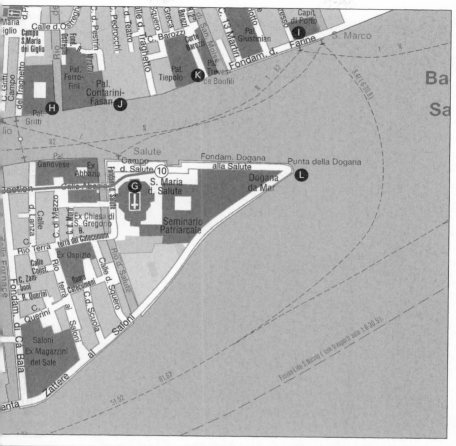

C. Gritti
Maria
iglio
Calle d. Ostreghe
Campo
S.Maria
del Giglio
Fond. Ostreghe
Calle d.O
Calle d. Pestrin
Calle d.Traghetto
Calle d. Piovan
Greca
Sguero
C. Barozzi
Corte
Barozzi
C. 13 Martiri
C. 2a
Barozzi
C. di San Moisè
Fondam. d. Farine
Capit.
di Porto
S. Marco
Ba
Sa

Pal.
Ferro-Fini
Minotto
Pedrocchi
Pal. Giustinian
di Porto

Pal.
Tiepolo
Pal.
Treves-
de Bonfili

Campo
S.Maria
dei Giglio
Pal.
Contarini-Fasan

Pal.
Gritti

H **J** **K** **I**

Pal.
Genovese
Ex
Abbazia
Calle Abbazia
Salute
Campo
d. Salute
Fondam. Dogana
alla Salute
Punta della Dogana

10

ozzetto
Calle
d. Lanza
C. t. Muti
Fondam. d. Salute
S. Maria
d. Salute
Dogana
da Mar

G

L

Ex Chiesa di
S. Gregorio
R.
terra dei Catecumeni
Seminario
Patriarcale

Rio Terrà
Ex Ospizio
Calle
Const.
G. Zam-
boni
R. Querini
Ramo
Catecumeni
Calle d. Squero
Calle d. Salute

C.
Querini
Calle d. Scuola
C.d. Scuola
Saloni

Saloni
Ex Magazzini
del Sale
al Saloni

Zattere

enta

Rio Terrà

Fondam. di Ca Bala

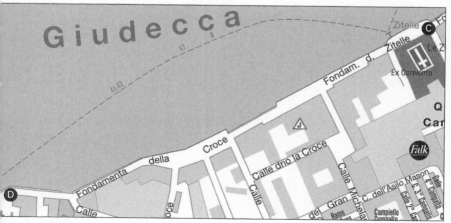

Giudecca

Zitelle
Zitelle
Le Z
Fondam. d.
Ex Convento

C

Q
Car

Falk

Croce
Calle drio la Croce
Calle Michiel
Calle dell'Asilo Mason
R. 1º Campalto
Calle 2º Campalto

della
Fondamenta
Calle
oce
Gran Michel
del
Ramo
Campiello
Campalto

D

In eastern Dorsoduro, the focus of this walk, Brunetti does not only solve crimes, he also merges into the world of artists, strolls through the legends he remembers and sees the Venice of foreign admirers who have made this glamorous *sestiere* their home. Curved between the Grand Canal to the north and the wide Giudecca Canal to the South, dotted with private art galleries and the Guggenheim Museum, crowned by the majestic Chiesa della Salute which Henry James once referred to as a 'great lady', the slender peninsula has for centuries possessed a charm irresistible to the expatriate lovers of Venice. Stunning views on both sides, the narrow *calli* divided by numerous canals, ample boat stops and a convenient *traghetto* all contribute to making this the most sought after address in the city, for the English and the American colonies. Brunetti, though more devoted to history than literature, indirectly gets a feel for Paola's beloved world of culture and writers.

Già Schiavi wine bar (1)

Since the nineteenth century, Dorsoduro has housed a series of well-known, though not always happy, foreign residents. The English writer John Ruskin was the first and most important foreign voice to call attention to Venice's distant architectural past, creating a new audience of visitors eager to admire the Byzantine and Gothic remains in the city. Between 1849 and 1853 he composed *Stones of Venice* the series that would increase both his and the city's fame. Returning around 1876–1877 for another stay, he rented a modest house overlooking the Giudecca Canal – a place from which he would attempt to stave off his descent into madness. His vow of silence for the last twelve years of his life was to be eerily echoed in the twentieth century by another Dorsoduro resident plagued by insanity, the American poet Ezra Pound. They are joined in this neighbourhood by a train of foreigners seeking a more permissive, sometimes promiscuous, atmosphere than that of their less tolerant home countries. The reports from foreign travellers, of islands populated by handsome *gondolieri*, gracefully rowing gentlemen around in the late hours, surrounded by crumbling palaces and mysterious lights, would attract numerous visitors, turning many into lifelong residents, especially artists leaving traces through their writing or painting – or as legend.

* * *

Enoteca Già Schiavi **(1)*** remains even today the special haunt where foreign artists and writers congregate on Friday and Saturday nights. It provides a convenient place either to meet compatriots after a solitary day in the studio or to buy bottles to take away from their extensive selection. The scene is often pure expatriate Venice: capes and walking sticks, aged suits and trilby hats, hennaed hair and turquoise eye shadow, leopardskin coats and oversized jewellery. The city's centuries-long reputation as a haven for exiles and eccentrics coalesces at this tiny wine bar. But it is popular with natives as well. In *Friends in High Places*, Brunetti has left the pitifully drugged Zecchino and tellingly heads *away* from home for a consoling drink at Già Schiavi. The area through which he walks seems to represent a place of rewards for him; a way to erase the sullen mood induced by crime. Yet in *Through a Glass, Darkly*, too early for wine, he finds no welcoming place to offer solace from the biting winds sweeping off the Giudecca Canal: 'Had it been warmer, he would have had his first ice-cream of the year, not at Nico's but at the little place down by Gia Schiavi.'

→

Fondamenta Maravegia to Squero di San Trovaso **(2)** Whatever his destination in Dorsoduro, Brunetti will often pass Venice's most famous gondola repair yard: the *squero* **(2)** across the Rio San Trovaso. In a city of pink brick and white marble, the boat builders' preference for working in wood creates this surprising setting reminiscent of chalets in the Dolomites, all pitched roofs and dark carved balconies.

Rows of upturned black gondolas sit awaiting repair, a mere shadow of the thousands that populated Venice in the 1500s. Most visiting artists, from the poet Shelley to the novelist Thomas Mann, have created memorable images of the gondola – from a coffin, black as death, to descriptions of the lithe rower delicately balanced on the asymmetrical *poppa*. Brunetti needs no reminder of hearse-like gondolas to make him think of death, crime, prisons, and greed. These themes preoccupied an earlier lover of Venice's incredible and improbable beauty. Maddened by the excessive interest charged by banks, the American poet Ezra Pound, like Brunetti, found the link between the civil and the criminal inescapable. Arriving in 1908 and in his early twenties, he lived in a tiny apartment on the Rio San Trovaso, a spot destined to haunt his later years. During his incarceration in Pisa by the US Army in World War II, he mused in *The Pisan Cantos* on his early formative residence where his view looked out onto the *squero*.

Once freed from St Elizabeth's insane asylum in Washington, DC, he did indeed return to Venice and Dorsoduro, move into a small gondolier's cottage near San Vio – close to Lele's gallery – and 'see the Giudecca again', taking his place among the gifted eccentrics perpetually drawn to the city and to this area.

$$\longrightarrow$$

The wide walkway along the Zattere has long been a place where Venetians like to stroll on a Sunday morning. More open-aired than the rest of the city, lined with cafés out on the water perfect for a lounge over coffee and the papers, and maybe one of the Nico's famous ice-creams, it also serves as the ideal setting for Italians to create a *bella figura* draped in the latest styles, squiring pampered dogs, their children finally let loose to race on bicycles without the frustration of endless bridges.

To Fondamenta Zattere left to Gelateria Da Nico (3)

While the walk along the Zattere certainly lures its share of both residents and foreign visitors, not all are eccentric artists. It has an additional appeal, especially among the young, for those in search of what they have heard are Venice's finest *gelati*. In *Acqua Alta*, freezing from the winter cold and hoping to escape the icy winds coming off the Giudecca Canal, Brunetti huddles in Nico's (3),* listening with amusement as two American girls order *gelati* to cup in their mittened hands:

'Oh, Kimberly, are you sure this is the place?' the first one said in English, sweeping the place with her emerald eyes.

'It said so in the book, Alison. Nico's is, like, famous.' (She pronounced 'Nico' to rhyme with 'sicko', a word Brunetti had picked up at his last Interpol convention.) 'It's famous for *gelato*.'

It took a moment for the possibility of what might be about to happen to register on Brunetti. The instant it did, he sipped quickly at his grog, which was still so hot it burned his tongue. (. . .)

'Do you think they'd have Heath Bar?'

'Nah, not in Italy.'

'Yeah, I guess not. I guess we're gonna have to stick to, like, basics.' (*Acqua Alta*, ch. 6)

→

Along Zattere over the bridges to Pensione Calcina (4)

The marble plaque on the nearby Pensione Calcina **(4)*** memorializes the genius of a man who gave his professional life – and his love – to Venice. Of all the eccentrics in the nineteenth-century strolling the *calli* of Dorsoduro, half-mad Ruskin seems the most tragic. When he rested here in 1877, then nearly sixty, he was bewildered into silence by the bizarre events of his private life: an unconsummated marriage of six years, ending in scandal; then, when he was almost forty, falling in chaste love with the ten-year-old Rose La Touche, who would herself go mad and die at the age of twenty-seven.

Young females and their tragic lives inhabit a central place in Donna Leon's novels, or perhaps it would be more true to say that Brunetti has unusually strong sympathy for the youthful victims of crimes he must solve. In *Wilful Behaviour*, an exceptionally bright and earnest university student of Paola's comes to Brunetti for help. Despite an enormous monthly stipend, the girl lives simply; her address may be in prestigious Dorsoduro, but the room is sparely furnished and lacks a view. Her earnest desire to clear her grandfather's name from infamy forces the Commissario into a murky swamp of Fascism, art theft, betrayal of Venice's Jews to the Nazis, sexual threat, and, of course, murder. When the girl is suddenly found dead, Brunetti rushes to phone Paola before the news spreads throughout the city's efficient network of gossip.

There was a noise in the background, a voice, two voices, and then Brunetti said, 'I've got to go. Don't expect me before tonight.' And then he was gone.

Gone perhaps from the sound of his wife's voice but not from the presence of death, an apartment in Dorsoduro, not far from the Pensione Seguso **(A)** but back two streets from the Canale della Giudecca. (*Wilful Behaviour*, ch. 9)

Another landmark café for Brunetti in the Dorsoduro has been the former Il Cucciolo **(B)** (now La Piscina)* perched above the water on a wooden deck in front of the Pensione Calcina. Like a returning bird, he uses it as a bellwether for a welcome change of seasons. Early in *Acqua Alta*, a book dominated by the vagaries of weather, Brunetti longs for a sign that the high waters which have washed the city's streets will eventually efface the violence as well. But he must wait.

(. . .) he turned left and ducked into the underpass that led out to the Zattere, the long, open *fondamenta* that ran alongside the canal of the Giudecca. Across the water he saw the Church of the Zittelle **(C)** and then, further along, that of the Redentore **(D)**, their domes soaring up above them. A strong wind came in from the east, stirring up whitecaps that knocked and bounced the vaporetti around like toys in a tub. (. . .) Il Cucciolo, the waterside bar where he and Paola had spent so many hours during the first weeks after their meeting, was open, but the vast wooden deck in front of it, built out over the water, was completely empty, stripped of tables, chairs and umbrellas. To Brunetti, the first real sign of spring was the day when those tables and chairs appeared after their winter's hibernation. Today, the thought made him shiver. The bar was open, but he avoided it, for the waiters were the rudest in the city, their arrogant slowness tolerable only in exchange for idle hours in the sun. (*Acqua Alta*, ch. 6)

By the end of the novel, Brunetti has 'had enough of death and violence, enough of pilfered beauty and the lust for the perfect. He longed for springtime and its many imperfections.' The perfect season lures him into returning to Il Cucciolo to meet the lovely Flavia and savour the canal-side views.

The water drew him now and the thought of sitting in the young sun with Flavia, having a coffee, talking of this and that, seeing the way her face went so quickly from ease to joy and back again. He was to meet her at Il Cucciolo at eleven, and he already delighted in the thought of the sound of the waters stirring under the wooden deck, of the desultory motion of the waiters, not yet thawed from their winter lethargy, and of the large valiant umbrellas which insisted on creating shade, long before there was any need of it. (. . .)

Ahead of him he saw the waters of the Giudecca Canal and, beyond them, the happy façades of the buildings on the other side. From the left, a tanker steamed into view, riding high and empty in the water, and even its streaked grey hull seemed bright and beautiful in this light. (*Acqua Alta*, ch. 28)

→

Across bridge left on to Ramo dietro gli Incurabili **(5)**, to fountain **(6)**

The far eastern end of Dorsoduro is inhabited by the city's cadre of artists, writers, and the journalist Padovani. First seen in *Death at La Fenice*, the highly entertaining character returns in *The Anonymous Venetian*, willing both to help Brunetti understand the world of the male prostitutes in Mestre and to provide an evening meal in Paola's absence. But first the uniquely Venetian directions to his house:

'I'm down in Dorsoduro. Do you know the Ramo dietro gli Incurabili?' **(5)**.

It was a small *campo* with a running fountain, just back from the Zattere. 'Yes, I do.'

'Stand with your back to the fountain looking at the little canal, and it's the first door on the right.' Far clearer than giving a number or street name, this would get any Venetian to the house with no difficulty. (*The Anonymous Venetian*, ch. 14)

While Padovani's enjoyably arch pose resurfaces – he refers to himself as Guido's 'gay consultant' – the intimacy of the art-filled house and the pleasures of a home-cooked meal reveal another side: the perfect host and engaging conversationalist. Well informed about both the high and the low – the politics of Venice and the rent boys on Via Cappuccina in Mestre – he serves as an acute source of detail. While Padovani cooks, Brunetti's native fascination with property registers accurately all the details of a typical artist's home in eastern Dorsoduro:

At eight that evening, Brunetti, freshly showered and shaved and carrying a bottle of Barbera, rang the bell to the right of the small fountain in the Ramo degli Incurabili. The front of the building, which had only one bell and which, consequently, was probably that greatest of all luxuries, a separate house owned by only one person, was covered by jasmine plants which trailed up from two terracotta pots on either side of the door. (. . .)

The central part of it soared up two floors to a roof inset with skylights. This open space was surrounded on three sides by an open loggia reached by an open wooden staircase. The fourth side was closed in and must hold the bedroom. (. . .)

Paintings filled two walls; there was no attempt to order them into styles or schools: they hung on the walls and fought for the viewer's eye. The keenness of the competition gave evidence of the taste with which they had been selected. He spotted a Guttoso, a painter he had never liked much, and a Morandi, whom he did. There were three Ferruzzis, all giving joyous testimony to the beauty of the city. Then, a little to the left of the fireplace, a Madonna, clearly Florentine and probably fifteenth-century, looked adoringly down at yet another ugly baby. One of the secrets Paola and Brunetti never revealed to anyone was their decades-long search for the ugliest Christ Child in western art. (*The Anonymous Venetian*, ch. 14)

Brunetti and Padovani's talk turns from sex and crime to the fate of the environment and the inevitable threat to Venice. For Brunetti, however, property and history trump even nature.

'(. . .) since the *laguna* is just a gut hanging off the Adriatic, which is itself a gut hanging from the Mediterranean, which . . . well, you get the idea. I think the water will simply die, and then we'll be forced either to abandon the city or else fill in the canals, in which case there will no longer be any sense in living here.'

It was a novel theory and certainly no less bleak than many he had heard, than many he himself half believed. Everyone talked, all the time, of the imminent destruction of the city, and yet the price of apartments doubled every few years, and the rents for those available continued to soar ever higher above what the average worker could pay for one. Venetians had bought and sold real estate through the Crusades, the Plague, and various occupations by foreign armies, so it was probably a safe bet that they would continue to do so through whatever ecological holocaust awaited them. (*The Anonymous Venetian*, ch. 14)

Venice is a place of masks, so the Commissario will not be astonished to find a Lega della Moralità secretly involved in transvestite crime. Certainly his discussion with Padovani about an underworld of misfits occurs in an ironic location, so near the home for the incurables (**E**) founded by the Jesuits in 1522, a time when Venice was rife with plague, syphilis, and leprosy.

→

Today, Ramo dietro gli Incurabili is the residence of a wide variety of artists – painters, sculptors, journalists – the houses nestling in cosy proximity. Some have even left their artistic mark on the nearby buildings. Padovani has three of his former neighbour's paintings on his walls; while visitors must go to the nearby Guggenheim or the galleries along the canal to see art, all he had to do was knock on the door of the detached house next to the fresco, now vanished despite the city's efforts to save it, and be welcomed for a tiny glass of *fragolino* and a look at the artist's works.

Outside the Questura he gave himself over to what was left of the day. He went out to Riva degli Schiavoni and took the Number One to Salute, then headed west with no destination in mind, turning that decision over to his memory and his mood. He cut through the underpass by the abbey, down past building site after building site then left, down towards the Incurabili. Only a fragment of Bobo's fresco remained, glassed in now in order to save what was left from the elements. (*Through a Glass, Darkly*, ch. 18)

In Dorsoduro, Brunetti often enjoys the city's centre for modern art, although he'll avoid the Peggy Guggenheim Foundation, which draws crowds outnumbered only by the Accademia Gallery nearby and the Palazzo Ducale in Piazza San Marco. The Guggenheim's former owner, another art-loving expatriate, once dominated this area, presiding over talented artists and fostering the group of galleries that line the Fondamenta Venier. Before leaving this *sestiere*, Brunetti often makes a stop to see an old friend of his father's at his waterside gallery, Lele Cossato, one of the modern *vedute* (view) painters who still records and celebrates Venice's beauty. The *vedute* belong to a prestigious tradition that has contributed to making Venice the most physically visual city in the world. Before mechanical devices made taking tourist photos an easy feat, requiring no particular artistic genius, the Grand Tourists in the eighteenth century suffered the same frustrating desire: how to export Venice, at least visually. Ever financially alert to opportunity, the city became home to a never-ending series of view painters. From the Venetians who invented the industry – Canaletto, Bellotto, Guardi – to the foreigners who elected to record La Serenissima – Monet, Whistler, Turner, Sargent – the practice continues into the twenty-first century with new generations of *vedute* painters who can be seen, brushes in hand, all over the city.

To Calle Navaro, left on Calle del Forno, right on Corte delle Mende, to canal

In *Acqua Alta*, Brunetti has come to an old friend for information about the art world and the murder of Director Semenzato in the Palazzo Ducale. Although the painter Lele Cossato, another 'lover of beauty', is a fictional invention of Leon, the location of his gallery (**F**) and the style of his works are similar to those of the current master Venetian scene painter, whose works fill the home of the journalist Padovani in *Death at La Fenice*. Lele's connections, too, are pure Venetian.

If anyone would know about Semenzato's reputation, it was Lele. Gabriele Cossato, painter, antiquarian, lover of beauty, was as much a part of Venice, it seemed, as were the four Moors, poised in eternal confabulation to the right of the Basilica of San Marco. For as far back as Brunetti could remember, there had been Lele, and Lele had been a painter. (. . .) his passion for the beauty of the city remained, that and his limitless familiarity with the art world and all it encompassed: antiquarians and dealers, museums and galleries.

(. . .)

Brunetti looked automatically at the paintings hanging on the walls of the gallery, vividly coloured scenes of the city, alive with light and filled with Lele's energy. (*Acqua Alta*, ch. 5)

→

Over bridge (**7**) right on Fondamenta Venier, past Guggenheim (**8**), along Calle San Cristoforo to back of Ca' Dario (**9**)

In Brunetti's world the grand and the squalid often compete, and the trendy Dorsoduro is certainly not exempt from the unholy mix. Burdened with its beauty and the superstitious curse that claims all owners have died violently, the Ca' Dario (**9**), one of the oldest *palazzi* on the Grand Canal, has exerted a special fascination for its foreign residents. From writers Rawdon Brown and Henri de Régnier in the nineteenth century to figures from finance and film stars like Woody Allen in the twentieth, many prospective buyers have been tempted by the loveliness of its roundel ornamented façade on the canal, and the charm of its large back garden. But almost as many have fled the curse. Sadly, this small *palazzo* stayed empty for years. A recent purchase may bring new residents to enliven the neighbourhood again.

Palazzo Dario's sale has been further hindered by its location: in this area of Dorsoduro, residential character is diminishing as it is increasingly being taken over by galleries and shops at the expense of local cafés and markets. Even some of the Venetians here seem to suffer the pretensions of the art-lover, if Signor da Prè in *The Death of Faith* is anything to go by. As Brunetti begins his search for the diminutive snuffbox collector and only heir to his sister's sizeable fortune, he must endure yet another lecture on the ecology of the lagoon from the boat driver:

'Anyone who eats a fish from out of that water is crazy,' the pilot said.

Late last year, there had been numerous cases of cholera reported, but in the south, where that sort of thing happened. Brunetti remembered that the health authorities had closed the fish market in Bari and warned the local people to avoid eating fish, which had seemed to him like telling cows to avoid eating grass.

The autumn rains and floods had driven the story from the pages of the national newspapers, but not before Brunetti had begun to wonder whether the same thing was possible, here in the north, and how wise it was to eat anything that came from the increasingly putrid waters of the Adriatic.

When the boat pulled up at the gondola stop to the left of Palazzo Dario, Vianello grabbed the end of a coiled rope and leaped on to the dock.

(. . .)

'Dorsoduro 723. It's up near the Guggenheim, on the left.'

The men walked up the narrow *calle* and turned right at the first intersection. Brunetti found himself still wanting a coffee, then surprised that there were no bars to be seen on either side of the street. (*The Death of Faith*, ch. 3)

Always quick to employ his useful Veneziano dialect and Castello accent in an investigation with locals, Vianello also proves to be ingenious at manipulating witnesses. By book six, *The Death of Faith*, he is beginning to take over from Brunetti if he sees an advantage he can use to loosen a suspect's tongue. Even the otherwise malignant little man da Prè has his passion, snuffboxes, and the policeman sees a benefit in upstaging his Commissario boss:

Vianello, who had nodded in silent assent through all of this speech, said to Brunetti, 'I'm afraid you don't understand, Commissario.'

Brunetti, who had no idea how he had deserved to be sent this clever man who could so easily disarm even the most antagonistic witness, nodded in humble agreement. (ch. 3)

To Campo Santa Maria della Salute **(10)**

Chiesa Santa Maria della Salute **(G)** and her immediate surroundings have lured many curious walkers in Venice away from her more famous sister across the water, the Basilica di San Marco. On any sunny day Henry James' description of the Salute seems especially apt: 'some great lady . . . her wide steps disposed on the ground like the train of a robe'. The church's marble steps are dotted with people admiring the spectacular views, heads nodding over guidebooks to identify the famous landmarks across the Grand Canal. The Gritti Hotel **(H)** where Hemingway stayed and Harry's Bar **(I)** where he drank are both immortalized in his novel set in Venice, *Across the River and into the Trees*. The lacy-balconied narrow *palazzo* the Venetians call 'Ca' Desdemona' **(J)** contributes to Venice's ever-growing legend industry, which seems to produce fakes just as much as the glass and lace businesses. The pretty, yellow Hotel Europa Regina **(K)** sits nearby: here American expatriate Kay Bronson kept rooms empty for Robert Browning and served both as hostess to Henry James and as the model for Mrs Prest in *The Aspern Papers*. In this book of James, Paola's favourite writer, as in the Brunetti novels, the high-minded and the low-motived hypocritically coexist.

The old customs house, the famous Dogana **(L)**,* sits with its dome just visible out on the furthest point, surmounted by a nude female statue that only the sexually timid Henry

James could describe as 'divested [of] her rotary bronze loveliness'. Like so many of Venice's abandoned buildings which once housed the riches of the world, the Dogana was for centuries the main customs house for all foreign goods entering by ship. More recently it has served as a battleground for foreigners competing to acquire this unmatched location in order to create another tourist venue.*

Not every view from the Salute steps is a grand vista. In a city often dependent on window boxes filled with flowers for signs of the seasons' change, the attractive houses that line the small canal opposite the side of the church with their long rows of hundreds of yellow marigolds ritually changed by their owners into banks of winter white calendula are a special delight. But even in the shadow of the Salute the Venetian dichotomy between lovely façade and rotten interior surfaces. In *A Venetian Reckoning*, Eastern European women have been forced into prostitution, and even snuff videos play a role. So it is with especial loathing that Brunetti turns his back on the Salute and approaches the expensive house of the elegant Signora Ceroni, who has been assisting in the women's ruin.

He couldn't remember the home address that they had got for Signora Ceroni beyond that it was in San Vio and that, when he had seen it, he had wondered how close it would be to the Church of La Salute. (. . .) He found the house not only near the church but looking out at it from the other side of the small canal that ran along the side of the church. Her name was on the bell. He rang it and, after a minute or so, heard a woman's voice asking who it was. He gave his name and, with no further questions, she buzzed him in.

He paid no attention to the hallway, to the stairs, or to what sort of greeting she gave him at the door. She led him into a large living room, one wall of which was covered with books. Soft lighting glowed down from lights which must have been concealed behind the beams that ran across the ceiling. None of this interested him. Nor her loveliness nor the soft elegance of her clothing. (*A Venetian Reckoning*, ch. 26)

Fatal Remedies continues the focus on violence to women, in this case sex tourism. The lawyer Zambino is defending the tourist agency vandalized by Paola Brunetti. Because it is Venice, and money is involved, the search for information includes the city's finest neighbourhoods.

Vianello must have learned their names in some other way, for his answer was immediate. 'Zambino lives in Dorsoduro, not far from the Salute. Big place, must be three hundred metres. He specializes in corporate and business law. Most of his clients are out on the mainland: chemicals and petrochemicals, pharmaceuticals and one factory that manufactures heavy earth-moving equipment.' (*Fatal Remedies*, ch. 8)

Illicit sex and violence to the young continues in *Uniform Justice*, this time when a young male cadet is found hanged. Brunetti, dubious about the claim of 'suicide', goes to interrogate the dead boy's father, Dottor Moro. Calling Signorina Elettra for information, he waits as his mind scans his geographic memory of the city and its residents.

When she answered, he told her where he was and asked that she check the phone book for Moro's address, which he thought must be in Dorsoduro, though he couldn't remember why he associated the man with that *sestiere*.
She asked no questions, told him to wait a moment, then said the number was unlisted. There elapsed another minute or two, then she gave him the Dorsoduro address. She told him to wait, then told him the house was on the canal running alongside the Church of Madonna della Salute. 'It's got to be the one next to the low brick one that has the terrace with all the flowers,' she said. (*Uniform Justice*, ch. 5)

Doubt turns to despair at the thwarting of justice, both to the victim and to his destroyed family. Brunetti wanders across Venice in the deepening night to await the Dottore's arrival at home. Best to leave him in this lovely *campo*, grateful once again that the incredible beauty of the Salute's views across the Grand Canal give him a consoling lift from his grim task.

As Brunetti walked through the quiet city, his imagination took flight again.

(. . .) he crossed the bridge to the broad *riva* in front of the Salute. Moro's house, off to his right, was dark, though all the shutters were open. (. . .)

He turned and looked across the still waters at the disorderly domes of San Marco and the piebald walls of Palazzo Ducale, and thought of the peace their beauty brought him. How strange it was: nothing more than the arrangement of lines and colours, and he felt better than he had before he looked at them. (*Uniform Justice*, ch. 19)

---

*Già Schiavi, long a family business, this spot at the foot of a bridge is crowded with locals and foreigners sipping outside on the steps or at the bar with the city's most extensive selection of *crostini* and *cicheti*.

*Gelateria Nico serves some of the city's best *gelati*, as well as being a meeting place out on the waterside terrace on Sundays.

*Pensione Calcina has a magical setting for views across the Giudecca Canal and offers the pleasure of staying where Ruskin lived and chopped wood in the courtyard.

*Pensione Seguso next to the Calcina sits on a tiny side canal, so drinks or breakfast outside are a particular delight.

*Il Cucciolo (now La Piscina) bar on the water in front of the Calcina also offers full meals.

*In 2007 an announcement claimed that the Dogana property for an art venue had been awarded to Francois Pinault to expand his collection now housed in the Palazzo Grassi.

WALK 7: *Rich and Poor*

Salute—San Vio—Ponte dell'Accademia—Santo Stefano—San
Maurizio—Calle larga XXII Marzo—San Moisè—San Marco

1 hour

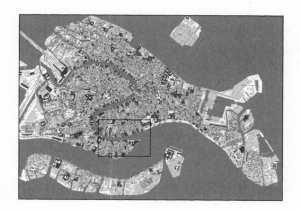

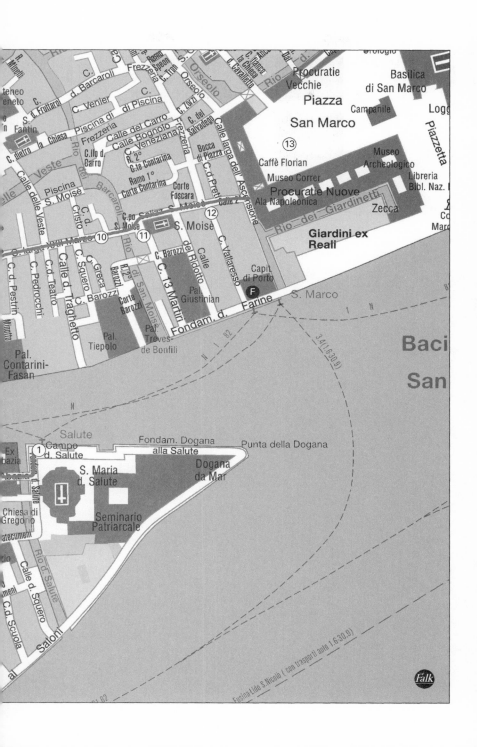

This walk from the gallery-filled area of the Church of Campo Santa Maria della Salute (1) the Salute **(1)** in Dorsoduro, over the arc of the Accademia Bridge, to the edge of Piazza San Marco opens and ends with famous and familiar Venice. Yet in between, in Campo Santo Stefano, the world of legitimate commerce coexists with the world of the African street sellers unknown even to Brunetti. This walk reveals that not only remote *sestieri* like Castello can be mysterious and filled with danger but the very heart of Venice herself.

* * *

Probably no visitor's comment on Venice is heard more often than the lament about perpetually getting lost. None of the residents' assurances that wandering aimlessly is part of this unique city's charm eases the tourists' confusion. No confession that residents too wind up in dead ends assuages the visitors' frustration. In spite of all consolation from the natives, tourists persist in seeing their failed grasp of the city's geography as, somehow, their own personal failure. The locals are more cavalier; in fact, a favourite pastime of some Venetian residents, both native and foreign, is to attempt an unfamiliar journey across the city without getting lost – no mean feat.

Donna Leon creates a game out of the venture for Brunetti, much as Hemingway does for his hero Colonel Cantwell in *Across the River and into the Trees*; it is a peculiarly Venetian adventure and one the Colonel enjoys and calls a *'solitaire ambulante'*.

Even natives like Brunetti delight in sights never noticed before, with every discovery meriting a reward:

Usually as he walked, he glanced at the fronts of buildings, up at their windows, down narrow streets, always alert to something he might not have noticed before. Like many of his townsmen, Brunetti never tired of studying the city, every so often delighting himself by discovering something he had never noticed before. Over the course of the years, he had worked out a system that allowed him to reward himself for each discovery: a new window earned him a coffee; a new statue of a saint, however small, got him a glass of wine. (*Death in a Strange Country*, ch. 12)

→

Over wood bridge right to *traghetto* landing (2)

Brunetti cannot always call up his sensitive response to beauty. In *Uniform Justice*, as he leaves the solace of the Salute area and crosses over the small bridge between vine-covered and flower-bedecked houses to the *traghetto* (2) that will take him across the Grand Canal to Santa Maria del Giglio, he proves immune to Dorsoduro's beauty. He is so much affected by the young cadet's gruesome death that it continues to haunt his every move. Later, the change in his mood is even recognizable to Paola, who finally asks the unthinkable: 'How much longer can you do this, Guido?'

But Venice has always sustained and rewarded him with her beauty – even in the face of appalling violence and the death of innocents. It is one faith he has not lost.

He looked ahead as they made their slow passage across the Canal Grande, struck by just how jaded a person could become: ahead of him lay Palazzo Ducale, and behind it popped up the gleaming domes of the Basilica di San Marco: Brunetti stared as though they were nothing more than the painted backdrop in a dull, provincial production of *Otello*. How had he got to the point where he could look on such beauty and not be shaken? (. . .)

Long experience had taught him that his sense of wonder was still intact and would return, bringing back with it an almost painful awareness of the beauty that surrounded him at every turn. (*Uniform Justice*, ch. 15)

→

Past Guggenheim to Campo San Vio (3)

Between murder and mayhem, art and beauty, Brunetti always appreciates food, especially in *Blood from a Stone*, when he feels abandoned by the devoted Paola, who is heartlessly going to her family's Christmas lunch. Since no scent of rosemary after a climb up the four flights to home and hearth will await him, he decides to enjoy a meal in the fashionable district of Dorsoduro.

The walk passes small Campo San Vio **(3)** with its Anglican church so important to the earlier expatriate community from England. The view from the edge of the Grand Canal is highlighted by Palazzo Barbaro **(A)**, another important gathering place for foreign artists in Venice, with its grand ballroom providing the final scene in Henry James' *Wings of the Dove*. In Venice, both underpaid writers and salaried policemen, like Brunetti, often have the privilege of working in exalted settings.

Brunetti could not give himself over wholeheartedly to playing the role of the neglected spouse. He could, however, treat himself to a good lunch. Aunt Federica, apart from her temper, was known for the skill of her cook, so Paola was sure to arrive at their meeting sated not only with the latest family gossip but with the results of the recipes the Faliers had spent the last four centuries enjoying.

This he found at Cantinone Storico **(B)*** in the form of a risotto with tiny shrimp which the waiter promised him were fresh and a grilled orata served with boiled potatoes. Asked if he'd like dessert, Brunetti thought of the heavy eating that lay ahead of him in the next weeks and, feeling quite pleased with himself, said all he wanted was a grappa and a coffee. (*Blood from a Stone*, ch. 17)

$$\rightarrow$$

Venice's unique geography has always been further complicated by the scarcity of bridges across the serpentine Grand Canal – today only three exist until the new bridge linking Piazzale Roma and the train station designed by the Spanish architct Calatrava is finished. The Rialto, first built on pontoons, later a drawbridge, has, with its prestigious history, managed to keep its latest white marble status since the sixteenth century. The wooden Accademia bridge **(5)** has not

To Rio terrà Antonio Foscarini **(4)** to Ponte dell'Accademia **(5)**

fared so well. *Friends in High Places* begins with Brunetti facing the illegality of his own apartment; later he is forced to see how much of the entire city's building is a product of questionable deals.

At the foot of the Accademia Bridge he hesitated for a moment but decided to make a wide circle and pass through Campo San Luca. He started over the bridge, eyes on his feet, and noticed how many of the strips of white facing were broken or torn off the front edge of the steps. When had it been rebuilt, the bridge? Three years ago? Two? And already many of the steps were in need of repair. His mind veered away from contemplation of how that contract must have been awarded. (*Friends in High Places*, ch. 20)

→

Into Campo Santo Stefano (6)

The Ponte dell' Accademia is not just a span over water but a move to a less prestigious and protected world. In *Blood from a Stone*, Brunetti leaves behind the Dorsoduro of elegant galleries and posh cafés, and crosses the bridge to enter one of the illegal commercial centres of the *vu cumprà*. In this eastern *sestiere* of San Marco, street sellers may enjoy a certain tolerance from the local police, who have been known to whistle in advance of their arrival as comradely warning, but that affords *extracomunitari* no safety from the threat of criminal violence. *Blood from a Stone* opens with a young African victim of a contract killing in crowded Campo Santo Stefano **(6)**.

They were in Italy illegally and stood on the street during the day, selling counterfeit bags. They lacked the funds to buy or rent shops, restaurants, or bars, so the resulting protection of wealth would not be offered them. (*Blood from a Stone*, ch. 11)

Donna Leon sets many scenes in Santo Stefano, the largest *campo* after Piazza San Marco on this side of the Grand Canal. Much visited by the Venetians for festivals, holidays, and political rallies, its former dangerous bullfights have now been replaced by tame outdoor Christmas stalls from all over Italy, with bands and pageants during Carnevale. Ringed with outdoor cafés and restaurants, made beautiful by the pale façade of Palazzo Loredan (C), today's Institute of Science and Arts, adorned by a marble statue of Niccolò Tommaseo, who aided Daniele Manin in fighting the Austrians, it is a perfect place to watch the crowds.

Brunetti often stops in the *campo* – for a coffee, a rest, or even to check on the city's current political climate, while he listens to the loudspeaker vainly haranguing the city's indifferent citizens into moral outrage.

He abandoned any thought of hurrying and allowed the flow to carry him towards Campo San Stefano. From the bottom of the closest bridge, he heard amplified sound but could not distinguish it clearly.

Down the narrow slot of the last *calle* they pulled him and then, suddenly, freed him into the darkening *campo*. Directly in front of him was the statue Brunetti had always thought of as the Meringue Man, so starkly white and porous was the marble from which he was carved. Other people, seeing the pile of books that seemed to issue from beneath his coat, called him something more indelicate.

To Brunetti's right, a wooden platform had been erected along the side of the Church of San Stefano. A few wooden chairs stood on it; the front corners held enormous speakers. From three wooden poles at the back of the platform hung the limp flags bearing the Italian tricolor, the lion of San Marco, and the newly minted symbol of what had once been the Christian Democratic party. (*A Venetian Reckoning*, ch. 22)

Brunetti is so familiar with Campo Santo Stefano that he knows not only the faces of people he has never met, but also their dogs. History records they have always been a pampered presence. Nowhere else in Italian Renaissance art can be found the numerous dogs immortalized in Venetian paintings, most in highly improbable settings: impatient in the middle of Saint Jerome's study in Carpaccio's series of frescos; snoozing at the delicate feet of Titian's luscious *Venus of Urbino*; waiting for bones from the table of Veronese's *Feast in the House of Levi*; listening patiently to the music in Longhi's *Concerto*, and many more.

A common scene today is that of Venetians stopping and chatting with the dogs they know by name and see frequently, usually a much more intimate exchange than with their owners. Campo Santo Stefano has its own menagerie in residence, and Brunetti frequents his chosen café there both to register the animals' changes and to inspect the scene:

(. . .) Lazing in the pale sunlight was a pink-and-white bulldog whose lack of muzzle always made Brunetti uneasy. Then there was that odd Chinese thing that had grown from what looked like a pile of furred tripe into a creature of surpassing ugliness. Last, lolling in front of the ceramics store, he saw the black mongrel that remained so motionless all day that many people had come to believe he was part of the merchandise.

He decided to have a coffee at Caffè Paolin **(D)**.* Tables were still set up outside, but the only people at them today were foreigners, desperately trying to convince themselves that it was warm enough to have a *cappuccino* at a table in the open air. Sensible people went inside. (*Death at La Fenice*, ch. 13)

In *Blood from a Stone*, Donna Leon creates the annual scene of Christmas shopping in this busy *campo*, making the street seller's murder all the more shocking. No air of menace disturbs the holiday atmosphere until the two anonymous killers arrive unnoticed.

Two men passed under the wooden arch that led into Campo Santo Stefano, their bodies harlequined by the coloured Christmas lights suspended above them. Brighter light splashed from the stalls of the Christmas market, where vendors and producers from different regions of Italy tempted shoppers with their local specialities: dark-skinned cheeses and packages of paper-thin bread from Sardinia, olives in varying shape and colour from the entire length of the peninsula; oil and cheese from Tuscany; salami of all lengths, compositions, and diameters from Reggio Emilia. Occasionally one of the men behind the counters shouted out a brief hymn to the quality of his wares: 'Signori, taste this cheese and taste heaven.' (. . .)

The two men passed the stalls, deaf to the blandishments of the merchants, blind to the pyramids of salami stacked on the counters on either side. (*Blood from a Stone*, ch 1)

In a city with a low crime rate, it is not by chance that one of only two murders by professional killers described in Donna Leon's whole series takes place in Santo Stefano. Few *campi* in Venice could so successfully conceal armed criminals. Between the noisy, boisterous stalls and the street musicians, the sound of the silencer-armed guns barely registers, even to the nearby American tour group bargaining for purses. Venice's confusing geography further abets the killers' easy escape, since they have a multitude of possible routes, all crowded, none straight.

'It has that feel about it, the work of professionals. They appeared out of nowhere, executed him, and disappeared.'

'So what does that tell you about them?'

'That they're familiar with the city.'

She gave him a questioning glance, and he elaborated, 'To know which way to leave. Also to know where he was.'

'Does that mean Venetian?'

Brunetti shook his head. 'I've never heard of a Venetian who works as a killer.' (. . .)

Paola (. . .) closed her eyes and considered the geography of the area and finally said, 'Afterwards, getting away would be easy. All they'd have to do is go back towards Rialto, or up towards San Marco, or over the Accademia.'

When she stopped, Brunetti continued, 'Or they could go into San Vidal and then cut back towards San Samuele.'

'How many places could they get a vaporetto?' she asked.

'Three. Four. And then they could have gone either way.'

'What would *you* do?' she asked.

'I don't know. But if I wanted to leave the city, I'd probably go up towards San Marco and cut in towards the Fenice and then to Rialto.' (*Blood from a Stone*, ch 4)

In the days after the crime, the African *vu cumprà* all disappear from Campo Santo Stefano, their absence quickly filled by other varieties of precarious pedlars. The area's central position between the Accademia bridge and San Marco will forever keep it busy and profitable.

He did see some sheets on the ground. At first he thought they must be the forgotten groundsheets of the crime scene, but then he saw the line of wind-up toys and linked wooden train carriages, carved to look like individual letters, spelling names across the sheet. The men stationed behind the sheets were not Africans but Orientals and Tamils, and off to the left he saw a band of poncho-draped Indios and their strange musical instruments. But as for Africans, the more Brunetti looked, the more they were not there. (*Blood*, ch. 17)

Still, ubiquitous though the street sellers seem to visitors to Venice, for residents they constitute a shadowy and uncertain presence, as Signorina Elettra reminds Brunetti:

'I simply think it's very strange that they can live among us and yet, for the entire time they aren't on the street, selling things, remain invisible.' She looked to see if he realized how serious she was, then added, 'That's why I say they live on a different planet. The only attention we pay to them on this planet, it seems, is when we arrest them.' (. . .)

He decided to accept her point and said, 'Then that's a way to begin: see if you can find out where it is they go when they disappear.' (*Blood*, ch. 6)

→

Calle dello Spezier **(7)** into Campo San Maurizio **(8)**

The poor and the rich are never so close as in this section of the city; this is especially evident when leaving the *ambulanti*-filled Campo Santo Stefano and entering the nearby

Campo San Maurizio **(8)**. This smaller square, with its jewellers and small antique shops, sits at the beginning of an artery leading to San Marco that still has the good fortune to be dotted with traditional shops filled with the elegant Venetian wares that have contributed so much to the city's renown. This atmosphere of sophistication makes the *campo* the understandable location of the occasional weekend street market for high quality craftsmen. And the rare crimes which the novels set in this *campo* demonstrate the same exacting standards: imaginative planning, no violence.

The only interesting crime had taken place at a jewellery store in Campo San Maurizio two days before, when a well-dressed couple pushed in their baby carriage, and, new father blushing with pride, asked to see a diamond ring to give to the even shyer mother. She tried on first one, then another. Finally, selecting a three-carat white diamond, she asked if she could go out and look at it in the light of day. The inevitable followed: she stepped outside the door, flashed her hand in the sunlight, smiled, then waved to the father, who dipped his head into the carriage to rearrange the covers and, with an embarrassed smile to the owner, stepped outside to join his wife. And disappeared, of course, leaving the baby carriage and doll behind, blocking the door. (*The Death of Faith*, ch. 1)

→

Campo Santa Maria del Giglio **(9)** hosts the landing stage of one of Venice's busiest *traghetti*, the quickest and easiest path across the Grand Canal from the city centre to the residential area of Dorsoduro. Before leaving for their quiet gallery-laden neighbourhoods, Dorsoduro residents can drink at Haig's bar, shop for expensive clothes along Calle larga XXII Marzo, then retreat to their costly properties far from the crowded centre. A brief gondola trip, offering resplendent views on either side; it is a rare and inexpensive treat to be rowed for half a Euro.

For Brunetti, both sides of this portion of the Grand Canal are areas he enters mainly on police business. In *A Venetian*

Calle Zaguri to Campo Santa Maria del Giglio **(9)**

Reckoning, a successful lawyer, Trevisan, has been found shot on a train from Padova, so the Commissario must try to prise information from the callous accountant brother-in-law and the grieving wife. Their wealth in ample evidence, their help in scant supply, Brunetti occupies himself with the views across the canal as they keep him waiting.

He got off at Santa Maria del Giglio, made a left at the Hotel Ala **(E)**.* (. . .)

'You can wait here,' Lotto said and left the room. Brunetti stood still for a moment, then walked over to one of the windows and pulled back the drape. Beyond him lay the Grand Canal, sunlight playing on its surface, and off to the left Palazzo Dario, the golden tiles of the mosaic that covered its façade catching the light that shot up from the water below, only to shatter it into fragments and sprinkle it back on the waters of the canal. Boats floated by; minutes went with them. (*A Venetian Reckoning*, ch. 9)

→

Calle delle
Ostreghe to Calle
larga XXII Marzo
(10)

The approach to Piazza San Marco along the Calle larga XXII Marzo **(10)** offers the most expensive shopping and business addresses in the city. The lawyer Trevisan conveniently has his office on this street, as Brunetti notes, 'above the Banca Commerciale d'Italia, about as good a business address as one could hope to have in Venice'.

Home to all the major Italian designer shops with their knock-off African competitors standing sentinel outside, it perfectly epitomizes the Venetian attitude to trade. So long as it brings money to the city, all will be accommodated. And this even includes an advantage for the *vu cumprà,* as Signorina Elettra explains:

'Where's the shop?' Brunetti asked, not because he was particularly interested but to show them that he really was listening.

'Off Ventidue Marzo. On that *calle* that goes up towards the Fenice, down from the bridge.'

Brunetti sent his memory walking towards Campo San Fantin, down the narrow *calle* towards the bridge, past the antique shop. 'Opposite the bar?' he asked.

'I think so,' she answered. 'I haven't checked the address, but it's the only one there, I think.'

'And these two rent to *extracomunitari*?' Brunetti asked.

'That's what Leonardo tells me. No long-term contracts, no questions about how many people will eventually live in the apartment, and everything paid in cash.' (*Blood from a Stone*, ch. 9)

→

In the streets around the main shopping artery, the tackier establishments haunt Brunetti's walks. Unlike the peace of his late night stroll across the city in *Death at La Fenice*, the bliss evaporates in the daylight hours when Brunetti is forced to see the deterioration of the city reflected in the quality of the wares that now fill the shops.

Into Campo San Moisè (11)

Along the way, he paused to look into shop windows, shocked, as he always was when in the centre of the city, by how quickly their composition was changing. It seemed to him that all the shops that served the native population – pharmacies, shoemakers, groceries – were slowly and inexorably disappearing, replaced by slick boutiques and souvenir shops that catered to the tourists, filled with luminescent plastic gondolas from Taiwan and papier-mâché masks from Hong Kong. It was the desires of the transients, not the needs of the residents, that the city's merchants answered. He wondered how long it would take before the entire city became a sort of living museum, a place fit only for visiting and not for inhabiting. (*Death at La Fenice*, ch. 9)

Brunetti's various struggles with the city are compounded by his constant manoeuvring with his difficult boss, Vice-Questore Patta. Any hint that persons of wealth, status, or station might be inconvenienced will hurl Patta into threats to remove the Commissario from an important case. In *Death at La Fenice*, anxious to appear at the conductor's funeral, Brunetti endures the latest harangue without resistance.

His meeting with Patta kept Brunetti from getting to the Church of San Moisè until just a few minutes before ten. The black boat carrying the flower-covered casket was already moored to the side of the canal, and three blue-suited men were busy placing the wooden casket on the wheeled metal platform they would use to take it to the door of the church. In the host of people who crowded around the front of the church, Brunetti recognized a few familiar Venetian faces, the usual reporters and photographers from the papers, but he didn't see the widow; she must already have entered the church. (*La Fenice*, ch. 11)

→

Along Salizzada San Moisè, to Calle Vallaresso **(12)**

It seems only fit that Salizzada San Moisè, the most expensive of Venice's streets leading to Piazza San Marco, should have as its neighbour the city's most famous bar. But Venetians are snobs not only about tourist restaurants run by foreigners or serving ethnic cuisine. In recent times, some have come to resent their own local institutions that have been co-opted by visitors – none more so than the famous Harry's Bar **(F)**.

They found themselves in the Piazza, and it was only then that Brunetti realized that he had been leading Vianello away from his house. He stopped and said, 'I'm going to go up and take the Number One. Would you like a drink?'

'Not around here,' Vianello said, his eyes taking in the Piazza and its hosts of pigeons and tourists, one as annoying as the other. 'Next thing, you'll be suggesting we go to Harry's Bar.'

'I don't think they let anyone in who isn't a tourist,' Brunetti said.

Vianello guffawed, as Venetians often do at the thought of going to Harry's Bar, and said he'd walk home. (*Wilful Behaviour*, ch. 16)

In this area with magnificent views of San Marco from the right addresses, native places increasingly become residences for foreigners, rich palaces find themselves hemmed in by more and more poor street vendors. When the death of Conductor Wellauer means the end of his wife's nearby residence on the Canal Grande, Brunetti goes to pay his last respects to the Belgian maid he has come to know. Their parting creates a poignant reflection on the pain of exile and the price of beauty:

'The signora will have to decide what she wants to do with the apartment. I will stay until she does that, and then I will go home, where I belong.' Saying that, she opened the door for him and then closed it silently behind him. On his way down the steps, Brunetti stopped at the first landing and gazed out the window. Off in the distance, the angel on top of the bell tower spread his wings in benediction above the city and all those in it. Even if exile is spent in the most beautiful city in the world, Brunetti realized, it is still exile. (*Death at La Fenice*, ch. 15)

→

Despite all Brunetti's grumblings about modern Venice with her inescapable changes, usually it takes amazingly little to remind him of the glory he was born into. Time to leave him with his joy and his pride.

To Piazza San Marco **(13)**

He turned right and walked up towards the Piazza **(13)**, and Brunetti found himself, to his own vast surprise, looking kindly upon the tourists who strolled past him, mouths agape and steps slowed by wonder. She could still knock them down, this old whore of a city, and Brunetti, her true son, protective of her in her age, felt a surge of mingled pride and delight and hoped that those people who walked by would see him and somehow know him for a Venetian and, in that, part heir to and part owner of all of this. (*A Venetian Reckoning*, ch. 7)

*Cantinone Storico, with its alfresco tables on a small canal, specializes in vegetables and porcini as well as seafood.

*Paolin, a popular place for *gelati* on this side of the Grand Canal, has sunny tables spread out into the *campo*.

*Hotel Ala, reasonable for its advantageous location, has views of the *campo* and its quiet back canal.

WALK 8: *Piazza San Marco*

San Marco—Riva degli Schiavoni—Pietà

1 hour

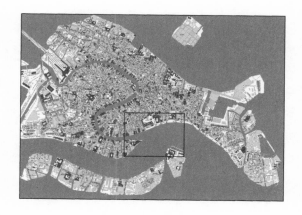

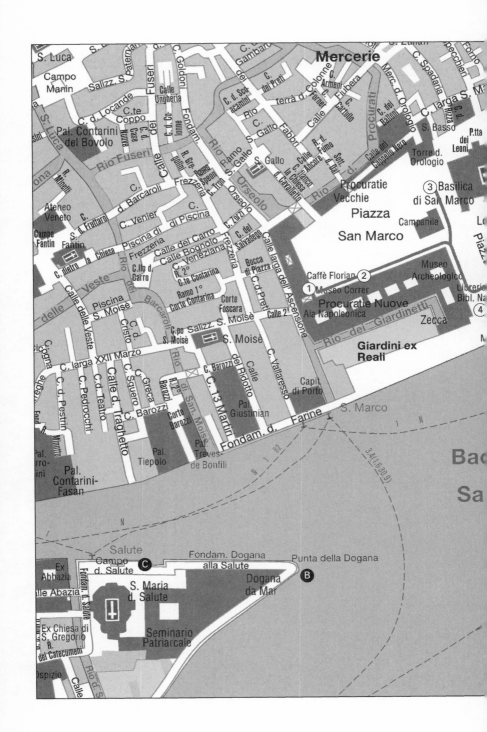

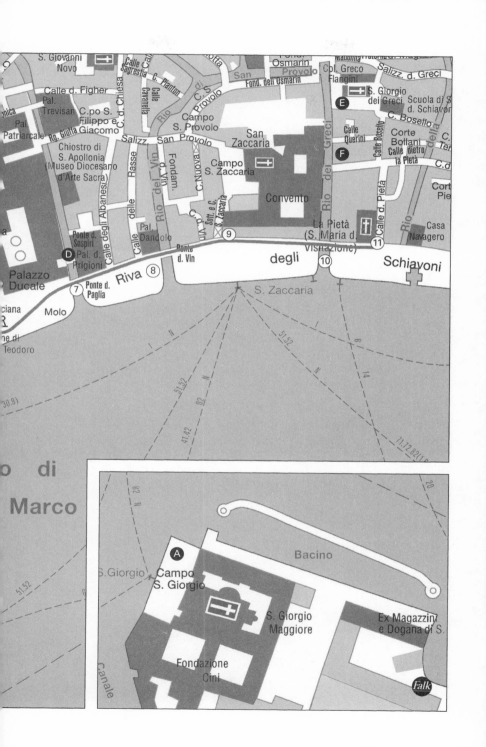

Unlike the rest of Italy, Venice names her open squares *campi*, gracing only San Marco with the honour of Piazza San Marco, front of Museo Correr (1) Piazza. Flanked by the Leoncini on one side of the Basilica and Piazetta San Marco on the other, fronting the lagoon, this famous area occupies most of walk 8. Palazzo Ducale, one of the loveliest secular buildings from medieval Europe – part Islamic, part Romanesque, part Gothic – anchors one corner of Piazza San Marco. Facing it across the *piazzetta* sits the Marciana Library, a Renaissance masterpiece that Palladio called the most beautiful building since antiquity. And in the centre reigns the grand Basilica with its overlay of architectural styles and the massive loot of Venice's extensive 'acquisitions' from the entire Mediterranean. Piazza San Marco never fails to amaze, though, ironically, it does not always please. Whether the visitor finds it the pinnacle of man's achievement in beauty or dismayingly over the top depends on many things. As one of the few open space landmarks in Venice and the lowest point in the city, the Piazza presents a bewildering series of faces: a mirror during *acqua alta* when the architectural façades duplicate themselves in the water-covered pavement; an inferno in the *ferragosto* heat when the buildings seem to quaver in the haze and lose all outline; and finally a masked meeting place when people cover the square during Carnevale, when the Piazza is more intimate and raucous than the 'drawing room' Napoleon once called it.

Centuries of foreign writers' spilt ink and artists' painted scenes have left ample evidence of a dizzying train of visitors' reactions to La Serenissima, but the views most often come from outsiders' eyes. For Commissario Brunetti, Venetian to the core, any walk across the enormous square will elicit a variety of private responses he can neither control nor escape. Haunted as he is throughout the rest of the city by changes he laments but cannot avoid, he remains hostage to his passion for beauty and thus vulnerable to the Piazza's allure.

* * *

More than any other place in Venice, Piazza San Marco both tests Brunetti's tolerance and inspires his loveliest raptures. Being in the world's most beautiful urban spot and man-oeuvring through the floods of visitors who congregate there sometimes creates an almost schizophrenic reaction in Brunetti. In *The Death of Faith*, his unsavoury investigation into the workings of a secret society only just beginning, his mood is still optimistic.

The great builders of the Serene Republic had had only manpower at their disposition: rafts, ropes, and pulleys, yet they had managed to create a miracle like that. He thought of some of the horrid buildings with which modern Venetians had defaced their city, (. . .) and he mourned, not for the first time, the cost of human greed.

He came down off the last bridge and then out into the Piazza, and all gloom fled, driven off by the power of a beauty that only man could create. The spring wind played with the enormous flags flying in front of the Basilica, and Brunetti smiled to see how much more imposing was the lion of San Marco, raging across his scarlet field, than were the three parallel bars of Italy. (*The Death of Faith*, ch. 17)

→

To Caffè Florian
(2)

His journeys into the miracle of the Piazza are not always so benign. On the rare stroll across to Caffè Florian **(2)*** for one of Venice's most expensive luxuries, a tiny thimble of perfect *espresso*, his moods will be affected by the size of the crowds, the pigeons, the condition of the weather, the severity of the latest crime he must face. Whether he chooses the glamorous interior or selects one of the elegant tables in the Piazza filled with the idle, he'll be sitting in history. Since it was the peripatetic Venetians who first brought coffee from the Ottoman Turks to Europe, it is appropriate the continent's most famous café opened in this city, in 1720. During the eighteenth century, when Venice was invaded by Grand Tourists from the North, over two dozen coffee-houses ringed the Piazza, including Florian's, its doors never to close. Today, although it shuts down by midnight, Caffè Florian inhabits a place of special moment. In the late hours when the surrounding area is nearly empty, with the buildings still lit and the moon over the Basilica, few places can match the Piazza's magic.

Silence and solitude, however, were not the primary charms most sought by the famous foreigners who flocked to the tables spread out into the square: Lord Byron sat studying Armenian grammar and eyeing the ladies; Wagner grumbled about the Venetians' refusal to applaud his music when the Austrians played in the Piazza; Goethe gazed at the campanile from Florian's before climbing it for his first view of the sea; even Proust felt the social ambience conducive to his devoted hours translating Ruskin.

The *caffè* also possessed an aura of respectability, as the English novelist Anthony Trollope appreciated, for it allowed the native female aristocracy to appear in public. And on occasion it served as a place of romantic allure, or at least illusion. Henry James has his narrator of *The Aspern Papers* take the middle-aged niece to Florian for her first night away from the crumbling Ca' Capella in decades: a seductive journey by gondola – with the seduction aimed not at hapless Miss Tina but at the letters of a dead poet he believes to be in her possession.

Donna Leon joins the ranks of writers sensing in Florian's an extravagant glamour no other café in the city offers. So, even a native like Brunetti can find the place ripe with promise as he waits for Signorina Elettra's sister in *A Venetian Reckoning*. The magic of the day and the majesty of the surroundings make this no ordinary interrogation for the Commissario, as he surveys the scene.

He went up the three low steps and through the etched-glass double door of Florian's. Though he was ten minutes early, Brunetti looked through the small rooms on the right and then through those on the left, but he saw no sign of Dottoressa Zorzi.

When a white-jacketed waiter approached him, Brunetti asked for a table near one of the front windows. Part of him, this splendid day, wanted to sit with an attractive young woman by a window at Florian's, and another part of him wanted to be seen sitting with an attractive young woman by a window at Florian's. He pulled out one of the delicate, curved-back chairs and took a seat, then turned it to allow himself a better sight of the Piazza. (*A Venetian Reckoning*, ch. 7)

Brunetti is part of a long Venetian tradition, in wanting to be seen in Florian's window. The custom of the finest costumed figures during Carnevale being seated at the most prominent tables continues today, and the residents still make certain to stroll by for a glimpse. But, whether the day is splendid or not, even Venetians must eventually put their tiny cups of *espresso* aside, pay the extravagant bill to the formal waiters, leave the sheltered *caffè* and brave the tumultuous piazza. It is unclear whether Florian's magic lingered for Brunetti, or if the company of a lovely young woman in delightful weather lightened his mood, but his normally sober take on modern Venice is nowhere in evidence – in spite of the Dottoressa's accusation that they now stood in their own Disneyland.

(. . .) together they went out into the Piazza, there to discover it had grown even warmer. (. . .)

'We are a pessimistic people, aren't we?' Brunetti asked.

'We once had an empire. Now all we have,' she said (. . .) encompassing the Basilica, the campanile, and below it, Sansovino's Logetta, 'all we have is this Disneyland. I think that's sufficient cause for pessimism.'

Brunetti nodded but said nothing. She hadn't persuaded him. The moments came rarely, but for him the city's glory still lived. (*A Venetian Reckoning*, ch. 7)

No matter the crowds, whatever the weather, from the privileged perch of Florian's tables Venice offers Brunetti a continuation of centuries of beauty and activity: the campanile bells boom, the two bronze figures known as the Moors bang away atop the clock tower, the two stone lions to the left of the Basilica tumble with children, and the whole façade of the church sparkles with golden mosaics and sculpted marble.

But Florian's has never been just about the exalted views. It has always insisted on hosting a prestigious clientele. If the modern day *caffè*, admittedly surrounded by pigeons and jeans, ever needed indisputable evidence of its continuing social status, the select presence of Vice-Questore Patta is advertisement indeed. His personal list of favourite bars and restaurants is a perfect indicator of where VIPs might gather. Even though Patta's Sicilian blood seems 'incompatible with that of Venice', placing him for ever beyond the truly chosen, he is always welcomed for 'a long coffee' at Florian's on winter mornings.

Cavaliere Giuseppe Patta had been sent to Venice three years before in an attempt to introduce new blood into the criminal justice system. In this case, the blood had been Sicilian and had proved to be incompatible with that of Venice. (. . .) The vice-questore's work schedule included a long coffee each summer morning on the terrace of the Gritti, and, in the winter, at Florian's. Lunch was usually taken at the Cipriani pool or Harry's Bar, and he usually decided at about four to 'call it a day'. Few others would so name it. (*Death at La Fenice*, ch. 6)

Yet, after the coffees and the companionship, the views and the energy of the Piazza, any crossing forces Brunetti into varying encounters with both pigeons and those aliens who adore and feed them – all recorded for posterity.

The pigeons, usually stupid and hateful, appeared almost charming to him as they bobbed up and down at the feet of their many admirers. Suddenly, for no reason, hundreds of them flocked up, swirled around, and settled back right where they had been, to continue with their bobbing and pecking.

A stout woman stood with three of them on her shoulder, her face turned away in delight or horror, while her husband photographed her with a video recorder the size of a small machine-gun. A few metres away someone opened a small bag of corn and threw it out in a wide circle, and again the pigeons swirled up and around, then settled to feed in the centre of the corn. (*A Venetian Reckoning*, ch. 7)

→

To front of
Basilica di San
Marco **(3)**

For nearly two hundred years writers and artists have been lamenting the impossibility of finding anything original to say about Venice, any new views to capture, and then, of course, they have proceeded either to lavish Venice with praise or damn it with complaint; often both. The temptation to admire is too great, the sights too awe-inspiring to resist, especially facing the Basilica of San Marco **(3)**.* But the opportunity often turns sour and the church is alternately derided for seeming nothing but a façade, a mere turnstile for a tourist site, an architectural folly, a temple to the Republic's glory instead of a holy church, or for some visitors even an immoral expression of Venetian worldliness. In Thomas Mann's tribute to the city's seduction, *Death in Venice*, poor Aschenbach is finally unhinged both by his attraction to the young boy Tadzio and by Venice's morbid charms; no longer able to persuade himself of the loftiness of his feelings, it is after a particularly sensual response to the Basilica of San Marco that he leers for the first time in obvious lust.

For Brunetti, the setting never fails to provoke a bewildering set of conflicting responses. In the course of the novels, he reminiscences on the changes since his childhood, laments how the façade of the Basilica seems forever covered with scaffolding, mocks the lunacy of the church's design, rhapsodizes over the surface beauty, and bewails the long lines of tourists waiting to enter the Basilica and do even more damage to the marble mosaic floors.

In *Suffer the Little Children*, this conflict comes to a climax – until the Basilica stuns both Brunetti and Vianello into silence.

As they entered the Piazza, the Inspector, who appeared not to have registered the tourists, said, 'The whole world's gone mad with fear of avian flu, and we have more pigeons than people.'

'I beg your pardon,' Brunetti said, his attention still on the tourists.

'I read it in the paper two days ago,' Vianello said. 'There's about sixty thousand of us, and the current population of pigeons – well, the one given in the paper, which is not the same thing – is more than a hundred thousand.' (. . .)

Brunetti was about to mention his surprise that such talk could come from the Questura's own paragon of all things environmental, when his eye shifted to the façade of the Basilica and those absurdly asymmetrical cupolas, the whole lopsided glory of it.

Brunetti stopped walking and put his hand up to quiet Vianello. In an entirely different voice, almost solemn, he asked, 'We're lucky, aren't we?'

Vianello glanced aside at Brunetti and then followed his gaze to San Marco and the flags whipping in the breeze, the mosaics above the doors. The Inspector stood there for some time, looking at the church, then glanced to the right, across the water and towards San Giorgio with its ever-vigilant angel. In an entirely uncharacteristic gesture, Vianello raised his free arm and moved it in an arc that encompassed the buildings around them as well as those across the water, then he turned to Brunetti and patted his arm, quickly, twice. For a moment, Brunetti thought the Inspector was going to speak, but he remained silent and moved away towards the Riva degli Schiavoni and the sun-splashed walk down to the Questura. (*Suffer the Little Children*, ch. 17)

In *The Death of Faith* Brunetti is about to begin his unpleasant research into the machinations of a secret society in the nearby library. This time his circular view out to the sparkling waters of the *bacino* and back to the façade of the church does little to compensate for the influx of crowds.

Out in the Piazza, Brunetti stood and looked out over the Bacino of San Marco, then turned and studied the ridiculous domes of the Basilica. He had read once about some place in California where the swallows return every year on the same date. St. Joseph's Day? Here, it was much the same, for the tourists all seemed to reappear in the second week of March, led by some inner compass that brought them to this particular sea. (*The Death of Faith*, ch. 17)

→

Marciana Library (4), front of the statues

The subject of his investigation in *The Death of Faith* is especially unpleasant for secular Brunetti: a Catholic secret society founded in Spain in the early twentieth century to achieve political dominion and the spread of Christian principles. Delaying the investigation, he stops in front of the Marciana Library (4),* admiring the pagan glory of its Renaissance architecture, the Doric and Ionic orders recalling the much-loved Classical past, the monumental statues flanking the entrance pointing to a former grandeur. Waiting inside for information on the crime he must research, he finds peace on this quiet island of learning at the very heart of Venice.

Before taking his degree in law at the university of Padova, Brunetti had spent three years studying in the department of history at Cá' Foscari, where he had been turned into a reasonably competent researcher, as much at home among the many volumes in the Marciana as in the meandering aisles of the Archivio di Stato.

As Brunetti walked up the Riva degli Schiavoni, Sansovino's library came into sight in the distance, and as it always did, its architectural unruliness gladdened his heart. (. . .)

He walked across the Piazza and under the Loggetta, then into the Library, a place which seldom saw a tourist, not the least of its many attractions. He passed between the two giant statues, showed his tessera at the reception window, and went into the reference hall. (. . .)

He made his way to a seat at one of the long tables (. . .) While he waited, he pulled down one of the Loeb Classical Library volumes completely at random and began to read the Latin text, curious to see how much of that language, if any, remained. He had chosen the letters of Pliny the Younger and paged through it slowly, looking for the letter describing the eruption of Vesuvio in which the writer's uncle had lost his life. (*The Death of Faith*, ch. 17)

→

Acqua Alta's murder takes place in the very core of Venice: in the museum inside Palazzo Ducale **(5)**.* This deceptively lovely rose and white marble Gothic wonder is one of the few famous places which has for centuries been the occasion for ruminations on violence, crime, and imprisonment: from its dungeons Casanova fled over the *piombi*, the appalling 'leads', leaping across the roofs to freedom – a flight that inspired artists like Schnitzler and Fellini. As Brunetti enters the chilly palace, Donna Leon recreates the ancient atmosphere of menace and intrigue, the sweating walls and the stairway that seems to resonate with the heavy steps of criminals.

To Palazzo Ducale
(5)

When Commissario Brunetti of the Venice police arrived at the scene of the murder of the director of the most important museum in the city, (. . .) [he] turned away and started down the corridor. His steps echoed eerily, reverberating back at him from both sides and from the staircase at the end. Cold, the penetrating damp cold of winter, seeped out from the pavement below him and from the brick walls of the corridor. Behind him, he heard the sharp clang of metal on stone, but no one called out, so he continued down the corridor. The night mist had set in, painting a slippery film of condensation on the broad stone steps under his feet. (. . .)

From off to the left, Brunetti heard a siren shriek out and shatter the tranquillity of the night, and for a moment he thought it was the lab team, arriving in a boat and being stupid about it. But the siren rose in pitch, its insistent whine ever louder and more strident, and then it wailed its slow way down to the original note. It was the siren at San Marco, calling out to the sleeping city the news that the waters were rising: *acqua alta* had begun. (*Acqua Alta*, ch. 9)

→

To Bacino di San
Marco between
the columns **(6)**

In Venice, whether inconvenient *acqua alta* or glorious Grand
Canal, the waters demand unique attention – especially at
this lowest point in the city. The perplexity of visitors is best
recorded by the American humorist Robert Benchley, who
famously cabled on first arrival, 'Streets full of water. Please
advise.' The awe of Venetians is best captured as they take
their habitual refuge from the crowds to view their Piazza
safely from boats on the Bacino di San Marco **(6)**. Brunetti
and Vianello, returning to the Questura from Pellestrina in
A Sea of Troubles, glide past the island Church of San Giorgio
Maggiore **(A)** into the *bacino* to witness Venice's long history
still visually extant in stone, marble, and golden mosaic, apparently floating on the water, dizzying to even the most jaded
of observers. But the sight from the water also reveals flanks
of vendors with their shoddy wares, making painfully obvious
the choices of modern Venetians, forever loyal to the
Republic's pursuit of gain.

The launch turned left into the main canal leading back
towards San Marco just as Vianello finished giving his account,
and spread before them was the sight that had welcomed
most arriving eyes ever since the great centuries of the
Serenissima. Bell towers, domes, cupolas – all disported themselves for the eyes of the passengers and crew of the arriving
boat, each one seeming to jostle the others aside, in the
manner of small children, the better to catch the attention
of the approaching visitors. The only difference between what
the two policemen saw and what would have been visible to
those who followed the same channel five hundred years ago
was the flock of construction cranes which loomed above the
city and, on top of every building, television antennae of
every height and configuration. (. . .)

Both of them stopped talking and watched the city draw
near. No city is more self-regarding than Venice: cheap and
vulgar self-portraits lined the sides of many streets; almost
every kiosk peddled garish plastic gondolas; hacks whose
berets falsely proclaimed them to be artists sold horrible
pastels at every turn. At every step she pandered to the worst
and flashed out the meretricious. (. . .) And yet her beauty

remained unblemished, just as it remained supreme. (*A Sea of Troubles*, ch. 6)

Many monuments disport themselves for Brunetti's affection, but he seems to hold the Church of San Giorgio Maggiore, lying in serene solitude on her island across the *bacino*, in special regard. With its Classical white façade soaking up the light, it has the rare virtue of isolation, must be reached by boat, offers little else to see, has no restaurants or hotels nearby. No, the visitor must possess determination – and since few do, it floats protected from the crowds visible across the water.

Few people were out, and those who were all seemed lifted almost to joy by the unexpected sun and warmth. Who would believe that, only yesterday, the city had been wrapped in fog and the vaporetti forced to use their radar for the short ride out to the Lido? Yet here he was, wishing for sunglasses and a lighter suit, and when he walked out to the waterside, he was momentarily blinded by the reflected light that came flashing up from the water. Opposite him, Brunetti could see the dome and tower of San Giorgio – yesterday they hadn't been there – looking as though they had somehow crept into the city during the night. (*A Venetian Reckoning*, ch. 7)

Several years later in *Wilful Behaviour*, Brunetti's lingering gaze over to San Giorgio moves right to the point of the Dogana **(B)**, and on to the church next to it, forcing him to consider the differences between the historical city's response to calamity and the modern version. After thousands of inhabitants had been killed, the soaring Church of the Madonna della Salute **(C)** built in 1630 was a tribute in gratitude to the Virgin Mary for saving the city from yet another plague. Today's needs are more prosaic.

He didn't hasten his steps but strolled along the *bacino*, taking the opportunity offered by a day cast in silver to look across to San Giorgio, then turned completely around and looked at the cupolas of the churches that lined the water on the other side of the canal. The Madonna had once saved the city from plague, and now there was a church. The Americans had saved the country from the Germans, and now there was McDonald's. (*Wilful Behaviour*, ch. 24)

→

Left along the Bacino di San Marco to Ponte della Paglia **(7)** down Riva degli Schiavoni **(8)**

Ultimately, Brunetti will leave the Piazza, Basilica, and Palazzo Ducale behind him in his daily journeys from or to the Questura. Whether he is moving towards the Piazza along the Riva degli Schiavoni, or away with the *bacino* on his right, the route offers no escape from the throngs of people and vendors. Lord Byron's famous boast, in *Childe Harold's Pilgrimage*, 'I stood in Venice, on the Bridge of Sighs;/ A palace and a prison on each hand' certainly creates no nostalgic feelings. From the perpetually crowded Ponte di Paglia **(7)** along the *bacino*, hordes of people struggle to snap photos of Byron's Ponte dei Sospiri **(D)** gracefully arching a few metres away.

But once over the bridge, on to the *riva* **(8)** the path widens and the bracing water to his right offers Brunetti some relief. In *The Death of Faith*, however, the stale taste left by his research into the Church's greed continues as he laments the residents' loss of their city to the increasing numbers of tourists. The *passarelle* had previously protected the Venetians from *acqua alta*; now the portable walkways are more often moved from residential areas to provide escape from the rising waters for visitors, and the complexion of entire neighbourhoods undergoes change to suit the invaders' desires.

Each year, there were more and more of them, and each year the city made itself more and more hospitable to them rather than to its citizens. Fruit dealers closed, shoemakers went out of business, and all seemed transformed into masks, machine-made lace, and plastic gondolas.

Brunetti recognized this as his most unpleasant mood, no doubt exacerbated by his encounter with Opus Dei, and knew that, to counter it, he had to walk. (*The Death of Faith*, ch. 17)

Brunetti seems able to shrug off some of his negative reactions to modern Venice so long as he has just one cause to ponder. However, when appalling climate and horrendous crowds combine, he has scant resources to cope with them. On any summer weekend, the major floating boat stops that serve the Piazza pitch and sway with their increased loads; some boats are so full they slow down only to drop passengers and chug on; others allow entry, but squeezed in between stacks of luggage and bulky backpacks, passengers find little room to stand.

Mercifully, *The Anonymous Venetian* is the only novel Donna Leon sets during *ferragosto*, Italy's major summer holiday and a time of unyielding heat in the pizza oven that brick and stone Venice becomes. With his family gone to the cooling mountains, the Commissario is miserable as he races for a boat along the *riva*, knowing he cannot escape the tangle of passengers but unwilling to face the brutal walk home:

He glanced around him and saw the half-naked tourists, the men and women with their bathing suits, shorts, and scoop-necked T-shirts, and for a moment he envied them, even though he knew the impossibility of his appearing like that any place other than a beach.

As his body dried, the envy fled, and he returned to his normal state of irritation at seeing them dressed like this. (. . .) He was not what Paola called a 'beauty snob', but he did believe that it was better to look good than bad. He turned his attention from the people on the boat to the *palazzi* that lined the canal, and immediately he felt his irritation evaporate. Many of them, too, were shabby, but it was the shabbiness of centuries of wear, not that of laziness and cheap clothing. The city had grown old, but Brunetti loved the sorrows of her changing face. (*The Anonymous Venetian*, ch. 3)

The winter weather is not much kinder to the population, whether they are struggling on foot or pitching about in a boat. The increased discomforts along the *riva*, with its vast exposure to strong winds, can turn any normally calm ride across the *bacino* into a rough affair, as Brunetti discovers.

The Piazza is not the only place for Venetians to meet near San Marco. But in search of information about the underworld of the *vu cumprà* in *Blood from a Stone*, and since conflict diamonds may be the issue, Brunetti must turn to someone with connections in the world of wealth – his father-in-law, Orazio Falier. However, the Count is a busy international businessman, so struggling through horrendous weather to meet on the Count's private boat close to deserted Piazza San Marco is Brunetti's only option.

When he emerged on to the Riva degli Schiavoni, huddled behind his umbrella, the wind coming off the *bacino* yanked the umbrella over his head and behind him, then ripped the material free of the thin struts and left it hanging shredded in his hands. Brunetti grabbed at it, gathering it up into a bulky, prickly lump, and made his way through the driving rain to the dock. The Count's boat was there, Massimo draped in a yellow slicker, waiting for him on deck. The pilot extended his hand and half pulled Brunetti forward, against the force of the wind, on to the boat. His foot slipped on the top step and he bounced down the other two, landing beside Massimo, who steadied him with both hands.

'*Buona sera*, Commissario,' the pilot said and relieved him of the umbrella. (*Blood from a Stone*, ch. 22)

→

Over Ponte del Vin to Hotel Paganelli **(9)**

In Venice, addresses as well as wealth matter: for private residences, businesses, offices, but especially hotels. For Brunetti a visiting witness's chosen location is just one more piece of evidence, one more clue to character. In Donna Leon's first novel, *Death at La Fenice*, Dardi, the esteemed baritone, when queried about where he can be reached in future, replies with astonishment, 'The Gritti', doubtful that other hotels are an option. Charles Dickens, Proust, George Sand, Balzac and Cocteau all chose to stay at the Danieli. But not just the major hotels, made famous by the likes of Hemingway, have value: if location is all in the city, so is the wisdom to know what place to choose, a decision crucial around Piazza San Marco. Although the entire Riva degli Schiavoni is lined with hotels and their cafés snaking towards the water, clamouring for customers, on the other side of the Ponte del Vin the seemingly endless rows of tourist stalls finally end, and the opportunities for peace and a quiet *caffè* at one of the outdoor bars increase.

In *Blood from a Stone*, there had been few witnesses to the murder of the African street seller, and those had been Americans busy bargaining for bags. But Brunetti finds the pair of doctors he interviews immediately after the murder exceptionally helpful, and hopes to meet them the next morning at their hotel for further questions with the rest of their group.

'Where are you staying?' he asked.

'At the Paganelli,' **(9)*** he answered. Brunetti was surprised that a group that large could find room there, and that Americans would have the good sense to choose it (. . .)

The Paganelli was a narrow hotel, slipped in, like an architectural dash separating two capital letters, between the Danieli and the Savoia & Jolanda. *(Blood from a Stone*, chs 3 & 5)

Here the sweep of the *bacino* can offer its full grandeur – views, breezes, the company of boats not meant for tourism.

He didn't know where the tugs had been sent, nor could he recall how many years it was since they'd disappeared, leaving the space along the *riva* clear for other boats, no doubt boats more useful to the tourist industry.

What wonderful Latin names they'd had, floating there red and proud and ready at an instant to chug off to help the ships up the Canale della Giudecca. The boats that sailed into the city now were probably too big for those brave little tugs to be of any help: monsters taller than the Basilica, filled with thousands of ant-like forms crowded to the railings, they sailed in and docked, hurled down their gangplanks and set free their passengers to wander into the city. (*Friends in High Places*, ch. 16)

→

From the top of the Ponte della Pietà **(10)**, on the right, the leaning campanile of the Church of San Giorgio dei Greci

To Ponte della Pietà **(10)**

(E) in pristine white marble juts into the sun. Its little onion dome is further evidence of the strong connections between the Orthodox East and the Republic of Venice so evident in the nearby Piazza – an influence not admired by everyone. When Wagner visited the church in 1882, his wife Cosima records in her diary, he was unsettled by its Eastern qualities, its absence of the feelings of Christianity.

→

To Chiesa della Pietà (11)

The two closest palaces lining the Rio dei Greci once housed the orphanage (F) for girls whose musical education would eventually be conducted by Vivaldi. But Brunetti's walks from the Piazza, along the chaotic *riva*, to the Questura allow him little opportunity to reflect on the pleasures of music. Instead, eager to leave the uncomfortable area of San Marco for the more familiar Castello, Brunetti even copes with cloaking mist:

The mist had not cleared. In fact, it appeared to have grown thicker, so Brunetti was careful to keep the façades of the buildings on his left in sight as he walked down the *riva*. The mist caused him to pass through the rows of *bancarelle* without seeing them. This added to the uneasiness he always felt when he walked past them and their vendors, so unlike the comfortable familiarity he felt in the rest of the city. He did not bother to analyse this sensation, was aware of it only in some atavistic, danger-sensing part of his mind. Once beyond them and past the façade of the Pietà (11), the feeling disappeared, just as the mist was beginning to do. (*Blood from a Stone*, ch. 5)

Ultimately Venetian residents will be asked if all *this* – usually accompanied by the sweep of a foreigner's arms – ever gets stale. Brunetti offers a spirited reply as he cruises past the city's glory in a boat, safe from the distractions of tourists, his uneasiness evaporated like the mist. Just returning from investigating the murder of the African street seller, he thinks about how much – and how little – times have changed in a city traditionally more mixed than the rest of Europe, a historic Venice that housed and possibly celebrated Shakespeare's *condottiero* Othello.

Enough of beautiful and busy San Marco: Brunetti heads for the Questura and his other 'family'.

Palazzo Ducale approached from the left, and its beauty pulled him to his feet. 'Come on,' he said to Vianello and went back up on deck. The cold hit him like a blow and the wind pushed tears from his eyes, distorting his vision and transforming the *palazzo* into a shimmering, shivering form suspended in the light reflected from the dancing waves.

Vianello came up the stairway and stood beside Brunetti. The flags on the tall poles in front of the *basilica* flapped wildly in the wind; boats and gondolas tied to the moorings bounced up and down and side to side, creating a series of booms so loud they could be heard above the wind. The Piazza seemed filled with huddled, bent shapes; the tourists kept their heads down, as protected from glory as they were from the wind.

Had it been better once, he wondered, when all of this was new and La Serenissima controlled the seas? Or had it been just as easy then to arrange the murder of some nameless Moor, certain that his insignificance and anonymity would serve to protect his killers? He closed his eyes for a moment, and when he opened them again, the *palazzo* had given way to the Bridge of Sighs and then to the façades of the hotels that lined the *riva*. (*Blood from a Stone*, ch. 9)

---

*Caffè Florian, closed Tuesdays in winter.

*Basilica San Marco, closed to tourists Sunday morning.

*Marciana Library, permission through Museo Correr. Closed Saturday & Sunday afternoon.

*Palazzo Ducale, guided or audio tours recommended.

*Hotel Paganelli, a small hotel with Venetian style rooms, many with views, is far less expensive than others on the *riva*.

At the end of Walk 8 visitors have a choice.

Walk 9 continues east into *sestiere* Castello and the Questura. This can then be followed by Walk 10, which moves further east from Arsenale to the Giardini.

Alternatively, after a return to Piazza San Marco, the journey continues west into Cannaregio for Walks 11 and 12.

WALK 9: *Questura World*

Pietà—Campo Bandiera e Moro—Greci—Questura—San
Lorenzo—Vigna—Celestia

1.5—2 hours

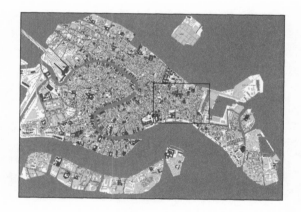

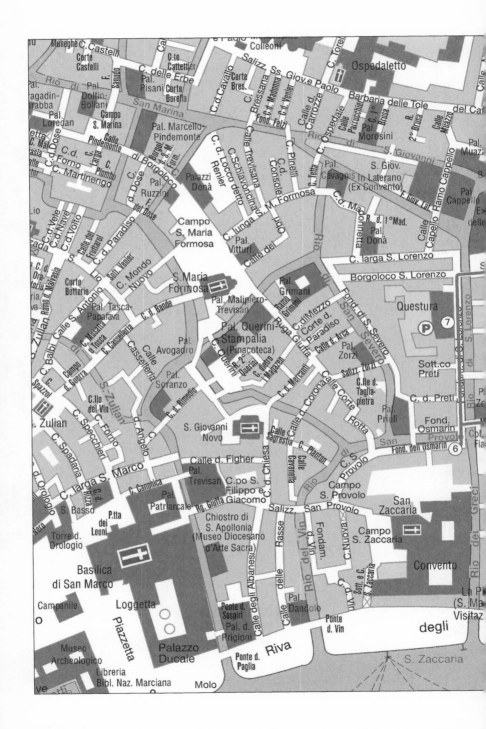

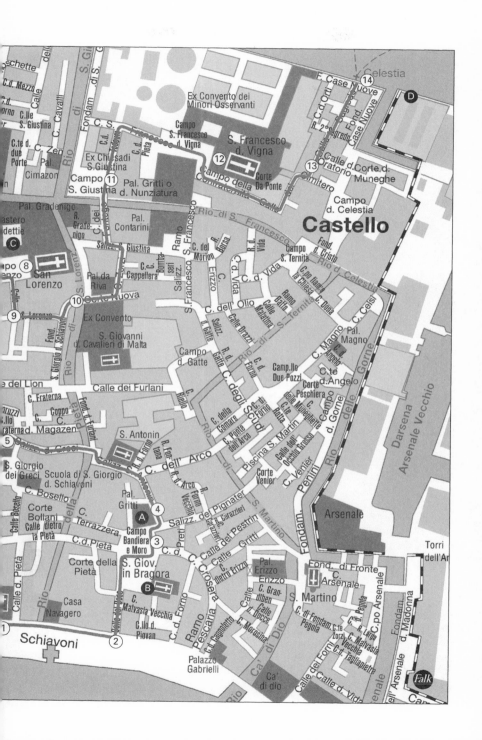

The western end of *sestiere* Castello is not far from Piazza
San Marco, but it could not differ more in atmosphere
from the glamorous centre. The rows of tourist gondolas
switch to passenger vaporetti; the marble and mosaics are
traded for more subdued ancient brick; the Piazza view out
to the glistening white façade of San Giorgio Maggiore moves
around to its long barn-like side, offering shelter to the tall
white masts of the residents' pleasure boats. For Venetians,
the area possesses a remote allure; it feels local and authentic;
the streets ring with shouted Veneziano dialect; the small
trattorie menus sound and taste home-made. Walk 9 from
the Church of the Pietà **(1)**, ending at the lonely and quiet
Celestia boat stop **(14)** with its views across the lagoon to
the Dolomite mountains, reveals a quieter, more domestic
Venice, though still adorned with all her history, from the
numerous churches all the way to the western corner of the
majestic abandoned Arsenale.

Chiesa della Pietà **(1)**

Anchoring the whole area for Brunetti is, of course, his
second home, the Questura. No matter what parts of Venice
he traverses during the day, eventually he must return to the
duty of work. Certainly the location of the Questura in
seemingly peaceful Castello provides no insulation from the
miseries of crime, although both the mundane and the
appalling are mercifully relieved by a colourful cast of friends.
Throughout the novels, Donna Leon uses these characters
to create a world apart: colleagues feel like another family;
enemies disrupt the professional dynamics; spies lurk in the
offices; rumour controls the scene. However, the Castello
walk also displays more than any other the numerous changes
Venice continues to endure. The actual Questura has been
moved to prosaic Piazzale Roma, the area clogged with buses.
The long-abandoned Church of San Lorenzo has now been
restored. Even the little bar Ai Greci has altered beyond

recognition. But in Brunetti's Castello the walk is through a past where fantasy and literature can still preserve us from all those changes.

Leon's Castello has a local reputation for a remoteness that can also serve a variety of unsavoury needs. Just far enough from the normal traffic of the city, it is a convenient home for some of Venice's shadier elements. Notaries cloak their greed behind a mask of piety, shy officials live in friendless isolation, nuns flee from oppressive church hierarchies, and melodramatic criminals like Ruffolo insist on the remoteness for meeting the police.

* * *

The Church of the Pietà (now open mainly for concerts) is often referred to by the locals as 'Vivaldi's church' in honour of the fame he brought to the city through the music he wrote for the orphaned girls whose musical education he oversaw. Nearly three hundred years after Vivaldi's triumphs, the area will serve as an ironic background to the murder of a very different abandoned girl in *Wilful Behaviour*, when Brunetti's investigation leads to another church once renowned for its piety.

→

To Calle del Dose (2) into Campo Bandiera e Moro (3)

Campo Bandiera e Moro (3) is one of the most inviting small spaces in Venice. The house on the corner of Calle del Dose, with its deep brown brick and white marble trim, every window adorned with seasonal flower boxes, looks across to a well-restored fifteenth-century Gothic *palazzo*, (A) now a hotel. The Church of San Giovanni in Bragora (B) is the *campo*'s star, its pale brick simplicity heightened by the beauty and harmony of its scalloped façade and white surrounds. Donna Leon uses both this delightful *campo* and the church ironically to situate a family armed with alarming hypocrisy and more than dubious morality.

In *Wilful Behaviour*, Brunetti and the newly promoted Ispettore Vianello are certain the brutal stabbing of a young university student of Paola's was no simple robbery gone wrong. Their investigation into Claudia Leonardo's seemingly unblemished life reveals her steady donations to charity organizations, but in her address book they find the phone number of one of Venice's most infamous families of notaries – the Filipettos. Because the Filipettos are known more for their financial acumen than their sense of charity, the address perplexes Brunetti enough for him to pay a visit. Instead of seeing the aged *notaio,* Brunetti is met at the door that opens on to the pretty pink *campo* by the old man's daughter, Eleonora, a woman devoid of feminine softness.

The address was in Campo Bandiera e Moro, in a building just to the right of the church where Vivaldi had been baptized, and from which, according to common belief, many of the paintings and statues had disappeared into private hands during the tenure of a previous pastor. They rang, then rang again until a woman's voice answered the speaker phone, asking them who it was. (. . .)
    She met them at the door, a woman composed of strange angularities: jaws, elbows, the tilt of her eyes all seemed made of straight lines that sometimes met at odd angles. No arcs, no curves: even her mouth was a straight line. 'Yes?' she asked, standing in the equally rectangular doorway. (*Wilful Behaviour,* ch. 15)

It is the Commissario's first image of an otherwise colourless and disappointed woman, who will propel a saga involving several deadly sins. When Brunetti returns to the *campo* for Filipetto's funeral, the exaggerated tribute is being held in the church most known for the relics of St John the Almsgiver and not far from the Pietà, a church celebrating the virtue of human pity: irony hovers in the hypocritically reverent air.

Gianpaolo Filipetto died quietly in his sleep and, having been a parishioner of the Church of San Giovanni in Bragora, he was buried there with all the pomp and ceremony due to his advanced years and his stature in the city.
    Brunetti arrived late and missed the Requiem Mass, but he was on time to mingle with the people who emerged from the church and stood, respectful and silent, waiting for the

coffin and the mourners to appear. (. . .) The first to emerge from the dimness of the church was the pastor, a man bent under the weight of years almost as heavy as those of Filipetto. Behind him came Filipetto's daughter, (. . .) she had grown even more angular and stick-like. (*Wilful Behaviour*, ch. 27)

→

Salizzada Sant' Antonin (4) to da Remigio (5)

When the preoccupations of crime cannot be ignored, and Brunetti finds himself trapped in Castello at lunchtime, too far from home to enjoy a family meal, he still manages to soothe himself with the food and drink that, as Paola laments, are so crucial to his happiness: 'How did this happen to me? I married a man, and I find myself living with an appetite.'

Although numerous lunch places exist near the Questura, Brunetti confines himself to his two options. The first is a sandwich at his third home, the Greci Bar. And if he's been cruelly denied a family meal by work or by Paola, he will most likely choose da Remigio (5),* which at least offers sufficient pampering to allow him to survive till dinner.

When there had been no sign of Signorina Elettra before lunchtime, he left the Questura without calling her, though he did call Paola to say he would not be home for lunch. He went to da Remigio and ate insalata di mare and coda di rospo in tomato sauce, telling himself that, because he drank only a *quartino* of their house white wine and limited himself to a single grappa, it was a light meal and would entitle him to have something more substantial that evening. (*Uniform Justice*, ch. 24)

→

Left on to Calle della Madonna, over Ponte dei Greci, left over tiny bridge to bar (6)

Although the former Ai Greci is now called Greci Moka Efti Crazy Bar and filled with green neon light and young hip people far different from the Questura crowds, in the Leon books it retains its old charm. As early as *Death in a Strange Country*, the bar at the foot of Ponte dei Greci (6)* becomes a fixture for Brunetti: it provides escape from the Questura, informal chat outside the office, and a litmus test for what

Venetians think about crime before any official version is published.

(. . .) he decided not to go home for lunch, nor spend the time going to a restaurant, though he was hungry after the long morning. He decided to go down to the bar at the foot of Ponte dei Greci and make do with a few *tramezzini*.

When he walked in, Arianna, the owner, greeted him by name and automatically placed a wine glass on the counter in front of him. Orso, her ancient German shepherd, who had developed a special fondness for Brunetti over the course of the years, hauled himself arthritically to his feet from his regular place beside the ice-cream cooler and tottered over to him. (. . .)

'What would you like, Guido?' Arianna asked, meaning *tramezzini* and automatically pouring him a glass of red wine.

(. . .) When the sandwiches came, he asked for another glass of wine and drank it slowly, thinking of the way things would be complicated if the dead man did turn out to be American. He didn't know if there would be questions of jurisdiction, decided not to think about that.

As if to prevent him, Arianna said, 'Too bad about the American.'

'We're not sure that he is, not yet.'

'Well, if he is, then someone is going to start crying "terrorism", and that's not going to do anyone any good.'
(*Death in a Strange Country*, ch. 2)

Throughout Italy, bars also serve as centres for news, whether through conversations filled with gossip and rumour or the equally questionable information found in the local papers. No matter what residents may think of the *Gazzettino*'s quality, or how many people actually buy the local paper of Venice, everyone still seems compelled to read it in bars. Across the city, the scene repeats itself: glance at the front page, turn to the sports, quick gulp of *espresso* or an early morning *ombra*, maybe a mumbled exchange about the dire state of things or the weather, and off. Brunetti, however, frequently pauses to canvass section two, in search of clues to recent crimes, sometimes falsely planted by himself as bait:

(. . .) he went down to the bar at the bridge and had a glass of mineral water and a toasted cheese sandwich. He picked up that day's *Gazzettino* from the counter and saw, in the second section, the article he had planted. As he expected, it said far more than he had, suggesting that arrest was imminent, conviction inescapable, and the drug trade in the Veneto effectively destroyed. (*Friends in High Places*, ch. 21)

By book sixteen, *Suffer the Little Children*, Vianello has fully emerged as the Questura's reigning voice of moral outrage, his denunciations a predictable part of the currency of gossip. At last the *Gazzetino* comes in for his special scorn.

Vianello was in the bar, reading the paper at the counter, when Brunetti arrived. A half-full glass of white wine stood in front of him. (. . .)

His eyes on the headlines, which blared news of the latest infighting among the various political parties as they attempted to butt one another aside in their frenzy to keep their trotters in the trough, Vianello said, 'You know, I always used to think it was all right to buy this, so long as I didn't read it. As though buying it was a venial sin and reading it a mortal.' He looked at Brunetti, then again at the headlines. 'But now I think I might have got it the wrong way round and it's a mortal sin to buy because it encourages them to keep on printing it. And reading it's only a venial sin because it really doesn't make any impression on you.' Vianello raised his glass and drank the rest of his wine.

'You'll have to talk to Sergio about that,' Brunetti said, nodding his thanks to the approaching barman for his plate of *tramezzini* and glass of wine, more interested in quelling his hunger than in listening to Vianello's vilification of the press. (*Suffer the Little Children*, ch. 11)

No matter how many daily trips Brunetti may make to the Greci bar for *un caffè*, only on a rare occasion will he use the bar as a place for investigating a crime – the atmosphere is too intimate to sully it with menace, the Questura easily nearby. But when his old friend Marco arrives at Brunetti's office in *Wilful Behaviour*, unwilling to admit why he has come, it seems prudent to have the conversation away from official ears.

Marco glanced down at his watch. 'Time for *un' ombra?*'
For most Venetians, any time after eleven was time for *un' ombra*, so Brunetti didn't hesitate before assenting.

On the way to the bar at the Ponte dei Greci, they talked about nothing and everything: their families, old friends, how stupid it was that they so seldom saw one another for longer than to say hello on the street (. . .).

Once inside, Brunetti walked towards the bar, but Marco put a hand on his elbow and pulled him to a bench at a booth in front of the window; Brunetti sat opposite him, sure he'd find out now what it was that had brought his friend to the Questura. Neither of them had bothered to order anything, but the barman, from long experience of Brunetti, brought them two small glasses of white wine and went back to the bar.

'*Cin cin*,' they both said and took small sips. Marco nodded in appreciation. 'Better than what you get in most bars.' He took another small sip and set the glass down.

Brunetti said nothing, knowing that this was the best technique to induce a reluctant witness to speak. (*Wilful Behaviour*, ch. 2)

Even in the early morning hours when most bars are closed, dei Greci will open its welcoming doors to the caffeine-desperate officers. In *Suffer the Little Children*, after their dreadful call to the hospital, they find the nearby Rosa Salva in Campo SS. Giovanni e Paolo still shut tight and head for the Greci, certain Sergio will already be at work:

When they reached the bar, the metal grille that protected the door and front windows was raised a few centimetres, enough to suggest that coffee was available inside. Brunetti tapped on the grille, calling out, 'Sergio, you in there?' (. . .)

'Don't you guys ever sleep?' Sergio asked, more bark than bite. He retreated into the bar and went behind the counter. (. . .)

Brunetti heard the hiss of the coffee machine, and a banging at the door; he looked up to see a tall African in a light blue jellaba and woollen jacket carrying a paper-covered tray of fresh pastries. Sergio called out, 'Take it over to the men at the table, Bambola, would you?'

The African turned towards them, and when he saw Marvilli's uniform jacket gave an instinctive jerk of recognition and fear. (. . .)

Vianello made a casual gesture. 'It's before work,' he called. Bambola looked from Vianello to the other two, and they nodded in agreement. His face relaxed and he walked over to their table and set the tray down; then, like a magician, he whipped back the paper, filling the space between them with the aromas of cream, eggs, sugar, raisins, and fresh baked dough. *(Suffer the Little Children,* ch. 5)

Along Fondamenta di San Lorenzo to Questura **(7)**

Although the novels understandably focus on crime and the various squabbles inside the Questura, the walk between the Greci bar and the office provides the Commissario with ample opportunities to indulge his passion for beauty. The canal alongside the Fondamenta di San Lorenzo is lined with *trattorie* terraces on the water, facing the early Gothic Palazzo Zorzi-Liassidi, now a hotel. Nearby, easily seen across the canal from Brunetti's office window, sits a large tree-filled garden, the perfect view by which to assess the passage of the seasons:

Brunetti stood at his window and flirted with springtime. It was there, just on the other side of the canal, evident in the shoots he saw popping up from the earth. Over the last few days, someone – in all these years, he had never seen a person working in the garden – had raked the earth, though he noticed it only now. Tiny white flowers were visible amidst the grass, and those fearless little ones that hugged themselves close to the ground, the names of which he could never remember – the little yellow and pink ones – sprouted from the freshly turned earth.

He opened the windows and felt fresh air flood into his overheated room. It brought with it the scent of new growth or rising sap or whatever it was that led to spring fever and an atavistic urge towards happiness. *(Through a Glass, Darkly,* ch. 1)

In *Wilful Behaviour,* Brunetti has returned to the Questura (7) after his meeting with his old friend Marco, a meeting that forces him to consider who in his life and work he can trust –

He (. . .) was brought up short by how few names he could put on any such list: Vianello, Signorina Elettra, Pucetti, and one of the new commissari, Sara Marino.

The fact that Marino was Sicilian had at first made Brunetti wary of her. (. . .) But then he had seen her honesty and enthusiasm for work; moreover, Patta and Lieutenant Scarpa both disapproved of her and so Brunetti had come to trust her. Aside from those four . . . there was no one else at the Questura in whom he could place blind trust. Rather than put his security in the hands of colleagues, all sworn to protect and uphold the law, how much sooner would he trust his life, career and fortunes to someone like Marco Erizzo, a man he had just advised to commit a crime. (*Wilful Behaviour,* ch. 6)

Brunetti's most important ally in the pursuit of justice is the dependable and honourable Vianello, first seen in *Death in a Strange Country.* Initially, simply a diligent police officer, over the years he develops into a foil for Brunetti in a variety of ways: increasingly accomplished computer hacker, model of fitness and health, concerned critic of environmental pollution. But his personal character and good nature seem the most valuable traits he brings to the partnership. And, as with Brunetti, his pleasure in both the seasons and the city is always celebrated when they are freed from the stifling Questura, but especially so when the police launch await them outside the glass doors for a ride across a Venice renewed by spring weather.

For no reason other than the light, Vianello spread his arms wide and smiled.

The pilot's attention was drawn by the movement, and he stared. Caught between embarrassment and joy, Vianello began to turn his motion into the tired stretch of a deskbound man, but then a pair of amorous swifts flashed by, low to the water, and Vianello dropped all pretence. 'It's springtime,' he called happily to the pilot and leaped on to the deck beside him. He clapped the pilot's shoulder, his own joy suddenly overflowing. *(The Death of Faith*, ch. 3)

Although Signorina Elettra does not arrive until the third novel, *The Anonymous Venetian*, she quickly becomes the bright spot in Brunetti's office life. She enlivens the visual scene at the dreary Questura, both with her colourful sense of style and her regular delivery of flowers, serves as a guard for Brunetti in his dealings with Patta, their immediate superior, and most importantly opens up the mysterious world of the computer through her skills and connections. But not until book ten, *A Sea of Troubles*, is she seen in a role outside the Questura; and later, in *Suffer the Little Children*, she travels to Verona to aid Brunetti in uncovering a criminal ring. It is at their first meeting, however, that Brunetti witnesses her cavalier independence, making them immediate allies:

'The flowers are beautiful. Are they to celebrate your arrival?'

'Oh, no,' she replied blandly. 'I've given a permanent order to Fantin; they'll deliver fresh flowers every Monday and Thursday from now on.' Fantin, the most expensive florist in the city. Twice a week. A hundred times a year? She interrupted his calculations by explaining, 'Since I'm also to prepare the Vice-Questore's expense account, I thought I'd add them in as a necessary expense.' (*The Anonymous Venetian*, ch. 11)

The Questura has been the workplace of Brunetti for over a dozen years. Even though the actual Questura has recently been moved to Piazzale Roma, Donna Leon continues to use this attractive and traditional site. In the first book, Vice-Questore Patta, sent to Venice from Sicily three years before, quickly establishes his reputation for his caustic treatment of subordinates, insufferable pretensions, and craven ambition. By book thirteen, *Doctored Evidence*, poor Patta is still struggling for his place in Venice and the Questura; yet, annoying as such a superior might be, Brunetti realizes that any replacement could only be worse.

In the years he had been in Venice, Patta had been unable to find his way alone through the narrow *calli*, but he had at least learned to send Venetians ahead to lead him through the labyrinth of rancours and animosities that had been built up over the centuries, as well as around the obstacles and wrong turnings created in more recent times. No doubt any replacement sent by the central bureaucracy in Rome would be a foreigner – as anyone not born within earshot of the waters of the *laguna* was a foreigner – and would flail about hopelessly in pursuit of straight roads and direct ways of getting somewhere. Aghast at the realization, Brunetti had to accept the fact that he did not want Patta to leave. (*Doctored Evidence*, ch. 20)

$$\rightarrow$$

Once ensconced in his private office at the Questura, Brunetti is safe from the predations of Patta and away from the prying of Lieutenant Scarpa, the Vice-Questore's resident spy. Stifling as Venetian police office life can sometimes seem, Brunetti often looks out of the nearly cloistered Questura only to discover two more closed worlds: the Church of San Lorenzo (8) and the old people's home.

To Chiesa di San Lorenzo (8)

Any gaze from the window forces him to encounter the seemingly eternal saga surrounding the restoration of the Church of San Lorenzo, its fate as unsolvable as many of the crimes he faces. Built in the ninth century, rebuilt in the sixteenth, the church reputedly once housed the illustrious remains of Marco Polo – a historic resonance undoubtedly pleasing to Brunetti. Even with the scaffolding recently removed and the old people's home refurbished in sparkling white, the façade still remains as impenetrable as the criminal world of Venice:

He stood at his window to shave, staring out at the façade of the Church of San Lorenzo, still covered, as it had been for the last five years, with the scaffolding behind which extensive restoration was said to be taking place. He had no proof that this was happening, for nothing had changed in all these years, and the front doors of the church remained forever closed. *(Death in a Strange Country*, ch. 2)

Years pass, and his vigil begins to take on a poetic air, as the idle cranes over the church remind him of a hovering angel; however, the secular Brunetti has little hope that either the cranes or any angels will save San Lorenzo:

He stood at the window, gazing at the two yellow cranes that rose above the Church of San Lorenzo. They'd been there for so long that Brunetti had come to think of them almost as a pair of angel wings soaring up from either side of the church. He thought they'd been there when he first came to the Questura, but surely no restoration could possibly take that long. (*Wilful Behaviour*, ch. 14)

If Brunetti shifts his view, it is only to include the old men's home in Campo San Lorenzo, which makes him ponder the abandonment of both places and people: the closed Church of San Lorenzo can offer no hope of salvation, and it abuts a building equally hopeless in its mission to ease the lonely passage from life into death.

He got up from his desk and stood at the window. The sun beat down on Campo San Lorenzo. All of the men who lived in the old-age home had answered the summons to sleep, leaving the *campo* to the cats and the people who crossed it at this hour. Brunetti leaned forward, resting his hands on the sill, and watched the *campo* as if in search of an omen. *(Friends in High Places*, ch. 13)

In *Wilful Behaviour*, the rare arrival of Count Falier, bent on assisting his son-in-law in understanding the distant past, provokes a grim reaction to the present. As Brunetti gazes from his office window to the abandoned old men of San Lorenzo **(C)**, he is reminded of the eternal hypocrisy of people and governments.

'(. . .) San Servolo was a death pit.' The Count considered this for a moment, then added, 'Not that it's much better with the way things are organized now.'

The window of Brunetti's office looked across to the old men's home at San Lorenzo, and what he saw there was enough to confirm everything the Count believed about the fate of the old, the mad, or the abandoned who came to be cared for by the current public institutions. (*Wilful Behaviour*, ch. 6)

→

Yet often enough Brunetti must put aside his laments over San Lorenzo to go ever deeper into *sestiere* Castello. In *Friends in High Places*, he searches for information about the perhaps not accidental death of a man so terrified of heights that he was unlikely to have climbed up four flights of scaffolding – and then fallen. In *The Death of Faith*, he must investigate the truth of a young nun's dangerous accusations. These journeys will take him through nearly-abandoned areas, oddly erected gasworks alongside Renaissance buildings, a deconsecrated church covered in graffiti, and the spot where a vineyard planted in the thirteenth century once thrived.

In *Friends in High Places*, the Commissario's alarm at Signor Rossi's announcement that Brunetti's apartment is illegal, and his anger at the idiocies of government bureaucrats, eventually turn into a fondness for the man. Something about his timidity and his fear touches Brunetti, making Rossi's death more personal to the Commissario than is useful for an officer of the law. Donna Leon has selected an especially neglected part of Venice for the shy Rossi to live. The deconsecrated Church of Santa Giustina **(11)**,

Calle San Lorenzo **(9)** Corte Nuova, **(10)** left to Calle Zorzi, to Calle dei Fontego, to Campo Santa Giustina **(11)**

which gives the *campo* its name, could stand as a lonely symbol of the fragility of Venice's buildings. According to tradition, it was founded in the seventh century. This was followed by over a thousand years of being rebuilt, re-consecrated, made into a military school and finally a *liceo scientifico*; now its once-revered walls are casually decorated with students' graffiti.

(. . .) the sight of Rossi's battered face lingered, and he wanted nothing so much as to get out of the confines of the hospital. He . . , asked for Rossi's address . . .

It was a low number in Castello, and when Brunetti asked the porter if he knew where it was, he said he thought it must be down by Santa Giustina **(11)**, near the shop that used to be the Doll Hospital. (*Friends in High Places*, ch. 7)

$$\longrightarrow$$

Calle del Tedeum
to Calle San
Francesco into
Campo San
Francesco della
Vigna **(12)**

The physical site of the Church of San Francesco della Vigna **(12)** has made it hospitable to Venice's legend industry. With the lagoon easily visible in the distance, locals claim it was here that Saint Mark sailing by had his famous dream of returning to Venice. Once filled with grapevines and wine-making monks, a fairytale place in stone-floored Venice, the route along the side of the church also has a misplaced arcade: twin rows of Tuscan-looking columns in southern terracotta colours sit along a back canal across from tall cypresses.

More anomalies lurk in these backwaters, as Brunetti will discover when he enters the closed world of the Curia. In *The Death of Faith*, Brunetti's surprise visit from the former nun who had been the only person capable of calming his mother's rages has led him to investigate respected members of the Catholic hierarchy in Venice. But wanting first to convince himself that her suspicions are well founded, Brunetti goes to see her confessor:

The address Brunetti sought was toward the end of the *sestiere* of Castello, near the Church of San Francesco della Vigna.

The first two people he asked had no idea where the number was, but when he asked where he could find the Fathers of the Sacred Cross, he was immediately told they were at the foot of the next bridge, the second door on the left. So it proved, announced by a small brass plate that bore the name of the order beside a small Maltese cross.

The door was answered after his first ring by a white-haired man who could well have been that figure so common in medieval literature – the good monk. *(The Death of Faith*, ch. 8)

→

The history of Venice might easily be retraced by a look at the scale of the buildings from her millennium-long reign as Queen of the Sea – from her modest beginnings on Torcello Island with what Ruskin called her cattle-shed high church, to the days of the Republic's glory epitomized by the towering Arsenale. Likewise the vigour of the city's neighbourhoods traces the rise and fall of Venice's fortunes, especially evident in this section of lonely Castello, where the sense of abandonment increases yearly as the population flees back to the place it came from in the fifth century – the mainland.

Right of church to Calle del Cimitero, to Calle Sagredo **(13)** to Celestia boat stop **(14)**

In *Death in a Strange Country*, Brunetti leaves his cosy apartment across the city and makes a long late night trek through Venice to the abandoned west side of the Arsenale and the Celestia boat stop **(14)**. Under a full moon, as he approaches this desolate spot facing the northern lagoon, his mood grows grimmer when he senses his stupidity in agreeing to such a remote place to meet the young thief Ruffolo to discuss the theft of major Impressionist paintings. The area is guaranteed to be empty, the bridge makes anyone approaching visible, and the beach is despicably filthy – all elements mirroring poor Ruffolo's pathetic sense of high drama.

He passed along the right side of the Church of San Francesco della Vigna, then cut to the left and back to the Celestia vaporetto stop. Clearly outlined ahead of him he saw the metal-railed walkway (**D**) and the steps leading up to it. He climbed them and when he got to the beginning of the walkway, he looked ahead at the bridge that rose up, like the hump on a camel, over the opening in the Arsenale wall that let the number five boat cut through the middle of the island and come out in the Bacino of San Marco.

The top of the bridge, he could see clearly, was empty. Not even Ruffolo would be so foolish as to make himself visible to any passing boat, not when the police were looking for him. He had probably jumped down on to the small beach on the other side of the bridge. (. . .)

In the ensilvering light of the moon, he could see that it was empty, but he could also see that its surface was covered with fragments of discarded bricks, shards of broken bottles, all covered with a layer of slimy green seaweed. *(Death in a Strange Country*, ch. 24)

Views in Venice alter radically depending on the perspective. When seen from further west on the Fondamenta Nuova in crowded Cannaregio, the cemetery island of San Michele seems paradoxically lively, busy with flower-laden visitors clambering off the boats, leaving behind happy tourists heading to nearby Murano. From lonely Celestia, in isolated northern Castello, however, the sweeping views over the lagoon to the Dolomites can offer no one much comfort. On his way to this solitary spot, Brunetti would have walked past nearby Bar Alle Alpi, named to commemorate the bravery of the mountaineers in World War II, men with whom his father had fought and lost much of his soul. In *Death at La Fenice*, however, he makes the journey by boat through the desolate Arsenale. It is the perfect place to leave Brunetti to his thoughts about a death far more personal than any other. As he leaves the Celestia stop he sees the lonely cypress-ringed island of San Michele floating in the lagoon, temporary resting place for Venice's dead.

Brunetti (. . .) caught the number 5 boat, which would take him to the cemetery island of San Michele, cutting through the Arsenale and along the back side of the island. He seldom visited the cemetery, somehow not having acquired the cult of the dead so common among Italians. (. . .)

'*Ciao*, Papà,' he said, but then he couldn't think of anything else to say. (*Death at La Fenice*, ch. 7)

---

*Da Remigio, favoured by locals for its wide choice of seafood and a menu of meats is a lively choice.

WALK 10: Remote Venice

Celestia—Arsenale—San Biagio—Via Garibaldi—San Pietro
Di Castello—Giardini

1.5—2 hours

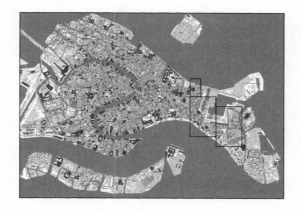

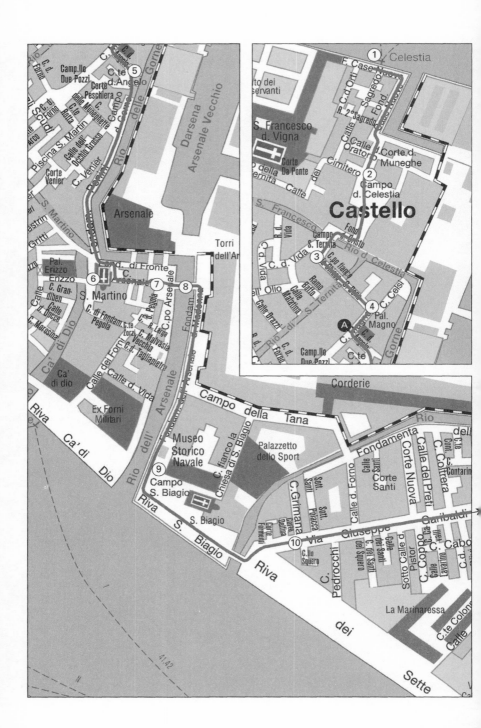

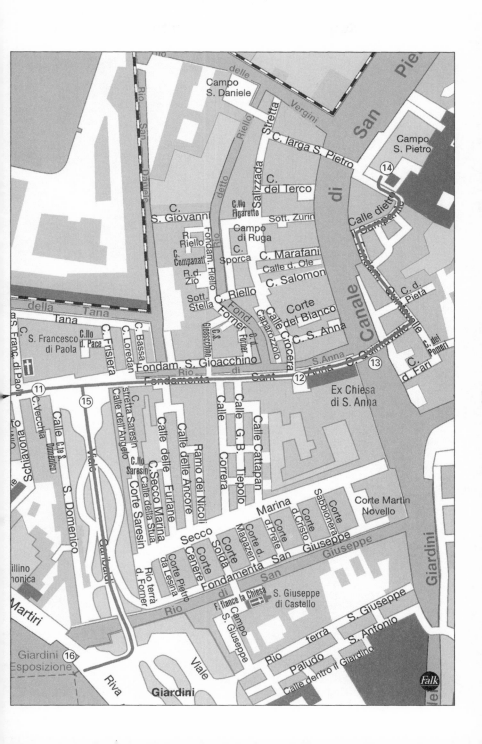

Walk 10 journeys from lonely Celestia (1), poised at the northern shore of the lagoon, to the Public Gardens (16), site of the world's most important contemporary art show, the Biennale. No walk around the city provides a clearer sense of Venice's important history than one through eastern Castello. The once-great medieval Arsenale looms as a symbol of her unmatched naval might; San Pietro di Castello functioned as the city's official cathedral from 1451 until Napoleon chose the Basilica of San Marco as strategically more convenient; the *calli* around wide Via Garibaldi are among the oldest in the city; and the national pavilions of the Venice Art Biennale have ensured the city's continued cultural prominence for over a hundred years.

Celestia boat stop (1)

Though Commissario Brunetti is a native, there remain areas of the city where even he feels like an outsider, where his Venetian proves no match for the locals' 'purest Castello', an asset Vianello conveniently possesses. The more recent arrival in Castello of the African bag sellers, secreted away in unregistered apartments, forces Brunetti to rely on colleagues for help; only those with generations of relatives still in residence seem able to penetrate Castello's network of unfamiliar contacts.

* * *

In the past, vaporetti would make frequent stops in remote Castello before entering the Arsenale Canal, a once convenient path from the lagoon to the Grand Canal avoiding the long detour around the most eastern edge of the city. Today the Arsenale has been put off limits to all but the military; its vast, impressive halls seen only during art exhibitions. Yet the historic buildings of Venice's 80-acre naval yards, even from the outside remain a potent reminder both for residents and visitors of Venice's earlier domination of the seas. During the sixteenth century, 16,000 men worked inside the Arsenale.

The Celestia boat stop, gazing across the still waters in this eastern part of the city, seems the ideal place to join Brunetti for a boat ride no longer available to mere residents or tourists, who now must accompany him in their imagination instead of boating through the Arsenale.

'I'd like to go to the Arsenale stop,' Brunetti said. He started to go down into the cabin, but as the boat swung out into the canal, he was stopped by the feel of the morning's softness on his face and decided to remain on deck. (. . .)

'We in a hurry, Commissario?' Foa asked as they approached Fondamenta Nuove.

Brunetti wanted this trip to last as long as possible; he wanted never to have to deliver this news. But he answered, 'Yes.'

'I'll ask if we can go through the Arsenale (7), then,' Foa said, taking out his *telefonino*. He (. . .) cut hard to the left, and then arched around to the right, under the footbridge and straight through the centre of the Arsenale.

How many years had it been since the Number Five did this every ten minutes? Brunetti asked himself. Ordinarily Brunetti would have enjoyed the sight of the shipyard that had fuelled Venice's greatness, but at this moment he could think of little save the cleansing wind. (*Through a Glass, Darkly*, ch. 16)

→

Fondamenta Case Nuove to Campo della Celestia **(2)** to Campo Santa Ternità **(3)** to Calle Donà to Calle Magno **(4)**

The walk between the Celestia boat stop and the Arsenale offers a pleasant diversion from the usual crowds of central Venice. Dotted with *palazzi*, sculpture-covered wellheads, austere churches, and crisscrossed by waterways garlanded with laundry like family-crested flags blowing in the wind, the area resembles a small village in its contentment. Even the sculpture has a domestic and intimate flair: on the left along Calle Magno at the entrance to tiny Calle dell'Angelo **(A)**, a stone relief angel hovers over the archway, sweetly guarded by two small hedgehogs, a touching contrast to the gigantic lions standing sentinel at the Arsenale nearby.

→

None of the modesty of the small Castello neighbourhoods can prepare the casual stroller for the immensity of the medieval Arsenale. Viewed from the Rio delle Gorne **(5)**, the western walls with their fishtail crenellation tower over the scene across the water, flaunting the faded ambitions of one of history's greatest naval forces. The sneering lion on the side wall speaks of a bygone imperial power rather than serving as a symbol of the evangelist Saint Mark.

Along Rio delle Gorne **(5)**, Fondamenta Penini to Chiesa di San Martino **(6)**

Certainly Brunetti cannot escape the lions that dominate the area around the great shipbuilders' yard. At the end of Fondamenta Penini, Sansovino's Church of San Martino **(6)** even provides a *bocca di leone*, one of Venice's lion's mouths, where citizens were encouraged to post anonymous denunciations for all kinds of crimes and sins. The lions' heads may no longer be in use, but Brunetti's own career has been much abetted by the Venetians' penchant for secretly reporting on their neighbours. The canal itself seems to mirror Venice's murkiness.

The water in the canal in front of the Church of San Martino was exceptionally low, and Brunetti paused to glance down into it. The slopes of viscous mud on either side gleamed in the sunlight, and the stench of corruption rose towards him. Who knew the last time the canal had been dredged and cleaned? (*Doctored Evidence*, ch. 11)

→

The inescapable contrast between the past and the present accompanies Brunetti on his trips to the Arsenale, mocking his historic sense of the city's glory. He may resuscitate Venice's majesty through memory, but the accumulation of lions that guard the twin tower-gates to the Arsenale **(7)** can no longer command respect. Stolen from their legendary perches throughout the Mediterranean, once powerful symbols of naval victory, they now invite scorn: 'he wondered, as he usually did whenever he looked at the statues, whether the men who had carved them had ever seen a real lion'. (*Doctored Evidence*, ch. 11)

Into Campo dell'Arsenale **(7)**

Seven hundred years before Brunetti stands on the wooden

crossing **(8)** to ponder Venice's 'terrible power', Dante walks
with Virgil 'from bridge to bridge', seeing ahead of him a
human vision of hell: 'As in the Arsenal of the Venetians, in
winter, the sticky pitch for caulking their unsound vessels is
boiling.' Since Dante gleefully condemns thieving public officials to the 'boiling oil' in the *Inferno* (Canto XXI), Brunetti
must feel a true *simpatia* with the dead poet. Dante describes
the scene of the shipbuilders at work in the harrowing fire-
light; Brunetti, too, imagines the men at their labour, their
ancient tools raised.

Facts, dates, pieces of information, fragments of rumour
swirled around, blinding him so that it wasn't until he found
himself at the entrance to the Arsenale, the goofy lions lined
up on his left, that he came back to the present. At the top
of the wooden bridge he allowed himself a moment to gaze
through the gateway into what had once been the womb
of Venice's power and the ultimate source of her wealth
and dominion. With only manpower and hammers and
saws and all those other tools with strange names that carpen-
ters and boat builders use, they had managed to build a ship
a day and fill the seas with the terrible power of their fleet.
(*Wilful Behaviour*, ch. 17)

In *Blood from a Stone*, the lions serve a more practical
function: to disguise a meeting between Brunetti and his
father's old friend, Claudio Stein, an expert in precious stones.
As so often, Brunetti's thoughts return to his own youth
whenever memories of his father arise, distracting him from
his immediate surroundings.

Brunetti remembered the bar, on a corner facing the pillared
gates of the Arsenale: Claudio must be out on the Riva degli
Schiavoni to be able to reach it in five minutes. Many times
in his youth, he had sat there, listening to his father's friends
talk about the war as they played endless, inconsequential
games of *scopa*, sipping at small glasses of a wine so tannic
it left their teeth almost blue. (*Blood from a Stone*, ch. 18)

Occasions arise when even native Venetians desire to appear as tourists, though not often. Brunetti watches the old jeweller cross over the bridge and disguise his purpose with the apparent casualness of a visitor admiring the scenery:

Brunetti barely noticed the lions when he reached the entrance to the Arsenale and walked directly into the bar, looking for the familiar face. When he saw no sign of Claudio, he checked his watch and found that it had been only six minutes since he left the Questura. He ordered a coffee and turned to face the door. After another five minutes, he saw the old man at a distance . . .

At the bottom of the bridge, Claudio went over and stood in front of the stone lions, studying them slowly, pausing in front of each one until he could have committed its face and form to memory. After that, he strolled back to the bottom of the bridge and looked left through the gates of the Arsenale and out towards the *laguna*. Then he turned and ambled alongside the canal in the direction of the *bacino*. To an idle spectator, the man with the cane could be a sightseer interested in the area around the Arsenale; to a policeman, he was someone checking to see if he was being followed. (*Blood*, ch. 18)

The Arsenale area this time, ironically, provides a perfect setting: a wide open space with everyone highly visible, two bustling cafés (one also a *trattoria*) filled with a combination of locals and tourists, enough artistic and historic works to invite examination and encourage lingering.

→

Everything along the delightful, open walk down the Fondamenta dell' Arsenale towards the lagoon gives further evidence of Venice's former maritime glories. The Museum of Naval History, a former warehouse used since the sixteenth century to store extra boat gear and oars for the city's vast fleet, is now filled with all the paraphernalia of a mighty war machine. So vast is the city's store of historical material that the little church at Campo San Biagio **(9)**, which served the

Bridge over Rio dell' Arsenale **(8)** on to Fondamenta to Campo San Biagio **(9)**

naval community since the 1100s, has been converted into an annexe for the museum. Like so many of the city's churches, its spiritual function has now been replaced by secular importance – a state of affairs that leaves Brunetti uncertain whether to shrug or lament.

He wondered how much longer they could continue to serve as places of worship, now that there were so few worshippers and young people were bored, as were his own children, by the irrelevance of what the Church had to say to them. Brunetti would not much regret its passing, but the thought of what little there was to replace it unsettled him. (*Wilful Behaviour*, ch. 17)

→

On to Via Garibaldi (10)

Via Garibaldi **(10)**, the widest street in the city and main thoroughfare for eastern Castello, was for centuries a sparkling canal dividing some of the oldest *calli* in Venice. Filled in by practical Napoleon two hundred years ago, it has continued as the social centre for residents and now increasingly for tourists, without, however, losing its reputation for a determined provincialism.

In *The Anonymous Venetian*, Brunetti reflects on the changes even Castello, with its staunch loyalty to the local dialect, has undergone. He discovers that Avvocato Santomauro of the 'charitable' Lega della Moralità lives, unsurprisingly, in the wealthy *sestiere* of San Marco. The banker, Leonardo Mascari, found murdered in women's clothing in Marghera, lives, surprisingly, in less fashionable Castello, only a block away from Via Garibaldi.

Castello was the least prestigious *sestiere* of the city, a zone primarily inhabited by solid working-class families, an area where children could still grow up speaking nothing but dialect and remain entirely ignorant of Italian until they began elementary school. Perhaps it was the Mascari family home. Or perhaps he had made a lucky deal on an apartment or house. Apartments in Venice were so hard to find, and those found so outrageously priced, either to buy or to rent, that even Castello was becoming fashionable. Spending enough money on restoration could perhaps provide respectability, if not for the entire *quartiere*, then at least for the individual address. (*The Anonymous Venetian*, ch. 13)

Not only the Castellani and the *nouveaux riches* occupy the *sestiere*, but in recent times the area has gradually become home ground for the African street vendors – no matter what prestigious addresses their landlords may possess across the city. In *Blood from a Stone*, Brunetti realizes his network of contacts, which has always seemed to encompass most of Venice, is woefully inadequate to penetrate the closed neighbourhoods of Castello. He must rely on his men at the Questura to gain access to the hidden byways behind the deceptive Via Garibaldi with its friendly cafés and shops, outdoor food stalls, fishmongers, and local restaurants.

'Yes. There's one I've arrested at least five times; I can ask him.'

'But what if he sees you coming?' Pucetti asked.

'No, no, it's nothing like that,' Gravini insisted. 'A bunch of them live in an apartment off Via Garibaldi, down near where my mother lives, so I see them when I go to visit her, when . . .' he trailed off, seeking a way to say it. 'Well, when we're both off work. He says he used to be a teacher, Muhammad. I can ask him.'

'You think he'd trust you?' Brunetti asked.

Gravini shrugged. 'No way to know until I ask him.' (*Blood from a Stone*, ch. 6)

It is not only for access that Brunetti seems suddenly dependent on his fellow officers to make Castello less alien. Grateful for steady Vianello's company and assistance when entering the shadowy world of the *vu cumprà*, Brunetti also gains helpful information from his neighbour in San Polo, the atypically generous and decent landlord Cuzzoni, who houses many of the *ambulanti*:

He didn't know how to tell Vianello that he thought his presence would have a calming influence on the Africans, as it so often did on witnesses. Nor did he know how to tell Vianello that he would himself find his company comforting when going into the presence of an unknown number of young men, most of them illegal immigrants working at illegal jobs and now somehow caught up in a murder investigation.

They got off at Giardini and started down Viale Garibaldi; as they walked, Brunetti recounted his conversation with Cuzzoni, though he said nothing more about the man than that he seemed undisturbed to learn that the police were interested in his tenants and indeed seemed almost proud to have them living in his apartments. (*Blood*, ch. 11)

Despite the attractions of *sestiere* Castello with its open spaces, wide avenues, and intimate neighbourhoods, its direct exposure to the lagoon causes it to suffer the vagaries of what Brunetti calls Venice's 'filthy climate'. The Christmas weather that opened *Blood from a Stone* continues to assail Brunetti as he leaves the Questura and heads into Castello in pursuit of information and evidence about the murdered bag seller. Greeted near the entrance to Via le Garibaldi by a statue of the hero of independence, Giuseppe Garibaldi, he seems to share the figure's imagined discomfort.

His memory of the map was clear: also, he knew the building because a former classmate of his in middle school had lived in the house next door. To spare his face from the wind, he kept his eyes on the pavement and navigated by radar more than vision. He walked past the Arsenale, the lions looking far more pleased than they should have been at finding themselves out in this cold.

He turned left into Via Garibaldi and walked past the monument to the hero who, gazing down at the frozen surface of the water in the pool at his feet, looked more concerned about the cold than had the lions. (*Blood*, ch. 10)

In *Doctored Evidence*, on the contrary, Brunetti is suffering the heat in Castello. Disorienting as medieval Venice can often seem to the bewildered visitor, for the residents the close-set buildings and tiny *calli* at least offer shade from the blistering summer sun. The normal pleasures of escaping on to wide, airy Via Garibaldi melt in the summer glare that bakes the unsheltered boulevard, now with no canals for relief.

He hurried down the last broad bridge and turned into Via Garibaldi. The sun had driven almost everyone indoors: even the shade under the umbrellas of the bars that lined the street was empty as people waited for the sun to move westward and put at least one side of the street in the shade. (*Doctored Evidence*, ch. 17)

Donna Leon's fifteenth novel, *Through a Glass, Darkly*, keeps Brunetti constantly on the move: physically between the island of Murano and Castello; professionally between the secretive world of the glass-blowers and the equally suspicious *Castellani*. No one trusts him and few will talk. In the hope of gaining information, he decides to head into the *sestiere* to contact the Dante-reading *uomo di notte*, who guards the glass furnaces during the late night hours. Giorgio Tassini lives, appropriately, alas, across the *calle* from the Church of San Francesco di Paola **(11)**, which for much of its history served as a hospice for the severely ill, like Tassini's daughter, who is languishing in a painful sickness no one can diagnose. But the family's tragedies will wait as the invigorating weather encourages Brunetti to take a long walk from the Questura.

Chiesa San Francesco di Paola **(11)**

It was only a little after eleven, one of the sweetest times of day in springtime, and so Brunetti decided to walk down to Castello to talk to Giorgio. (. . .)

His strides grew longer as he felt the sun begin to work the winter stiffness out of him. Days like these reminded him of what a filthy climate the city really had: cold and damp in the winter; hot and damp in the summer. He banished this thought as the remains of winter gloom and looked around him, his smile as bright as the day itself.

He turned into Via Garibaldi, leaving the warmth of the sun behind him. Tassini lived opposite the Church of San Francesco di Paola, and he slowed as he saw the church on his left. (*Through a Glass, Darkly*, ch. 7)

But Signor Tassini is away, and Brunetti, standing on one of the most ancient *calli* in Venice, must convince Tassini's suspicious mother-in-law to let him in and then to answer probing questions about her beleaguered family. Between his Veneziano and her Castello dialect, a sense of trust finally emerges, reminding Brunetti of his own family past.

She did not smile, but her face relaxed, and a thin tracery of wrinkles softened around her eyes and mouth. 'What can I do for you?' she asked in purest Castello, her voice almost as deep as his own. (. . .)

As he gave her his name and shook her hand, it occurred to Brunetti to wonder how much of what she said would be comprehensible to a person from, say, Bologna. A number of the teeth on the top left side of her mouth were missing, so her speech was slurred, but it was the *Veneziano stretto* that was sure to defeat any ear not born within a hundred kilometres of the *laguna*. Yet how sweet it was to hear that dialect, so much like the one his grandmother had spoken all her life, never bothering to have anything to do with Italian, which she had always dismissed as a foreign language and not worthy of her attention. (*Glass, Darkly*, ch. 7)

Knowing locations in Castello finally helps Brunetti to get access to the night-watchman himself:

'When do you want to meet?' Tassini asked.

'If you could possibly spare me the time right now, I could be there in about fifteen minutes.'

The line sang emptily for a long time, but Brunetti resisted the impulse to speak. 'All right,' Tassini said, 'but not here at the house. There's a bar opposite San Francesco di Paola.'

'On the corner before the park?' Brunetti asked.

'Yes.'

'I know it, the place that draws the little hearts on the cappuccino *schiuma*, no?'

'Yes,' said Tassini in a gentler tone. (*Glass, Darkly*, ch. 10)

→

In *Wilful Behaviour* the trail of crime and guilt leads from a young university student's corpse in fashionable Dorsoduro to a suspect library far across the city in the remote backwaters of Castello.

Straight to Ex-chiesa di Sant'Anna **(12)**

Venice, a city spangled with well over a hundred functioning churches, once had more than twice as many. Half have been destroyed, have collapsed, or been deconsecrated, making the decline of regular attendance a subject not easily ignored, even for the secular Brunetti. After ruminating on the murder of Paola's pupil, Brunetti moves further east into Castello to the deconsecrated Church of Sant'Anna **(12)**. The seemingly rude health of crime in the city only makes the spiritual malaise more troubling.

He turned both from these reflections and the gateway and continued, weaving back towards Via Garibaldi and then, keeping the canal on his left, down towards Sant'Anna. When he saw the façade of the church, he realized he had no memory of ever having been inside; perhaps, like so many others in the city, it didn't function any longer as a church. (. . .)

He crossed the small bridge on his left and saw, on his right, a single long building the back of which faced the church. He turned into Calle Sant'Anna and found himself in front of an immense green *portone*. To the right were two bells: 'Ford', and 'Biblioteca della Patria'. He rang the one for the library. (*Wilful Behaviour*, ch. 17)

→

The unusual absence of waterways around Via Garibaldi ends at the wide Canale di San Pietro, making the act of crossing the bridge feel like an entry into another world. The water

Across Canale di San Pietro **(13)** to Chiesa San Pietro **(14)**

lined with brightly painted family fishing boats and tiny docks would never suggest that a former castle here was important enough to give *sestiere* Castello its name. More unexpected, this remote location was once the site for Venice's original cathedral, Chiesa San Pietro di Castello **(14)**.

In *Through a Glass, Darkly*, Brunetti resists staying on Murano for Nanni's 'fresh fish and polenta' and instead settles for a lunch in Castello. After his unmemorable meal, he walks to the island of San Pietro to visit its church. Although Brunetti attends religious functions only on required occasions, this is a special place, supplying further evidence of the city's lucrative contact with the East. A strange marble slab of Arabic calligraphy, backing a stone throne, remains in the church. One more testimonial either to Venice's cosmopolitan history, or to her reputation for pillage, especially of objects with which to beautify the city.

Because Paola and the kids were at lunch with her parents that day, Brunetti ate at a restaurant in Castello, a meal he paid no attention to and forgot as soon as he left. After he had eaten, he walked down to San Pietro in Castello and went inside the church to have a look at the funeral stele with its carved Qur'anic verses. Continuing debate as to whether he was looking at evidence of cultural theft or multiculturalism in no way diminished his appreciation of the carving's beauty. *(Through a Glass, Darkly*, ch. 22)

→

Back along Via Garibaldi **(10)** to Viale Garibaldi **(15)** through park and right to Giardini boat stop **(16)**

In particularly hot weather, Brunetti often avoids the torturous unshaded Riva degli Schiavoni promenade, opting instead for a vaporetto to get him either from or to the Questura. In the area around Via Garibaldi, the Giardini boat stop **(16)** is closer and easier for him –and the location itself is stupendous. One side faces the fresh air and distant views across the end of the lagoon; the other side is backed by the only large park in the city, created by Napoleon. Scantily used by most Venetians, it comes alive during the summer Venice Art Biennale, now held in odd-numbered years. Filled with exhibition halls built by nearly thirty countries, it draws art followers from all over the world. The recently renovated Café Paradiso, at the gardens' main entrance facing the lagoon, offers one of the most enchanting vistas in the city, especially since it is so far away from the bulk of the crowds.

In former years the Giardini also offered ample places for youthful courting, as Signorina Elettra recalls in *Uniform Justice*. Despite the gardens' allure, however, they were not inviting enough to blind her to the appalling conceit of the cadets from the military academy on Giudecca, as she explains to Brunetti:

'Going out?' he inquired.

'For a coffee, for a walk, just to go down to the Giardini to sit on a bench and talk.' With a rueful smile, she corrected herself. 'To listen, that is.' She smiled across at him. 'I believe one could employ a new noun here, sir: a listen, instead of a conversation. That's what I had whenever we met: a listen.'

'Perhaps it was a quicker way for you to get to know him,' Brunetti suggested drily.

'Yes,' she said brusquely. 'I got to know him.' (*Uniform Justice*, ch. 8)

In the even-numbered years, when the art crowd has moved on to other venues and the local places taken over by tourist shops are empty, the gardens can have an abandoned feel. Summer temperatures soaring, their greenery fades and the views melt into the heat haze over the water.

His appointment with Avvocatessa Roberta Marieschi was set for ten the next morning. Because her office was in Castello, just at the beginning of Via Garibaldi, Brunetti took the Number One and got off at Giardini. The trees in the public gardens looked tired and dusty and greatly in need of rain. Truth to tell, much the same could be said of most of the people in the city. He found the office with no difficulty, next door to what had once been a very good pizzeria, now transformed into a shop selling fake Murano glass. (*Doctored Evidence*, ch. 10)

Beginning this walk with Brunetti ruminating on Venice and the salvation of fine weather, this journey comes full circle in *A Sea of Troubles* as he heads away from the city out into the *laguna* to faraway Isola di Pellestrina. Uplifting winds accompany him as he passes by in a police launch, the Giardini offering one more enchanting Venetian sight to gladden Brunetti's heart. In this final scene of the walk, he looks away from the bracing waters – as a good native son, he keeps his eyes on the beauty of the city that is his own.

The next morning, Brunetti and Vianello left for Pellestrina a little after nine. Though both knew they were engaged in the investigation of two savage murders, the glory of the day once again conspired to lighten their hearts and fill them with a schoolboy sense of adventure and fun. No office to be stuck in, no Patta calling to demand instant progress, and no fixed times to be anywhere; even the pilot, grumbling at the helm that they'd be slowed down by cross-tides, couldn't dim their mood. The morning did not disappoint. The trees in the Giardini were covered with new leaves, and occasionally a sudden breeze set them shimmering, their undersides twinkling in the light reflected from the water. (*A Sea of Troubles*, ch. 10)

WALK 11: *Artful Properties*

San Marco—Santa Maria Formosa—Palazzo Querini-Stampalia
Santi Giovanni e Paolo—Chiesa dei Miracoli
Santa Marina

1 hour

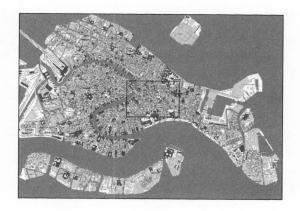

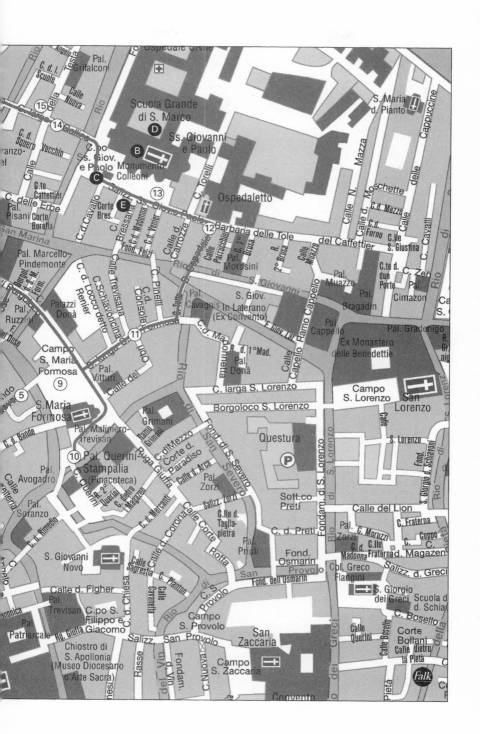

Walk 11 moves from Venice's central Piazza **(1)** into the northern part of the city highlighted by Campo SS. Giovanni e Paolo. Popular with visitors for its ample cafés, Gothic buildings, and airy views from the nearby bridge and *fondamenta* leading out to the lagoon, the *campo* is dominated by Venice's greatest bronze sculpture, the equestrian statue of Colleoni. It also houses a crucial necessity for the residents, the city's major hospital, a Renaissance property with a chequered past and present.

In Donna Leon's novels, Brunetti must approach the area from a variety of points across the city, since the nature of his work too often forces him to the *ospedale* to investigate the injured, maimed, and dead victims who require his attention in their search for justice. But this is also a neighbourhood with fine restaurants, delightful *trattorie*, and a Rosa Salva bar still open for his favourite *caffè*. Campo Santa Maria Formosa is the site of the only museum that Brunetti visits, delighting him with some of the city's loveliest paintings, although he also finds there grim reminders of the crimes he cannot escape. In nearby Calle della Testa he first visits the lavishly, and illegally, restored home of the American archaeologist, Brett Lynch, another property that astonishes him with the Venetians' canny ability to mask architectural transformation. Later in *Acqua Alta*, Brunetti reunites with Brett's soprano lover to cross the city, battling rising waters to save the young American. The walk ends with Brunetti enjoying another café he frequents in Campo Santa Marina – one more brief escape from the pressures of crime.

Piazza San Marco **(1)**

* * *

Torre dell' Orologio **(1)** is a glamorous entrance into a world preoccupied with commerce and gain. The 'Moors' who strike the bells on the hour, once beautiful bronze figures, have

Under Torre dell' Orologio **(1)** on to Merceria **(2)**

been tarnished by time and weather, losing their ancient splendour as have so many art objects and façades in the city. But if Venice is dubiously reminding visitors of her former glory, then the long shopping artery of the Mercerie (2) bears ample witness to her vital commerce in beautiful objects. Here the shop windows announce Murano's continuing status as glassmaker at least to the wealthy – chandeliers the size of small cars replace the tourist stalls' kitsch; shimmering silks, softest cashmeres, and hand-woven linen edge out the city's ubiquitous T-shirt sellers; pearls, diamonds, and emeralds garland the windows of shops, while all the semiprecious stones that helped make Venice so central a marketplace – jasper, porphyry, jade – are still on display in every shape.

$$\longrightarrow$$

Past Chiesa San Zulian (3), left on Salizzada San Lio (4) to Testiere (5)

Yet the allure of glamorous goods has little status in the Brunetti family; Paola finds most jewellery gaudy, and since Brunetti must enjoy his pleasures on a policeman's salary, he leaves the Merceria dell'Orologio to head away from the expensive emporia and into a 'jewel' of a restaurant for his midday reward. Yet the inescapable nightmare of youthful death haunts even his excellent meal at one of Venice's most popular fish *trattorie*, il Testiere (5).* The young cadet's death at the military academy in *Uniform Justice* and the resultant damage to the boy's family preoccupy his thoughts, erasing his usual appreciation of excellent food.

He walked down to Testiere, where the owner would always find him a place, and had a fish antipasto and then a piece of grilled tuna Bruno swore was fresh. For all the attention Brunetti paid to it, the fish could have been frozen or freeze-dried. At any other time, ignoring a meal this fine would have shamed Brunetti: today he could not drag himself away from his attempt to discover the connection between Moro's professional life and the suffering inflicted upon his family, and so the meal remained eaten but untasted. (*Uniform Justice*, ch. 21)

$$\longrightarrow$$

Venice's medieval layout, with its meandering narrow streets, not only provokes the unwary into getting lost, but also affects Venetian behaviour. The cramped *calli* and close-set buildings offer many opportunities for the prying eyes and ears of the residents to spy into the apartments of their neighbours. In a small city, where no one's business has a prayer of privacy, filled with an ageing population with little to occupy the long winter days, the activities of foreigners garner unwanted attention, and immigrants provide a special source of nosy gossip. And, of course, because it is Venice, everyone gets neatly slotted into groups – 'us', 'them', 'tourists', 'foreigners', 'immigrants'. In *Suffer the Little Children*, a pregnant teenage girl becomes an object of curiosity, until she disappears, when she becomes a source of worry.

To Salizzada San Lio (4) to Calle della Fava (6) to Calle degli Stagneri (7)

'Where did she have the baby, Signora?'

'Right there, in the *calle* across from my place. Not out in the *calle*, you understand. (. . .)'

'Where is this exactly, Signora?'

'Calle dei Stagneri (7). You know it. It's near San Bortolo, the *calle* that goes down to Campo de la Fava. I live down on the right side, and she was on the left, on the same side as that pizzeria, only we're both down at the end, near the bridge. The apartment used to belong to an old woman – I never knew her name – but then she died and her son inherited it, and he started to rent it out, you know, the way people do, by the week, to foreigners, or by the month.

'But when I saw the girl in there, and she was pregnant, I thought maybe he'd decided to rent it like a real apartment, you know, with a lease and all. And if she was pregnant, she'd be one of us and not a tourist, right? But I guess there's more money if you rent by the week, especially to foreigners. And then you don't have to pay the . . . ' (*Suffer the Little Children*, ch. 1)

In this medieval part of the city, marble tributes to the Madonna abound. Spanning the far end of Calle del Paradiso (8) is a fifteenth-century Gothic marble relief of a sheltering Madonna (A). Lovely at any time, the high pointed arch is

Back to Salizzada San Lio to Calle del Paradiso (8) into Campo Santa Maria Formosa (9)

especially magical at night when light filters through the lacy surround. It provides the perfect entry into the Campo Santa Maria Formosa (9), where Venice acquired its first church dedicated to the Madonna, in 1492. Although Ruskin detested the distorted marble face that leers out at passers-by at the base of the bell tower, the church itself with its marble interior and fine paintings attracts a large share of admirers.

The *campo*, broad and rambling, sits ringed by marble-clad *palazzi*, the former Communist Party headquarters with its ornamental brick façade, numerous cafés, a pizzeria, and outdoor markets for fresh food and flowers. A *campo* whose surface easily charms tourists also alerts Brunetti's radar for a property's potential:

Directly in front of him, on the other side of the *campo*, stood Palazzo Priuli, abandoned for as long as he could remember, the central prize of vicious litigation over a contested will. As the heirs and presumptive heirs fought over whose it was or should be, the *palazzo* went about its business of deteriorating with a singlemindedness that ignored heirs, claims and legality. (. . .) Brunetti the dreamer had often considered that Palazzo Priuli would be the ideal place to imprison a mad aunt, a recalcitrant wife or a reluctant heiress at the same time as his more sober and practical Venetian self viewed it as a prime piece of real estate and studied the windows, dividing the space beyond into apartments, offices and studios. *(Acqua Alta*, ch. 15)

This area has been residence to generations of Venetians, including Signorina Elettra's family the Zorzis, as Brunetti finally discovers. A character especially admired by readers of the novels, she almost never appears outdoors in the city; instead she is seen mostly occupying her throne at the Questura. There she dispenses judgement, controls Vice-Questore Patta, thwarts Lieutenant Scarpa, instructs Vianello, and abets Brunetti. Despite her colourful outfits and the brilliant flowers she orders to adorn the offices, she remains an enigma to her colleagues. In *A Sea of Troubles*, although she takes on a starring and dangerous role, once she arrives at a distant island in the lagoon she remains beyond Brunetti's control and bewilderingly invisible in her private life.

The weekend passed quietly. Brunetti had no clear idea of when Signorina Elettra planned to go out to Pellestrina. He thought of calling her at home, even looked up her number in the phone book, something he'd never done before. He found the listing, a low number in Castello that would put her home, he calculated, somewhere near Santa Maria Formosa. While he had the page open, he checked for other Zorzis and found at least two who lived within a few numbers of her address: family? *(A Sea of Troubles, ch. 13)*

So welcoming a place has attracted the attention of some new immigrant arrivals. As early Europe's most cosmopolitan city, Venice used to house her troublesome mix of foreign populations in specific areas or buildings designed to keep everyone easily watched and controlled. Whilst the Ghetto is the city's most ancient 'arranged' living space, the practice of semi-isolating various groups was common in Venice in medieval and Renaissance times: German merchants stored their goods in the Fondaco dei Tedeschi, which also accommodated visiting merchants; the Ottomans were mostly confined to the Fondaco dei Turchi, although none were so restricted as the Jewish colony.

Today, much of that clannish cloistering has been imposed by the immigrants themselves. As Brunetti discovers in *Blood from a Stone*, the African street sellers seem to disappear when not working the main shopping streets; the Chinese are highly visible in the bars they are gradually taking over throughout the city; the Albanians and Kosovars can be seen in heavily trafficked areas, entertaining with their street music; the Sri Lankans sell roses in good weather, umbrellas in bad. In *Wilful Behaviour*, Brunetti unexpectedly finds a group of Kurds keeping to their nomadic ways, yet camping in places where their political message will be most effective.

He passed through Campo Santa Maria Formosa and saw what looked like a tribe of Kurds camped in front of the abandoned *palazzo*, their meagre possessions spread in front of them as they squatted and stooped on bright-coloured carpets. The men wore sober suits and black skullcaps, but the women's long skirts and scarves flared out in orange, yellow, and red. Their uninterest in passers-by seemed total; all they lacked were campfires and donkeys; they could just as easily have been in the middle of the plains. (*Wilful Behaviour*, ch. 21)

To Palazzo Querini
Stampalia **(10)**

The Querini Stampalia museum **(10)**,* less grand than the ever-crowded Accademia which Brunetti routinely passes without entering, possesses an enviable collection of paintings that can still be visited without a noisy guide narrating in the background. It is patronized by Venetians, like Brunetti, who often see the historic and legendary figures as people they've come to know.

For all of Brunetti's sorrow at the waste of teenage death, to lose a child barely past infancy provokes unmatched anguish. In *Suffer the Little Children*, he ponders how any family – including his own – could cope when a baby is taken away, for whatever reasons. Just as food and wine have failed to reconcile him to the continuing joys of life, so his beloved art can do little besides remind him of a two-thousand-year-old history of family tragedy.

He let his feet and his whim take him where they pleased, and after a time he found himself standing at the foot of the bridge that led to the entrance to Palazzo Querini Stampalia. (. . .)

He went upstairs to the gallery, where he had not been for some time. How he loved to look at these portraits, not so much because of their beauty as paintings as but for the resemblance of so many of them to people he saw every day. Indeed, the portrait of Gerolamo Querini, painted almost five hundred years ago, bore an almost photographic likeness to Vianello – well, to what Vianello had looked like as a younger man. (. . .)

His favourite was the Bellini *Presentation in the Temple*, and, as always, he allowed himself to come to it last. And saw that child, the swaddled Jesus, being passed back to his mother by the high priest Simeon. The baby's body was bound tight by the encircling strips of cloth, his arms trapped to his sides with only the tips of his fingers wriggling free. At the sight of him, Brunetti's thoughts returned to Pedrolli's child, similarly bound, if by the decisions of the state. (*Suffer*, ch. 19)

→

With the years, outsiders become more central to Brunetti's concerns. *Ambulanti, stranieri, extracomunitari, clandestini, vu cumprà* – the labels may vary but their presence increases, and many are taking up positions in areas unaccustomed to foreign workers. Deducing where a person belongs and where not, one of the main tools Brunetti uses to track down suspicious transactions, becomes ever less evident. In *Suffer the Little Children*, an African deliveryman reacts with fright when he sees policemen idling over their coffee as he drops off his early morning tray of fresh brioche. Brunetti is equally intrigued to hear the owner calling the young man by an Italian nickname and to discover he works legally.

Calle lunga Santa Maria Formosa **(11)**, over Ponte Tetta to Barbaria delle Tolle **(12)**

Brunetti placed the bill on the counter then half turned to the door, where Vianello was already waiting for him. Over his shoulder, Brunetti asked, 'Bambola?'

Sergio smiled. 'I saw his real name on his work permit, and there was no way I was going to be able to pronounce it. So he suggested I call him Bambola, since it's as close as anyone can get to his real name in Italian.'

'Work permit?' Brunetti asked.

'At that *pasticceria* in Barbaria delle Tolle,' Sergio said, pronouncing the name of the *calle* in Veneziano, something Brunetti had never heard a foreigner succeed in doing. 'He actually has one.' (*Suffer*, ch. 6)

→

In *Death in a Strange Country*, Brunetti finds himself at the furthest reaches of *sestiere* Castello, for him an always unfamiliar and frequently unpleasant area. His shortest route

Campo SS. Giovanni e Paolo **(13)**

home would take him along the Barbaria delle Tole and into Campo SS. Giovanni e Paolo **(13)**, but the haunting image that opens *Death in a Strange Country* of the young American sergeant's body floating face down in the canal opposite the hospital forces him to detour around the *campo* in a vain attempt to dispel memory:

As he did whenever he was overcome by nervousness, Brunetti walked. He turned left and walked along the water until he came to the bridge that took him to Sant' Elena, crossed it, and walked around this farthest part of the city, finding it no more interesting than he ever had in the past. He cut back through Castello, along the wall of the Arsenale, and back towards Santi Giovanni e Paolo, where all of this had begun. Intentionally, he avoided the *campo*, refusing to look at the place where Foster's body had been pulled out of the water. (*Death in a Strange Country*, ch. 22)

Even without a dead body in the canal, Campo SS. Giovanni e Paolo can still haunt, as the three major monuments, despite their splendour, also create reminders of death – especially for Commissario Brunetti. The great Gothic preaching church of the Dominicans **(B)** serves as the funereal pantheon of Venice, home to twenty-five entombed doges. Next door, the city's major hospital sits conveniently along a canal for easy access to the cypress-crowned cemetery island of San Michele visible out in the lagoon. Even Verrocchio's bronze equestrian statue of Colleoni **(C)**, with its rearing horse's nostrils flared for battle, and the *condottiere*'s vicious face bent on military violence, immortalizes the cost in lives of Venice's power.

But when the sun is shining, and crowds stroll in the breezy open space, even death must take a holiday. Then it seems impossible not to stop at one of the cafés, all offering perfect views, for an *aperitivo* and a leisurely look around.

Although the Church of SS. Giovanni e Paolo dominates the *campo* by its size, its unadorned brick façade cannot compete with the marble *trompe-l'oeil* glory of the Scuola di San Marco **(D)** it abuts. By 1500 one of the most important *scuole* in the city – charitable institutions created by wealthy citizens to help the poor and abandoned, always decorated by Venice's finest painters and sculptors – its scalloped crown draws the eye skyward over a façade of pale marbles. In so exalted a setting, the lions ranged alongside the main portal seem simply to pose rather than fulfilling their duty to protect. The exterior is complemented by a colonnaded hall of marble columns inside, topped by ornate ceilings, walls covered with paintings by Tintoretto and Veronese – all leading today to the drab scrubs of the surgical staff, and the rubber clogs of the medical teams of the Ospedale Civile. For Brunetti, the *campo* rarely reveals the charm of its setting, allowing the luxury of exalted ruminations on Venice's past glories. Instead, he must face the wounded and the dying. 'Dante-like', he enters his own kind of hell that crime requires:

As he approached the hospital, Brunetti found himself thinking of all the times his work had brought him here; not so much recalling the specific people he had been called to visit as the times when he'd passed, Dante-like, through the yawning portals beyond which lurked pain, suffering, and death. Over the course of the years, he'd come to suspect that, no matter how great the physical pain, the emotional suffering which surrounded that pain was often far worse. He shook his head to clear it of these thoughts, reluctant to enter with these miserable reflections already in his care. (*Friends in High Places*, ch. 6)

Not even the beauty of the hospital's entrance can distract him from the misery ahead in *Suffer the Little Children*.

The *portiere* seemed to be asleep behind the window of his office: certainly he did not look up as Brunetti entered the hospital. Blind to the magnificence of the entrance hall though aware of the sudden drop in temperature, Brunetti worked his way right and left and then left again until he arrived at the automatic doors of the emergency room. (*Suffer the Little Children*, ch. 3)

Dante's eternal punishments meted out to corrupt officials might again have come to mind as Brunetti reflects in
Acqua Alta on the gross irresponsibility involved in the futile
modernizing of the *ospedale*, made worse by the neglect of
basic patient services.

He left the room and stood at a window in the corridor,
gazing down into the central courtyard that was a part of the
original fifteenth-century monastery. Opposite him he saw
the new pavilion that had been built and opened with such
public shouts of glory – nuclear medicine, most advanced
technologies to be had in all of Italy, most famous doctors,
a new age in health care for the exorbitantly taxed citizens
of Venice. No expense had been spared; the building emerged
an architectural wonder, its high marble arches giving a
modern-day reflection of the graceful arches that stood out
in Campo SS. Giovanni e Paolo and led the way into the
main hospital.

The opening ceremony had been held, there had been
speeches and the press had come, but the building had never
been used. No drains. No sewers. And no responsibility . . .
(. . .)

Did one laugh or cry? The building had been left unpro-
tected after the opening that was not an opening, and vandals
had already broken in and damaged some of the equipment,
so now the hospital paid for guards to patrol the empty corridors, and patients who needed the treatments and procedures
it was supposed to provide were sent to other hospitals or
told to go to private clinics. He could no longer remember
how many billion lire had been spent. And the nurses had
to be bribed to change the sheets. (*Acqua Alta*, ch. 3)

Not only does the hospital have to bear the weight of its
history, but the entire *campo* is entangled in repeated architectural change. Since the majority of Venice's monuments
date from several hundred years ago, the city is a constant
and rotating scene of repair, never more obvious nor long-
lasting than when this concerns the restoration of principal
attractions. Readers have grown accustomed to Brunetti's

laments over the eternally closed Church of San Lorenzo outside his office window at the Questura, but other architectural and sculptural delights in the city also remain shrouded in scaffolding for years, their eventual removal always an occasion for celebration. For a decade, whenever Brunetti escaped the confines of the hospital in Campo SS. Giovanni e Paolo he faced at least one of its three monuments undergoing extensive restoration. In *The Death of Faith* in 1996, 'He looked at the scaffolding that covered the front of the Basilica and saw that the shadows had crawled halfway up the façade.'

But even in slow-moving Venice the work gets done, the results applauded. By 2006, in *Suffer the Little Children*, 'Brunetti noticed that the statue of Colleoni was finally free of the scaffolding that had covered it for years: it was wonderful to see the old villain again.' But he is denied the chance to stop at a bar for a celebration since he discovers at this early hour nearby 'Rosa Salva' **(E)**,* still not open.' And for much of the ten years in between, even the silvery marble façade of the hospital itself stayed hidden under cover.

Scaffolding is only one way to camouflage a building; address is another. Venice's system was originally based on a plan of sequential numbering by *calle* within each *sestiere* – a system which quickly came to exist in name only. Confused further by the absence of consistent street signs, even residents are often baffled. In *Death at La Fenice*, Brunetti embarks on a typical experience when looking for Brett Lynch's apartment in a residential neighbourhood far from the more friendly areas of the city.' In Campo SS. Giovanni e Paolo he relies on the Venetians' interest in their neighbours to serve as the most available source of information:

The only way to find it was to get to the church and ask someone who lived in the neighbourhood. She ought to be easy to find. Foreigners tended to live in more fashionable parts of Venice, not this solidly middle-class area, and very few foreigners managed to sound as if they had grown up here, as Brett Lynch did.

In front of the church, he inquired first for the number,

then for the American, but the woman he had approached had no idea of where to find either. *(Death at La Fenice*, ch. 8)

Yet, unlike cities with cars, where it is understandable to admit ignorance, it is impossible for Venetians to accept defeat in the face of questions about location; they know their city, and if the address is unfamiliar, the next step is to refer the question to an authority, most often a bar owner. They may consult the city's directory in the privacy of their homes – but only as a last resort would anyone on the street ever consider anything but a local's advice.

→

On to Calle larga G. Gallina **(14)** to Maria's kiosk **(15)**

She told him to go and ask Maria, saying the name as if she expected him to know exactly which Maria she meant, and if Maria didn't know where she lived, then the American didn't live in the neighbourhood.

At the bottom of the bridge in front of the Basilica, he found Maria, a white-haired woman of indeterminate age who sat inside her kiosk **(15)**, dispensing newspapers as though they were fortunes and she the Sibyl. He gave her the number he was looking for, and she replied, 'Ah, Signorina Lynch,' saying it with a smile and giving the name the two syllables demanded by Italian and would he mind taking her newspapers along with him? (*Death at La Fenice*, ch. 8)

One of the perpetual surprises for visitors to Venice is the disparity between the exterior of buildings and their interior opulence. The outside walls may lose *intonaco* in slabs, brickwork may crumble, the staircases chip away, the shutters splinter in slivers; few residents have the resources or, more importantly, the optimism to battle the ravages wrought by Venetian waters. Even fewer possess the nerves to enter the fray with the gods who grant restoration permits. But in the modest neighbourhood of Calle della Testa at the beginning of eastern Cannaregio when Brunetti finally finds the address, the contrast between the exterior and the apartment at the top of the stairs is more than striking:

He was surprised to find himself in a vast open space, easily ten metres by fifteen. The wooden floor was made of the thick oak beams used to support the oldest roofs in the city. The walls had been stripped of paint and plaster and taken down to the original brick. The most remarkable thing in the room was the tremendous brightness that glared from the uncovered skylights, six of them, set in triple pairs on either side of the peaked ceiling. Whoever had received permission to alter the external structure of a building this old, Brunetti reflected, either had powerful friends or had blackmailed both the mayor and the city planner. (*La Fenice*, ch. 8)

→

In *Suffer the Little Children* Brunetti is not looking for house numbers but for a place to eat. With too little time to get from the hospital at Campo SS. Giovanni e Paolo for lunch at home, he must grab a bite where he can. Luckily, he can escape the scenes of misery and death to revive himself at nearby Da Alberto **(16)*** with its counters full of small *cicheti* to snack on or a dining room for a simple meal.

Kiosk **(15)** straight over bridge to Da Alberto (16)

Brunetti stopped in a trattoria at the foot of the second bridge between the hospital and Campo Santa Marina but, finding that there was no table free, contented himself with a glass of *vino novello* and a plate of cicchetti, standing at the bar to eat them. (. . .)

The *fondi di carciofi* were delicious, and Brunetti asked for two more, then another *polpetta* and another glass of wine. When he was finished, he was still not satisfied, though he was no longer hungry. These pick-up meals that he was often forced to eat were one of the worst things about his job (. . .) . He paid and left, cut behind the Miracoli and down towards Campo Santa Marina. (*Suffer the Little Children*, ch. 21)

→

Filled with trees and benches for the locals, cafés for the tourists, the little Campo Santa Maria Nova sits in peculiar

Straight into Campo Santa Maria Nova **(17)**

surroundings – glory on one side, madness on the other. Its neighbour, the Chiesa di Santa Maria dei Miracoli (**F**), excites as much praise as any church in the city, despite its treasure-chest size. A Renaissance temple, covered with vari-coloured marbles, adorned with serpentine and porphyry decoration, and highlighted by exquisite sculptures from the Lombardo family, it is sited on a small canal to reflect its beauty. A popular choice for Venetian weddings, in *Suffer the Little Children* it had been the setting for the earlier marriage between Dr Pedrolli and the daughter of the powerful head of the Lega Doge political party – a society event designed to arouse Paola's scorn: '"Chiesa dei Miracoli garlanded with flowers": the usual.'

Set back from the *campo* is the Palazzo Bembo-Boldù (**G**), now the city's treatment centre for the mentally ill. While it garners little praise from the residents of Venice, it is familiar to everyone in the city. In *Doctored Evidence*, a long-time patient of the psychiatric ward, an old, nearly deaf woman terrorizes her neighbours with the perpetual blaring noise from her TV.

'She's crazy. That's why. Mad as a horse. Believe me, Signore, I did my homework on this woman. I spoke to her lawyer, her doctor, her niece, the people at the psychiatric centre at Palazzo Boldù, to the neighbours, even to the postman.'

She saw his interest and went on. 'She was a patient at Boldù for years, when she could still manage the stairs and leave the house. But either she stopped or they threw her out – if a psychiatric centre can throw people out, that is.'
(*Doctored Evidence*, ch. 4)

Palazzo Boldù is also an outpatient clinic for depressives needing constant medication. In *Suffer the Little Children*, a young woman with emotional problems has been exposed by a moralistic pharmacist. Most matters are settled within Venetian homes, and care provided by the family; there could be little worse than a friend or relative abandoned to psychiatric treatment away from home.

'I'm not mistaken. He's that sort of man. He loves to impose his ideas on other people, loves to see them punished for their sins. Look what he did to Romina: she's a zombie, going in and out of Palazzo Boldù every day, drugged out of her mind. And all because she wanted to marry and have children, and Dottor Franchi decided that manic depressives should not marry and have children.' (*Suffer the Little Children*, ch. 26)

→

As Donna Leon readers know, her novels are filled with interesting female characters, most seen through the eyes and with the sympathy of Guido Brunetti. Despite Paola's occasional accusations that he misunderstands women's travails, he is amazingly alert to slights against women, and especially sensitive to their needs, whether for protection or comfort. After a tense and unpleasant phone conversation with a colleague of Paola's about her secret abortion that has suddenly been made public, Brunetti finds himself in front of the Santa Marina magazine stand unable to purge the vileness he feels at the invasion of the young woman's privacy. The sexual exploitation of women takes on new force as he views the evidence in front of him.

Calle Castelli into Campo Santa Marina (18)

It was as he was walking into Campo Santa Marina **(18)** that he realized his body had contracted into something that felt like a long, tight knot. He stopped at the *edicola* and stood quietly for a while, looking at the covers of the magazines on display through the glass, all the while rolling his shoulders in an attempt to loosen them. Tits and ass. Paola had again observed, months ago, that he should spend a day counting the times he saw tits and ass: in the newspapers, in magazines, in ads on the vaporetti, on display in every kind of shop window. It might help him understand, she suggested, the attitude of some women towards men. (. . .)

He pulled his eyes away and looked at the façade of Palazzo Dolfin **(H)**. 'She's right,' he said under his breath. (*Suffer the Little Children*, ch. 24)

The strong, brave Brett Lynch in *Acqua Alta* is a later development from the more indecisive, despairing lover first met in *Death at La Fenice* a few years earlier. After so much time in and out of Venice, Brett finds herself isolated with no one to turn to but an officer of the law. Late at night in dismal weather, she asks for the last thing Brunetti wants to do: cross the city and meet in the seclusion of an unappealing bar (now a successful *trattoria*) not far from Brett's apartment near Santa Marina. But chivalry and affection prevail.

Giro's was a smoky, dismal place, one of the few bars in the city that stayed open after ten at night. The management had changed hands a few months before, and the new owners had done their best to tart the place up, adding white curtains and slick music. But it had failed to become a hip pub, while ceasing to be a local bar where friends met for a coffee or a drink. It had neither class nor charm, only overpriced wine and too much smoke. (*Death at La Fenice*, ch. 22)

Charity dictates that Brunetti not be left in such grim surroundings, and, luckily, Campo Santa Marina also hosts Didovich **(I)**,* one of the city's best places for a morning snack – brioche light as feathers, various small vegetable tarts, a mere two delicious bites.

Paola and the children were long gone, so he left the house, glad of the chance to drink his coffee in the company of a familiar *pasticceria*, with conversation no more demanding than the idle comments someone might make to him. He bought both *Il Tempo* and *Il Gazzettino* at the *edicola* in Campo Santa Marina and went into Didovich for a coffee and a brioche. (*Uniform Justice*, ch. 10)

*Il Testiere has a special charm since it is one of the city's best places for fish, but has the atmosphere of a casual *trattoria*—no formal waiters or linen.

*Querini Stampalia is both a museum and a library, giving it an appealing musty feel. Besides the early Venetian paintings, it is a fine place to see eighteenth-century Venice at play, including combats on the Ponte dei Pugni.

*The Rosa Salva bar in Campo San Luca is no longer operating, but the same fine pastries and excellent coffee in an old-fashioned atmosphere prevail at the one in Campo SS. Giovanni e Paolo.

*Da Alberto is a favourite with locals and visitors for its abundant *cicheti* and casual dining room with a varied menu that loyally keeps to the seasons.

*Didovich is more than a café to its devoted locals. The dazzling array of pastries and small vegetable tarts—courgette, aubergine, spinach, and far more – lure residents from all over the city.

Hotel Santa Marina, across from Didovich, sits in a quiet *campo* a mere five minutes from the chaos of Rialto, making it a convenient place for Brunetti to reserve a quiet room for the dead boy's parents in *Friends in High Places*.

WALK 12: *The Most Beautiful Neighbourhood in the World*

Santa Marina—Santi Apostoli—Strada Nuova—Fondamenta della
Misericordia—Ghetto—San Marcuola

1.5–2 hours

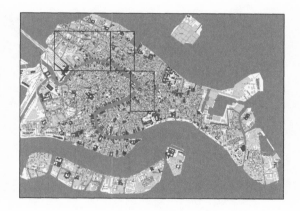

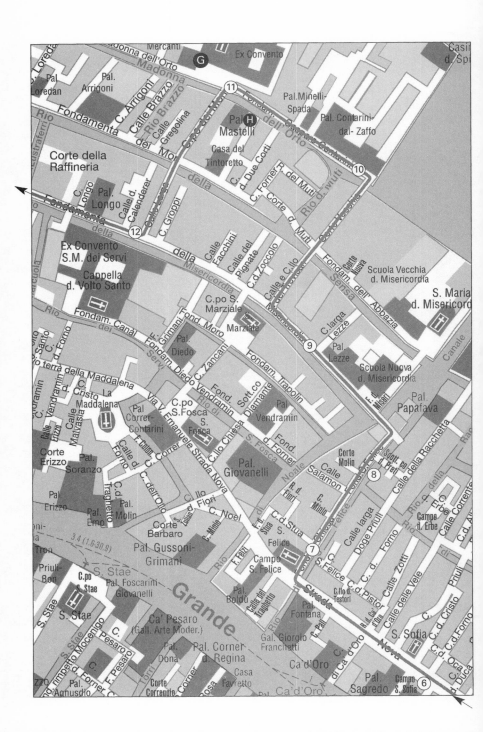

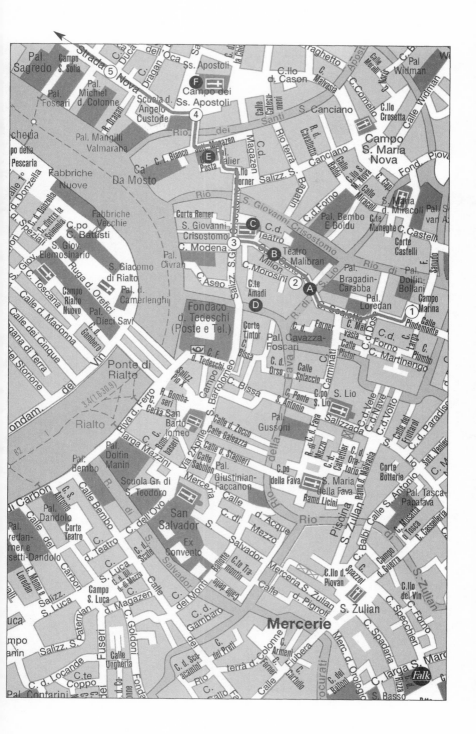

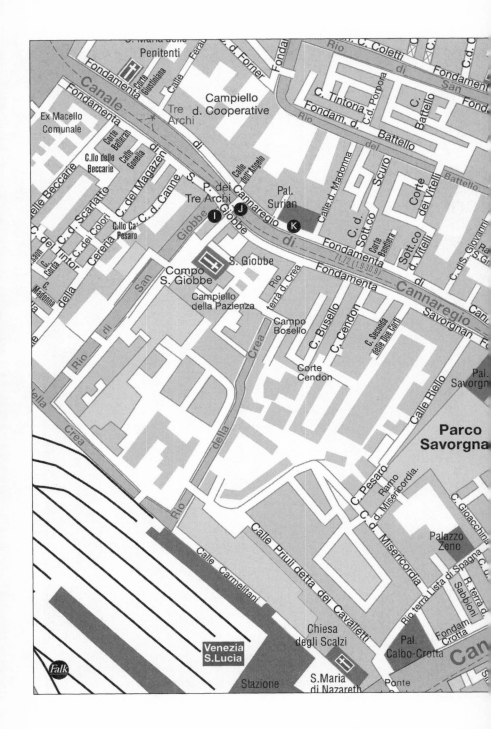

V enice's historically famous centre is enclosed in the cosy embrace of its two most authentically local areas: Castello to the east; Cannaregio in the west. Stretching from the central station to the Ospedale Civile, Cannaregio's eastern edge, this area is the Venice of the Venetians: besides the Gothic Church of the Madonna dell'Orto it contains mostly family-run shops, native-owned bars and *trattorie,* artists' workshops, and over one-third of the city's population – making it Brunetti's favourite *sestiere.* Although he lives in central San Polo, surrounded by fading *palazzi* and marble bridges, it is the idea of this area being a 'neighbourhood' that continues to enchant him: 'Cannaregio (. . .) [is] to him the most beautiful neighbourhood in the city. Which meant, he supposed, in the world.' (*Fatal Remedies,* ch. 20)

Campo Santa Marina (1)

* * *

It is no small a part of the city's charms for the historic-minded Brunetti that when he meanders through the most beautiful neighbourhood in the world, he never walks alone. For centuries, every traveller, every arriver, seems to have left a mark, and the ghosts remain, both in visible stone and in the air of legend; none more so than Marco Polo. Few Venetians have been enmeshed in so disputed a reputation as the Cannaregio-born Polo. His (fairly accurate) travel accounts, originally titled *Description of the World,* were called by locals in Veneziano 'il Milion' for their incredible claims; Marco himself was called 'il Milion' for his own fantastic boasting when he returned from the court of Kublai Kahn; 'il Milion' also stood for the masses of hidden jewels which poured out when he slit the lining of his robes. Venice valued him enough to name after him two courtyards where the Polo family lived: Prima and Seconda del Milion.

Today, remnants of the Case dei Polo are scattered around

Through Sottoportego and Calle Scaletta to Calle Corte Milion (2) the Corte Seconda del Milion **(A)**. Surrounded by unusually high domestic buildings for Venice, the ancient square possesses some of the oldest houses in the city, their façades decorated with a collage of architectural ornamentation from several centuries: ancient door and window arches, decaying marble friezes and roundels, and a recessed white cross enliven the surfaces. It is a strangely neglected spot, sitting so close to the busy Salizzada San Giovanni Crisostomo.

The nearby Corte Prima **(B)**, through a dilapidated *sottoportico*, is an inviting setting for the small Ristorante al Milion* that nestles on one side. Once a *bacaro* that drew the locals to this corner for *un' ombra* and some *cicheti* of shellfish, it now offers a modest menu, served in fine weather under the vine-covered arbour.

In *The Anonymous Venetian*, however, this spot merely offers Brunetti an escape from the miserable days of *ferragosto*, when his family is away in the cooling mountains and the broader *calli* of the city bake under the sun.

Because he was near the Rialto, it would have been easy for Brunetti to go home for lunch, but he neither wanted to cook for himself nor risk the rest of the *insalata di calamari*, now in its third day and hence suspect. Instead, he walked down to Corte dei Milion and had an adequate lunch in the small *trattoria* that crouched in one corner of the tiny *campo*. (*The Anonymous Venetian*, ch. 18)

→

To Salizzada San Giovanni Crisostomo **(3)**

Leaving the *corte*, Brunetti would have to pass beside the Renaissance Church of San Giovanni Crisostomo **(C)**, long-faded and mostly ignored by the hurrying shoppers. The exterior of the church has recently been blessed by a full restoration. Rose pink walls and trimmings of white marble now enliven the shopping street of Salizzada San Giovanni Crisostomo, running from the Coin **(D)** department store at one end to Campo Santi Apostoli at the other. Since this is Venice, the city's major department store sits facing a small canal always crowded with gondola traffic heading out into the Grand Canal, its Gothic palace façade restored after fire damages less benign than the inevitable passage of time. Venice spent the centuries of its glory insulated from fears of military invasion, indifferent to the wars that often raged up and down the peninsula, unconcerned by repeated excommunication from the papacy. However, the fear of natural disasters has been ingrained in the character of the Venetians for ever: no place to escape the plague, no means to quell the engulfing waters, and, most crucially, no effective way to quench the raging fires. The enormous disaster of the 1996 burning of La Fenice, which meant the loss of Europe's most beautiful opera house, will find a permanent place in the long list of historic events the city records. Any burning, especially of a public building, lingers in the residents' memories as a constant reminder of their fragile safety.

Brunetti, attempting to uncover clues to the mysterious wasting away and death of young Roberto Lorenzoni in *A Noble Radiance,* heads for a meeting with a salesgirl in Venice's main department store, Coin. Gutted in a fire in the 1980s, it is a modern touchstone for the perils of a city laced by clogged waterways with uneasy access for boats and no fire hydrant system. For the Commissario, it holds personally distressing memories:

He decided he would prefer to speak to her in person and so, telling no one what he was doing, he left the Questura and headed back in the direction of the department store.

Since the fire, almost ten years ago now, he had found it difficult to enter the store; the daughter of a friend of his had been one of the victims killed when a careless worker set fire to sheets of plastic that had, within minutes, turned the entire building into a smoke-filled hell. At the time, the fact that the girl had died from smoke inhalation and not from fire had seemed some consolation; years later, only the fact of her death remained. (*A Noble Radiance*, ch. 18)

→

The route into Campo Santi Apostoli goes through an underpass topped by the Veneto–Byzantine Palazzo Falier (**E**) – a family name that resounds through the Brunetti books. It is

Into Campo Santi Apostoli (**4**)

not surprising that Guido's father-in-law, Count Orazio, only 'numbered two doges on his mother's side', neglecting to include the third family doge, the infamous Marin Falier. Marin's reign of less than a year may have been too short; perhaps his plot to eliminate the powerful Venetian nobles seemed sheer lunacy to the Count; or his beheading unfit for genealogical chess; or the Venetian state's confiscation of this beautiful family palace may have left too deep a wound. Whatever the reasons, in the Brunetti novels the Faliers must inhabit an invented palace across the Grand Canal near Ca' Rezzonico. Marin Falier's *palazzo* is now a hotel, offering the modern Brunetti fan a chance to stay in at least one Falier home.

Foa, like most pilots, had the grace of silence and did nothing more than nod to acknowledge Brunetti's request. He seemed to feel no need to fill up the journey with words. By the time they reached Rialto, the broad-beamed boats that hauled produce to the market had turned the stillness into memory. Foa swung into Rio dei SS Apostoli and directly past the *palazzo* in which some distant ancestor of Paola's had lived before being beheaded for treason. They shot out into the *laguna* where the first thing Brunetti saw, off to the right, were the walls of the cemetery and, behind it, banks of clouds scuttling towards the city. (*Through a Glass, Darkly*, ch. 14)

The nearby Church of Santi Apostoli (**F**), repeatedly rebuilt, was begun in the ninth century, establishing this part of Cannaregio as one of the earliest residential areas in the city. Today, with its exceptionally tall campanile surrounded by trees and the lively entry on to Strada Nuova, the Church often seems disregarded by the thronging crowds, on their busy way somewhere else. Even Queen Caterina Cornaro of Cyprus, originally buried here in 1510, now has her elegant tomb at the Church of San Salvador.

→

Strada Nuova (**5**) to Campo Santa Sofia (**6**)

Figures vary on the exact number of buildings – including houses, and churches – Napoleon levelled to create Strada

Nuova (5). By 1871, a wide, straight, level street had replaced many of the former winding, quirky lanes. Dotted with palaces on the Grand Canal side, churches commandeering the *campi*, it is one of the few sections of the city with nearly ceaseless movement at all hours. Anyone walking either to or from the *stazione* will usually be directed along Strada Nuova, one of the only direct paths in the city: a long string of wine bars, shops, a major *traghetto* stop, a McDonald's all jostle with endless *gelati* stalls, banks, fabric stores, and restaurants — most with tables outside to enliven the scene even more. It is a friendly strip and one where people often meet more by chance than arrangement — just as Signora Gismondi in *Doctored Evidence* occasionally meets her neighbour's impoverished Romanian maid:

'I met her once on Strada Nuova. It was about six weeks ago and I was having a coffee in a bar, and she came in. It was that place just at the corner near the Santa Fosca *traghetti*. When I went over, she recognized me, you know, from the window, and she kissed me on the cheek, as if we were old friends. She had her purse open in her hands, and I saw that all she had were some coins. (. . .)' She stopped speaking, memory taking her back to that afternoon in the bar. 'I asked why she had come in, and she said she wanted an ice-cream. I think she said she loved ice-cream. I know the man who runs the place, so I told him I was offering and not to take her money, that I'd pay.' (*Doctored Evidence*, ch. 4)

Strada Nuova on the whole permits a more direct contact with people than the intricate, medieval *calli*, which follow their individual patterns, each with its own character. Brunetti finds the complexities of Venice's geography ironically mirrored in the relations between its residents:

The geographical inwardness of Venice was reflected in its social habits: the web of narrow *calli* connecting the six *sestieri* mirrored the connections and interstices linking its inhabitants to one another. Strada Nuova and Via XXII Marzo had the broad directness of the ties of family: anyone could follow them clearly. Calle Lunga San Barnaba and Barbaria de le Tole, straight still but far narrower and shorter, were in their way like the bonds between close friends: there was little chance of losing the way, but they didn't lead as far. The bulk of the *calli* that made movement possible in the city, however, were narrow and crooked, often leading to dead ends or to branches that took the unsuspecting in the opposite direction to the way they wanted to go: this was the way of protective deceit, these the paths that had to be followed by those without access to more direct ways of reaching a goal. (*Doctored Evidence*, ch. 20)

Campo Santa Sofia's **(6)** most important function for the residents of western Cannaregio is its invaluable *traghetti* route across the Grand Canal to the Rialto market, allowing shoppers to avoid the long walk around and over the bridge, hauling kilos of fish, fruit, and vegetables, and even flowers if it is Tuesday or Saturday. The *campo*'s value for tourists is as a welcome spot to rest. The marble wellhead with its wide base, always full of young travellers grateful for the quiet of the open space away from the Strada Nuova crowds, is surrounded by ample benches occupied by ageing locals. Facing the Grand Canal with the busy market across the water, the *campo* offers picturesque views of the wooden *traghetto* shack with its flower boxes and lounging, handsome *gondolieri*. One of the oldest *traghetti* stops in Venice, the Santa Sofia rowers guild opened before the earliest pontoon bridge of the Rialto in the late 1100s. Today it still sits unshadowed by a string of the city's finest palaces.

$\rightarrow$

Rio di San Felice to Fondamenta della Chiesa **(7)** to Ponte Chiodo **(8)**

As any visitor to the major painting galleries in the city notices, for centuries the Venetians made do with elegantly curved bridges with no parapets, the concern over public safety clearly subordinate to the grace of architectural shape. Eventually, progress came even to the isolated islands of Venice, linking each of them with the comfort of railings and walls. Only one bridge in the city remains without a balustrade, the private Ponte Chiodo **(8)**. And it is to this spot that the hapless, young *vu cumprà* in *Blood from a Stone* races to escape the police pursuing him from nearby Strada Nuova.

Pucetti interrupted suddenly, 'Gravini, you're one of the ones who went into the canal, aren't you?'

Gravini lowered his head, as if embarrassed at having been caught at some folly. 'What was I supposed to do? He was new, the one who fell in. It was probably the first time he'd been caught in one of our raids. He panicked, really just a kid, and he ran. What else would he do, with cops all over the place, running at him? It was over by the Misericordia, and he ran up that bridge that doesn't have a parapet. Lost his footing or something and fell in. I could hear him screaming all the way back by the church. When we got there, he was flailing around like a madman, so I did the first thing that came into my head: I went right in after him. Didn't realize until I was in the water that it wasn't very deep, at least not near the sides . . . (*Blood from a Stone*, ch. 6)

→

In *Wilful Behaviour*, Brunetti takes this walk from Santi Apostoli to one of the northern lagoon boat stops, passing Venice's largest supermarket, some of Cannaregio's Oriental oddities, and the area's most spectacular Gothic church, the Madonna dell'Orto **(G)**, amply supplied with Tintoretto masterpieces, for this was his parish. Looking across the *rio*, he sees the Palazzo Mastelli **(H)**, with its Eastern 'stone relief of the turbaned merchant leading his camel', causing the locals to rename the building Palazzo del Cammello.

In *Doctored Evidence*, Brunetti's return to the back *calli* of this delightful area is suddenly tainted by the brutal battering of an old woman much despised by everyone. The locals are not talking, the Romanian maid has run away, the heat of summer is punishing on the unsheltered walkways along the canal.

The police had little trouble finding the house, for the doctor had explained that the victim's home was at the beginning

Left on to Fondamenta della Misericordia **(9)**, right to Calle dei Trevisan and Corte Vecchia, left on to Fondamenta Gasparo Contarini **(10)**

of the *calle* to the right of the Palazzo del Cammello. The launch glided to a halt on the south side of the Canale della Madonna. (. . .) Sweat dripped from their faces, and their jackets soon began to cling to their bodies. Cursing the heat, wiping vainly at their sweat, four of the five men began to carry the equipment to the entrance to Calle Tintoretto and along to the house. (*Doctored Evidence*, ch. 1)

→

To Campo dei Mori **(11)**

For Venetians, the presence of the Orient is no unfamiliar intrusion but a reminder of their cosmopolitan past as conduit between East and West. Around the corner from Palazzo Mastelli sits Campo dei Mori **(11)** with its sculpted turban-wearing figures, 'Moor' having been applied in Venice to all kinds of foreigners coming from the East. Since it is less than a ten-minute journey to the Fondaco dei Turchi across the Grand Canal, it is not surprising that this area might have seen far more Silk Road visitors and traders than the rest of the city, nor that La Serenissima would honour with reliefs and statues a region of the world which brought it such extraordinary wealth.

→

Calle Larga to Fondamenta della Misericordia **(12)**

Not all the *fondamente* that run alongside the waterways of Venice offer the convenient clarity of a single title. The Fondamenta Misericordia **(12)** leading to the Ghetto has, over the centuries, acquired a sequence of varying names, but time has altered little else in this sleepy *sestiere* edged by the Cannaregio Canal to the west and the lagoon to the north. Although the area has recently blossomed with new restaurants to accompany the old favourites, not all the changes have been welcome. As Signorina Elettra laments in *Suffer the Little Children*, the twenty-first century is invading everywhere in Venice, and even the stones underfoot are no longer safe. The recently repaved walkways along these backwaters are examples of the changes that make her weep.

'During the repaving of the streets,' she continued (. . .), 'When they raised the sidewalks against *acqua alta*,' she added, raising her eyebrows in silent comment on the folly of that attempt. 'They dug up all the *masegni*, the ones that had been there for centuries.' (. . .)

'They replaced them with machine-cut, perfectly rectangular stones, every one a living example of just how perfect four right angles can be.' (. . .)

'And where did the old ones go, I wonder?' she asked, raising her right index finger in the air in a ritual gesture of interrogation. (. . .) 'there has been talk of a piazza somewhere in Japan.' (. . .)

'Even the French and the Austrians, when they invaded – and God knows they stripped us clean – at least they left us the paving stones. Just thinking about it is enough to make me weep.'

As it would, Brunetti realized, any Venetian. *(Suffer the Little Children*, ch. 15)

$\longrightarrow$

Although location always matters in Venice, where one lives and where one shops, there exists among residents of the various *sestieri* a sort of reverse snobbery about where to dine. To capture a reservation at tiny Da'a Marisa **(I)** near the Tre Archi Bridge, for example, qualifies as a triumph, for the place is always packed with Cannaregio locals. Still, Brunetti hardly expects his aristocratic father-in-law to choose Bentigodi (Bussola in the novel) **(14)*** in such an inconvenient working-class neighbourhood to meet for lunch.

Wooden bridge **(13)** over Rio della Misericordia to Rio terrà Farsetti to Bentigodi **(14)**

Confused, Brunetti said only, 'All right. Where shall we meet?' expecting the Count to name one of the famous restaurants in the city.

'There's a place over near Campo del Ghetto. The daughter of a friend of mine and her husband run it, and the food's very good. If it's not too far for you, we could meet there.'

'Fine. What's it called?'

'La Bussola. It's just off San Leonardo, heading towards Campo del Ghetto Nuovo. One o'clock?' (*A Noble Radiance*, ch. 6)

The lunch begins with more revelations for Brunetti than its unexpected location. Throughout the Donna Leon novels, he finds himself baffled by his eccentric in-laws. If he was impressed in *The Death of Faith* to discover Countess Falier reading Darwin's *Voyage of the Beagle*, he is surprised in the opposite way in *A Noble Radiance* as he sees the Count reading Venice's local newspaper, *Il Gazzettino*. With its intermittent grasp of fact and its appetite for scurrilous detail, the paper may be acceptable for a glance in a bar, but to bring it to lunch for more careful scrutiny might to most Venetians indicate a decided lack of intellectual seriousness.

He took the *traghetto* again, and when he came out at San Leonardo, he crossed the *campo* and took the first left. A few empty tables stood in the shade in front of the restaurant.

Inside, a counter stood to his left, a few demijohns of wine on a shelf in back of it, long rubber tubes flowing from their tops. To the right, two arched doors opened into another room, and there, at a table against the wall, he saw his father-in-law, Count Orazio Falier. The Count sat, a glass of what looked like prosecco in front of him, reading the local paper, *Il Gazzettino*. Brunetti was surprised to see him with such a newspaper, which meant either that his opinion of the Count was higher than he realized, or of the local newspaper, lower. (ch. 8)

$$\rightarrow$$

To Campo Ghetto
Nuovo **(15)**

The world's first ghetto was developing in Venice from 1516 onwards, its name culled from Veneziano *geto* – meaning foundry and indicating the area's original function. Although persecuted elsewhere, Jews from all over the world were welcome in Venice to work in commerce and as doctors. At night the Ghetto was isolated from the rest of the city behind locked gates until these were removed in 1797 by Napoleon. Housed on a small island enclosed by bridges, their numbers ever increasing and with nowhere to expand except up, the Jews of the Ghetto Nuovo **(15)** created the tallest domestic buildings in Venice, some reaching six or more storeys. The *campo*'s three Gothic marble wellheads, numerous trees, a café with tables spread out into the open space, and the constant activity of kids kicking a soccer ball make it an inviting place. And Brunetti traverses the city to its precincts in several of Donna Leon's novels.

In *Death in a Strange Country*, he tries to escape the sordid connections involved in mysterious toxic waste dumping with a walk across the city, winding up in the Ghetto with his black thoughts:

He suddenly found himself in Campo del Ghetto. He sat on a bench and watched the people going past him. They had no idea, none at all. They distrusted the government, feared the Mafia, resented the Americans, but they were all generalized, unfocused ideas (. . .) They had learned enough, from long centuries of experience, to know that the proof was there, amply, but those same brutal centuries had also taught the people that whatever government happened to be in power would always succeed in hiding any and all proof of its evildoing from its citizens. (*Death in a Strange Country*, ch. 22)

The Anonymous Venetian finds him so incapable of the patience needed to await crime results that he endures the punishing weather of *ferragosto* to get away from the Questura in eastern Venice and into Cannaregio: 'he went out for a lunch, deliberately choosing a restaurant in the Ghetto, even though this meant a long walk there and back in the worst heat of the day'.

The complicated mess created by Paola's attack on the travel agency in Campo Manin in *Fatal Remedies* has suddenly escalated into a bizarre murder that Brunetti, called back from home leave by Patta, must investigate. This time the trail leads to Campo del Ghetto and the victim's family home tucked away in quiet extravagance. Ever attuned to the value of property, Brunetti scans the rooms, hoping to get a sense of the victim's life and wealth.

A long central corridor led from the door to a bank of four Gothic windows at the other end. Brunetti's sense of orientation told him that the light must be coming in from Rio di San Girolamo, especially as the distance to the buildings visible through them was so great: the only open space that large must be the expanse of the Rio.

The girl led them into the first room on the right, a large sitting-room with a fireplace flanked by two windows, each more than two metres high. (. . .) A large gilded mirror sat above a table on which stood an enormous spray of red gladioli, their colour and number reflected by the glass, so that they seemed to multiply and fill the room. A silk carpet, Brunetti thought it a Nain, lay in front of the fireplace, so close to the sofa that whoever sat there would have to put their feet on it. An oak chest stood against the wall opposite the flowers, on its surface a large brass salver gone grey with age. The wealth and opulence, though discreet, were evident. (*Fatal Remedies*, ch. 14)

→

Calle del Ghetto Vecchio **(16)** to Canale Cannaregio **(17)**

Cannaregio Canal **(17)** is the third of Venice's waterways honoured with the name *canal*; all smaller ones are called *rio*. The serpentine Grand Canal and the expansive Giudecca lined with majestic palaces, raucous with boat traffic, both offer compelling views. The short Cannaregio canal seems like a modest relative, less showy but somehow more companionable. Instead of the tourist-loaded vaporetti, the smaller, black and white *motoscafi* serve the Cannaregio Canal. Crossed by two bridges, the canal boasts the only span in Venice with more than one arch, the lovely Ponte dei Tre Archi **(J)**. Ponte delle Guglie provides the first water crossing leading into Cannaregio: too low for public boats to pass under during *acqua alta*, the bridge forces the rubber-booted locals into a slow slog to the street markets that begin on the eastern side of the *ponte*. Because the canal's short distance floats out north into the refreshing waters of the lagoon, it even sports the, admittedly rare, sight of boys leaping in for a swim during the sweaty days of August, watched by the local crowds at the *trattorie* and cafés that line the western side of the canal.

Without any principal buildings of major interest, except

the Palazzo Surian (**K**) where Jean-Jacques Rousseau served as secretary to the French ambassador in 1743, the area retains a quality of community life unseen in Venice outside of faraway eastern Castello. Fewer crowds, lower prices, and the ring of Veneziano at every table make it an appealing place to stroll and dine, with boat owners pulling up to ask about the day's menu, or simply to be offered a quick *ombra* passed out over the water.

For Brunetti the neighbourhood's claims to attention also reveal an underside never far away in Venice, no matter how beguiling the surface. In *Friends in High Places*, one of the many university students living in Cannaregio close to the Facoltà di Economia has been found dead in an apartment, from an overdose.

'We've just had a call from the station over in Cannaregio.'
'The one by Tre Archi?' (. . .)
At the back of the Arsenale, Pertile swung sharply to the left and past the usual stops: the hospital, Fondamenta Nuove, La Madonna dell'Orto, San Alvise, and then turned into the beginning of the Cannaregio Canal. Just after the first boat stop, they saw a police officer standing on the *riva* and waving to them as they approached. (. . .)
'Where is he?' Brunetti asked as soon as his feet were again on firm ground.
'Down this *calle*, sir,' he said, turning away from Brunettii and into a narrow street that ran back from the water toward the interior of Cannaregio. (*Friends in High Places*, ch. 12)

→

The stroll from Ponte delle Guglie along the traffic-laden Rio Terrà San Leonardo to the end of this walk at the quiet Campo San Marcuola offers a study in the inhabitants and invaders of Venice – stereotypes, to be sure, but that's never stopped a Venetian from passing judgment. The Cannaregio locals, perched in the numerous cafés and bars that line both sides of the street, sip the favoured drink, *spritz con Aperol*, before the evening rounds of wine begin. From this privileged vantage point, they watch – and comment on – the

To Ponte delle Guglie (18), along Rio terrà San Leonardo (19)

parade of newcomers arriving from the nearby railway station, deliberating on their country of origin. The migratory patterns differ, as does the plumage: the Northern Europeans prefer cooler weather, avoiding the glare of summer, sensibly wrapped in jackets with practical pockets and comfortable shoes; the Americans seem to like any season that allows them to arrive in the briefest gear and the whitest sneakers; the Japanese struggle by in their designer clothes, dragging enormous bags on wheels. It is a harmless parlour game to help these insulated islanders wile away the early evening in idle amusement.

Luckily, the string of outdoor market stalls filled with the season's produce that continue up to San Marcuola offer a distraction from the crowds and the baggage that clog this long artery to the centre of Venice. Flower shops spill their beauty out on to the street, fish markets abound in the mornings, chestnuts roast in the winter evenings, *gelaterie* scoop until late into the night as day-trippers struggle by on their way back to the station, laden with masks and Murano glass.

→

Right at *traghetti* San Marcuola sign **(20)**, left on Calle del Cristo into Campo San Marcuola **(21)**

The grandest thing about Campo San Marcuola **(21)** is its setting. To the left of the vaporetto stop is Palazzo Vendramin-Calergi **(L)**, the home of Venice's Casinò and the place where Richard Wagner died in 1883 an event, apparently unmourned by a Venice still resentful of the fifty-year occupation by German-speaking Northerners. Though the Casinò was for centuries off limits to Venetians with the aristocrats forced to spend their money elsewhere, leaving the gambling to be done by exiles far from home, it has been restored to the residents, providing Brunetti with an excellent social cover for research on criminal cases.

The three men rose from the table, held the chairs of the women, and the six of them started for the Casinò gaming rooms on the floor below.

Because they couldn't all fit into the elevator, the women were put inside while the men decided to use the main staircase to go down to the main gambling hall. Brunetti found

Count Orazio on his right and tried to think of something to say to his father-in-law.

'Did you know that Richard Wagner died here?' he asked, forgetting now how it was that he knew this, since Wagner was hardly a composer he liked.

'Yes,' the Count answered. 'Hardly soon enough.' *(Death in a Strange Country*, ch. 9)

Directly across the Grand Canal sits the recently cleaned Fondaco dei Turchi **(M)** (now the Natural History Museum), a marvel of the Veneto-Byzantine style of the thirteenth century. With its ornamented grey and cream marble front, it must have seemed a melancholy last residence for the ambassador from Constantinople, with the Ottomans on the cusp of toppling the final capital of the Byzantine Empire, leaving him without a home, East or West.

It is a sight Brunetti passes on the vaporetto after a return by train from little America at the Vicenza military base. In *Death in a Strange Country*, his range of periods and worlds feels more complex than ever, as he leaves behind bowling alleys and bingo crowds for the long slow boat ride. Stationing himself on the outside seats to be near the water, he ruminates on the wealth of the packet of illegal white powder he is about to offer to the Grand Canal. As he uses one more occasion to ally himself with his ancient forebears, best to leave him to so extravagant and so Venetian a gesture.

The boat pulled away from the embankment and under the Bridge of the Scalzi, up the Grand Canal towards the Rialto and its final stop. (. . .)

He set his briefcase on the chair beside him, propped the lid open, and reached into his inner pocket, pulling out one of the envelopes. Carefully, touching only its corners, he peeled it open. Turning sideways, the better to examine the façade of the Natural History Museum, he slid his hand under the railing and emptied the white powder into the waters of the canal. He slipped the empty bag into his briefcase and repeated the process with the second. During the golden age of the Most Serene Republic, the Doge used to perform an elaborate yearly ceremony, tossing a gold ring into the waters of the Grand Canal to solemnize the wedding of the city to the waters that gave it life, wealth, and power. But never, Brunetti thought, had such great wealth been deliberately offered to any waters. *(Death in a Strange Country,* ch. 8)

---

*Ristorante al Milion, traditional Venetian food.

*Bentigodi da Francesca, tiny tables on the *calle,* imaginative dishes, especially vegetables.

Brunetti's Lagoon Islands

San Michele—Murano—Burano—Le Vignole—Lido—San Servolo—
Pellestrina

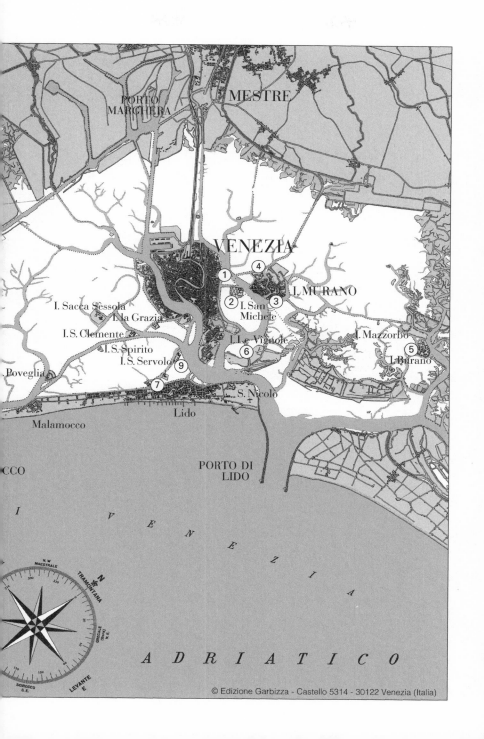

. . . you should choose the finest day in the month and have yourself rowed far away across the lagoon to Torcello. Without making this excursion you can hardly pretend to know Venice.

—Henry James, 'An Early Impression'
in *Italian Hours*

After a dozen walks through the city of Venice with Commissario Guido Brunetti, it is time to enter another part of his world, the islands of the *laguna*. The Venetian lagoon has always shared the city's Janus-faced reputation: a suspicious remoteness for residents; a romantic, mysterious allure for foreigners. Goethe crossed the *laguna* to claim in his *Italian Journey*, 'Now, at last, I have seen the sea with my own eyes.' Shelley immortalized the lagoon floating with 'funereal' gondolas, while Ruskin later cursed its 'dirty steam-engines'. Byron swam across it from the Lido to the Grand Canal; James made a journey through it a required adventure for any visitor. Mann's Aschenbach died on the Lido; Diaghilev, Stravinsky, Ezra Pound, and Joseph Brodsky are all buried on Isola San Michele.

Rather than a specific walk, this chapter journeys through the *laguna* to and past the islands used by Donna Leon in the Brunetti novels: from the cemetery island of San Michele, where Brunetti's father is buried, to Murano, the setting for *Through a Glass, Darkly*, to the Lido for *The Death of Faith*, and finally further south to Pellestrina and *A Sea of Troubles*. Brunetti has fewer of the familiar wide-ranging walks he takes in the other novels. Instead, he repeatedly finds himself a stranger in the *laguna*, constantly interpreting codes and manners far different from those of his world in Venice.

* * *

Nowhere is the Venetians' ambivalent attitude to their *laguna* more apparent than when Brunetti faces his utter ignorance of the locations of any but the most familiar islands, the arrangement of the various canals, the regions where his seafood meals originate. Never a boatman, he ponders a map of Venice's waters in total bewilderment that he should live in the centre of so mysterious a body of waters – the *palude*.

He dropped the other maps back into the box and took the map of the *laguna* out on to the terrace. Careful of the long-dried tape that held parts of it together, he opened it slowly and stretched it out on the table. How tiny the islands looked, surrounded by the vast expanse of *palude*. For kilometres in every direction, the capillaries and veins of the channels spread, pumping water in and out twice a day, as regular as the moon itself. For a thousand years, those few canals at Chioggia, Malamocco and San Nicolò had served as aortas, keeping the waters clean, even at the height of the Serenissima's power, when hundreds of thousands of people had lived there, their waste added to the waters every day. (. . .)

The immensity of the area depicted on the map reminded him how lost he was in it and how ignorant of how things were organized upon its waters, even in relation to the juris-diction of crimes. If cases were given out, rather in the manner of party favours, to the first comer, then how could one expect to find consistent records of what had happened there?

He assumed that large fish were taken from the Adriatic; where then did the clams and shrimp come from? He had no idea what places in the *laguna* could legitimately be used for fishing, though he assumed that all of the shallow waters lying just off the coast of Marghera would be closed. Yet if what the boat pilot said, and Vianello believed, was true, then even that area was still fished. (*A Sea of Troubles*, ch. 13)

→

ÍSOLA di SAN MICHELE (2)

Boating into the *laguna* from the most popular departure point, Fondamenta Nuove (1), the first sight, and the last truly familiar place for Venetians, is the cemetery island of San Michele surrounded by towering cypresses. Although Brunetti rarely goes simply to visit, 'not having acquired the cult of the dead so common among Italians', as he says in *Death in La Fenice*, he is pulled to the island for occasional autopsies. The grimness that accompanies Brunetti on his walks to the Ospedale Civile in Campo SS Giovanni e Paolo to attend to victims or identify bodies is made more acute when a watery journey out to the cemetery island is required. In *Death in a Strange Country*, a medical doctor from the nearby American Army base at Vicenza has arrived at Piazzale Roma to identify the corpse of the young sergeant found floating in a Venetian canal. Her sombre appearance and youth, added to her unawareness of where the body has been taken, makes his task more painful.

Without bothering to say goodbye to the men inside, Brunetti left the station and went towards the car. 'Doctor Peters?' he said as he approached.

She looked up at the sound of her name and took a step towards him. As he came up, she held out her hand and shook his briefly. She appeared to be in her late twenties, with curly dark brown hair that pushed back against the pressure of her hat. Her eyes were chestnut, her skin still brown from a summer tan. Had she smiled, she would have been even prettier. Instead, she looked at him directly, mouth pulled into a tense straight line, and asked, 'Are you the police inspector?'

'Commissario Brunetti. I have a boat here. It will take us out to San Michele.' Seeing her confusion, he explained, 'The cemetery island. The body's been taken there.' (*Death in a Strange Country*, ch. 4)

Introduced in *Death at La Fenice*, pathologist Ettore Rizzardi becomes a frequent ally in Brunetti's assault on the obstacles erected by bureaucracy to thwart the pursuit of justice. He reminds the Commissario that their relationship extends far beyond work to include shared family sorrows.

'Will you do it?'

Rizzardi thought for a moment before he answered. 'I'm not scheduled, but since I examined the body, the *questore* will probably ask me to do it.'

'What time?'

'About eleven. I should be finished by early afternoon.'

'I'll come out,' Brunetti said.

'It's not necessary, Guido. You don't have to come to San Michele. You can call, or I'll call your office.'

'Thanks, Ettore, but I'd like to come out. It's been too long since I was there. I'd like to visit my father's grave.'

'As you like.' They shook hands, and Rizzardi started for the door. He paused a moment, then added, 'He was the last of the giants, Guido. He shouldn't have died like this. I'm sorry this happened.' (*Death at La Fenice*, ch. 2)

Donna Leon uses Brunetti's professional visit to the cemetery island in *Death at La Fenice* for a more personal reason, to fill in his family background.

He had come here in the past; in fact, one of his first memories was of being taken here as a child to help tend the grave of his grandmother, killed in Treviso during the Allied bombing of that city during the war. He remembered how colourful the graves were, blanketed with flowers, and how neat, each precise rectangle separated from the others by razor-edged patches of green. And, in the midst of this, how grim the people, almost all women, who came carrying those armloads of flowers. How drab and shabby they were, as if all their love for colour and neatness was exhausted by the need to care for those spirits in the ground, leaving none left over for themselves.

And now, some thirty-five years later, the graves were just as neat, the flowers still explosive with colour, but the people who passed among the graves looked as if they belonged to the world of the living, were no longer those wraiths of the postwar years. His father's grave was easily found, not too far from Stravinsky. The Russian was safe; he would remain there, untouched, for as long as the cemetery remained or people remembered his music. His father's tenancy was far more precarious, for the time was arriving when his grave would be opened and his bones taken to be put in an ossuary in one of the long, crowded walls of the cemetery.

The plot, however, was neatly tended; his brother was more conscientious than he. The carnations that stood in the glass vase set in the earth of the grave were new; the frost of three nights earlier would have killed any that had been placed here before. He bent down and brushed aside a few leaves that the wind had blown up against the vase. He straightened up, then stooped to pick up a cigarette butt that lay beside the headstone. He stood again and looked at the picture displayed upon the front of the stone. He saw his own eyes, his own jaw, and the too-big ears that had skipped over him and his brother and gone, instead, to their sons. (*La Fenice*, ch. 7)

MURANO (3)

Murano, the island nearest San Michele, is the most often visited in the lagoon, primarily by tourists hoping to get a bargain when buying glass. While the Lido swarms with crowds in the summer months, Murano is awash year round. However, few visitors to Murano venture beyond the main boat stops of Colonna, Faro, and Museo to cross the causeway where the working-class Muranese work on dingy Sacca Serenella (4). Donna Leon uses this divide in *Through a Glass, Darkly* to explore a world unseen both by the visitors to Venice and by the city's residents.

For all of Brunetti's ingenuity and fortitude in getting around Venice on foot and in all weather, he must obviously rely on the boats to transport him to the islands. Long years of the company and assistance of pilots have developed in him an unspoken respect and the familiarity he will need to aid him in dealing with the difficult and taciturn boatmen on the islands.

Foa, like most pilots, had the grace of silence and did nothing more than nod to acknowledge Brunetti's request. He seemed to feel no need to fill up the journey with words. By the time they reached Rialto, the broad-beamed boats that hauled produce to the market had turned the stillness into memory. (. . .) They shot out into the *laguna* where the first thing Brunetti saw, off to the right, were the walls of the cemetery and, behind it, banks of clouds scuttling towards the city.

He turned away deliberately and faced Murano, stood with the warmth of spring on his body; the boat swung past the island then slipped around to the right and into the Serenella Canal. Brunetti glanced at his watch and saw that it was barely six o'clock. Foa made another silk-smooth landing, and Brunetti stepped up on to the ACTV *embarcadero*. (*Through a Glass, Darkly*, ch. 14)

Like most Venetians, Brunetti rarely visits the island, but the opening of an art gallery to which he and Paola have been invited provides a welcome lure from the onslaught of tourist Venice.

But his urge to escape Venice at the beginning of the huge tourist surge will unexpectedly reveal to Brunetti the enormous divide on Murano between the sparkling canal-side glass shops and galleries, and the poorer workers and factory owners like De Cal a mere causeway away.

The gallery was new, run by the friend of a colleague of Paola's at the university who suggested that they attend. The level of crime in Venice was as low as the waters of that year's spring tides, and so Brunetti was happy to accept; because the gallery was on Murano, he wondered if he would get to meet Ribetti and his wife: he hardly thought a gallery opening was the sort of place where he would re-encounter De Cal.

The opening was scheduled to begin at six on a Friday

evening, which would allow people time to see the artists' work, have a glass of prosecco, nibble on something, and then go out to dinner or go home on time to eat. As they boarded the 41 at Fondamenta Nuove, Brunetti realized that years had passed since he had been out to Murano. He had gone there as a boy, when his father had worked in one of the factories for a time, but since then he had been there infrequently, since none of their friends lived on Murano, and he had never had reason to go there professionally. (*Glass, Darkly*, ch. 4)

If the Leon novels explore the unfamiliarity of the lagoon for Brunetti and other Venetians, they offer an even fuller picture of how closed and hostile the residents can be to all outsiders – anyone not from their own island. The arteries of gossip that flow as easily through Venice as its canals shut down abruptly at the appearance of any 'foreigner' entering the island communities. Even boats from across the water alert the local boatmen to an intruder.

'I think your boat's coming,' Grassi said.

Brunetti's question was no more than a tilting of his head.

'I don't recognize the engine, and it's coming fast, out from the city,' the *maestro* said. He pulled some money from his pocket and left it on the counter; Brunetti thanked him and they headed for the door.

When they reached the canal, Grassi was right: the police boat was pulling up to the ACTV *embarcadero*. On board were Bocchese and the crime team. (*Glass, Darkly*, ch. 14)

In *Through a Glass, Darkly*, the De Cal family has owned a glass factory for generations. The mere suspicion that it may go to old man De Cal's son-in-law has brought his daughter to Brunetti for advice. Assunta explains that her husband has one mark against him that nothing can erase, and that may threaten his life:

'That he'd see him dead before he'd let him have the *fornace*. The man who told me this said my father was drunk when he said it and was talking about the history of the family and not wanting it to be destroyed by some outsider.' She looked at Brunetti and tried to smile but didn't make a very good job of it. 'Anyone who's not from Murano is an outsider for him.'

Trying to lighten the mood, Brunetti said, 'My father felt that way about anyone who wasn't from Castello.' (*Glass, Darkly*, ch. 6)

But even the Castellani allow marriages with those from other *sestieri*, and Brunetti can extract help from his colleagues who still have families resident in the area. On the islands, however, none of his men seem able to break the walls of silence; they are outsiders as well as 'cops'. And their presence is easily detected: by accent, clothes, education.

When the coffee came, Brunetti said, 'I'm looking for Paolo Bovo. His kid told me he was here.'

'Paolo,' the barman called towards a table at the back, where three men sat around a bottle of red wine, talking, 'the cop wants to talk to you.'

Brunetti smiled and asked, 'How come everyone always knows?'

The barman's smile was equal in warmth to Brunetti's, though not in the number of teeth exposed. 'Anyone who talks as good as you do has to be a cop.'

'A lot of people talk as well as I do,' Brunetti said.

'Not the ones who want to see Paolo,' he answered, wiping at the counter with an unusually clean cloth. (*Glass, Darkly*, ch. 9)

Young officer Pucetti's uncle lives on Murano and has agreed to speak to Brunetti as a favour to his nephew. The Commissario discovers that at Sacca Serenella it is not only his education and his language that mark him as an outsider.

'All right. I'll tell him to meet you at one-thirty.'

'Where?'

'Nanni's,' Pucetti answered. 'It's on Sacca Serenella, the

place where all the glass-workers eat. Anyone can tell you where it is.'

'What's your uncle's name?'

'Navarro. Giulio. He'll be there.'

'How will I know him?'

'Oh, don't worry about that, sir. He'll know you.'

'How?' Brunetti asked.

'Are you wearing a suit?'

'Yes.'

Did he hear Pucetti laugh? 'He'll know you, sir', he said and broke the connection. (*Glass, Darkly*, ch. 8)

Any understanding of Brunetti's Venice will depend in part on a grasp of the many attitudes to food and drink. Donna Leon uses the islanders' meals and drinking habits to remind Brunetti of the days of his father, and to force him to face yet once more the sweeping changes that have occurred in all of Venice. The old traditions are still precariously preserved in these isolated men clinging to their own class, as Assunta describes her father in *Through a Glass, Darkly*:

'People tend to say things they don't mean, especially when they're angry, or when they've had too much to drink.' He remembered De Cal's face and asked, 'Does your father drink more than he should?'

She sighed again. 'A glass of wine is more than he should drink,' she said. 'He's a diabetic and shouldn't drink at all, and certainly not as much as he does.'

'Does this happen often?'

'You know how it is, especially with workmen,' she said with the resignation of long familiarity. '*Un' ombra* at eleven, and then wine with lunch, then a couple of beers to get through the afternoon, especially in the summer when it's hot, and then a couple more *ombre* before dinner, and more wine with the meal, and then maybe a grappa before bed. And then the next day you start all over again.'

It sounded like the kind of drinking he was used to seeing in men of his father's generation: they'd drunk like this most of their adult lives, yet he had never seen one of them behave in a way that would suggest drunkenness. And why on earth should they change just because the professional classes had switched to prosecco and spritz? (*Glass, Darkly*, ch. 6)

Unlike the familiar *fondamente* of the tourist Murano, lined with cafés and places to eat, the Sacca Serenella area is used mostly by local people involved in glass-making. Its only *trattoria*, with a daily menu as unchanging as its clientele, even Venetian Brunetti needs help to find.

As he got off the boat at Sacca Serenella, he stopped a man behind him and asked where the *trattoria* was.

'You mean Nanni's?' he asked.

'Yes. I've got to meet someone there, but all I know is that it's the place where the workers go.'

'And where you eat well?' the man asked with a smile.

'I wasn't told that,' Brunetti answered, 'but it wouldn't hurt.'

'Come with me, then,' the man said, turning off to the right and leading Brunetti along a cement pavement that ran beside the canal towards the entrance to a shipyard. 'It's Wednesday,' the man said. 'So there'll be liver. It's good.'

'With polenta?' Brunetti asked.

'Of course,' the man said, pausing to glance aside at this man who spoke Veneziano yet who had to ask if liver was served with polenta. (*Glass, Darkly*, ch. 8)

At Nanni's, Brunetti enters again into the long-disappeared world of his youth. He finds a place indifferent to any of the innovations – cosmetic or culinary – found in the new market a mere causeway stroll away:

The man turned to the left, leaving the water behind them, and led Brunetti along a dirt trail that crossed an abandoned field. At the end, Brunetti saw a low cement building, its walls striped with what looked like dark trails of rust running down from leaking gutters. In front of it, a few rusted metal tables stood around drunkenly, their legs trapped in the dirt or propped up with chunks of cement. The man led Brunetti past the tables and to the door of the building. He pushed it open and held it politely for Brunetti to enter.

Inside, Brunetti found the *trattoria* of his youth: the tables were covered with sheets of white butcher paper, and on most tables lay four plates and four sets of knives and forks. The glasses had once been clean, perhaps even still were. They were squat things that held little more than two swigs of wine; years of use had scratched and clouded them almost to whiteness. There were paper napkins, and in the centre of each table a metal tray that held suspiciously pale olive oil, some white vinegar, salt, pepper, and individually wrapped packets of toothpicks. (*Glass, Darkly*, ch. 8)

Unlike their houseproud neighbours, the Buranese with their brightly painted buildings, the Sacca Serenella workers seem caught in a time warp: the twenty-first century obsessions with controlled smoking, moderate drinking, and constant renovation have passed them by.

Assunta had told him Bovo lived just on the other side of the bridge, in Calle drio i Orti, and he found the *calle* with little trouble. (. . .)

At the corner he came to a window covered to chest height with curtains that had begun life as a red-and-white check but had moved into a wrinkled, hepatic middle age. He opened the door and walked into a room more filled with smoke than any he could remember having entered in years. He went to the bar and ordered a coffee. He displayed no interest in the barman's tattoos, a pattern of intertwined serpents that encircled both wrists with their tails and ran up his arms until they disappeared under the sleeves of his T-shirt. (*Glass, Darkly*, ch. 9)

Sacca Serenella is dominated by ageing factories filled with giant furnaces belching fire, their workers' days spent in darkened halls amidst gruelling heat. From this setting Donna Leon creates an atmosphere that evokes Brunetti's imaginative grasp of the past recurring in the present, especially through books and art.

The sliding metal doors to the immense brick building had been rolled back sufficiently to allow room for a man to slip in or out. Brunetti stepped inside and found himself in darkness. It took his eyes a moment to adjust, and when they did they were captured by what, for an instant, he thought was an enormous Caravaggio at the other end of the dim room. Six men stood poised for an instant at the doors of a round furnace, half illuminated by the natural daylight that filtered in through the skylights in the roof and by the light that streamed from the furnace. They moved, and the painting fell apart into the intricate motions that lay deep in Brunetti's memory. (*Glass, Darkly*, ch. 12)

None of the Brunetti novels is so packed with, and dependent upon, reference to books and writers as *Through a Glass, Darkly*. The plot intertwines, appropriately, with Dante's *Inferno*, as the epic scenes from the late thirteenth century re-emerge in the furnaces of Murano. The night-watchman's obsessive readings drive him into instability. The tackiness of much of Murano's products (both fake and real), and the pollution spewing from the island, remind Brunetti of an earlier era.

Brunetti has acquired De Cal's night-watchman's copy of the *Inferno*, and as he struggles to decipher the cryptic marginal notes, the parallels between Dante's vision and the hellish world of the *fornaci* on Sacca Serenella begin to emerge:

He dipped in just as Dante, still new to Hell and still capable of pity, tried to leave a message for Cavalcante that his son was still alive, then followed his Guide deeper into the abyss, already sickened by the stench. He flipped quickly on and found Vanni Fucci's obscene gesture to God, and flipped on again. He read of Dante's violence toward Bocca Degli Abbati and felt a moment's pleasure that such a traitor was so viciously treated.

He turned back and found himself reading one of the passages bordered by the notes Tassini had made in red. Canto XIV, the burning sand and horrid stream and fiery rain, that whole grotesque parody of nature that Dante thought so well suited to those who sinned against it: the usurers and sodomites. Brunetti followed them as, beneath the flaming snow that fell all around them, Dante and Virgil moved deeper into Hell. (. . .) He flipped back to Tassini's heavy red lines under '. . . the plain whose soil rejects all roots . . . The wood itself is ringed with the red stream.' In the margin, Tassini had written, 'No roots. No life. Nothing.' In black ink, he had written 'The *grey* stream.' (*Glass, Darkly*, ch. 18)

Unfair to leave Brunetti in Murano on such a despairing note. The changes that he continually witnesses and ponders in Venice have their place in the *laguna* as well. Neither he nor Vianello has much hope for the future, but they can still find amusement in the chicanery surrounding them from the highest to the most trivial levels, and Venice's legendary Murano glass is no exception:

'I thought they were all made in China or Bohemia by now,' Brunetti said, repeating something he had heard frequently, and from people who should know.

'Lots of it is,' Vianello said, 'but they still can't do the big pieces, at least not yet. Wait five years and it'll all be coming from China.'

'And your relatives?'

Vianello turned his palms up in a gesture of hopelessness. 'Either they'll learn how to do something else, or everyone will end up like your wife says we will: dressing in seventeenth-century costumes and walking around, speaking Veneziano, to amuse the tourists.'

'Even us?' Brunetti asked. 'The police?'

'Yes,' Vianello answered. 'Can you imagine Alvise with a crossbow?' (*Glass, Darkly*, ch. 3)

BURANO (5)

North of Murano lies the pretty island of Burano, long famous for its hand-made lace and brightly coloured fishermen's cottages, as well as its remoteness from the tourist meccas of Murano and the Lido. So Brunetti, when forced to spend time in the *laguna,* does exactly what he does in Venice to reward himself with an escape from crime – he eats in a favourite *trattoria.* But even this solace is becoming a rarity in his world. Certainly once-reliable restaurants in Venice have been increasingly taken over by tourists . . . but on Burano?

He turned from the Piazza into Via Galuppi and headed for da Romano; he was sure he could reserve a place for one o'clock: a single person was always welcome in a restaurant. At worst, he might have to wait a quarter-hour, but on a day like this it would be a joy to sit at a table in one of the bars that lined the street, sip a prosecco, perhaps read the paper.

The small tables in front of the restaurant were all occupied; at many of them, three people sat at tables designed for two. He passed through the door and into the restaurant, but before he could speak, one of the waiters, hurrying past with a platter of seafood antipasto, saw him and called out, '*Siamo al completo.*'

For a moment, it occurred to Brunetti to argue and try to find a place, but when he glanced around inside he abandoned the idea and left. Two other restaurants were similarly full, though it was just after twelve, far too early for a civilized person to want to eat.

Brunetti had lunch in a bar, standing at the counter and eating toast filled with flabby ham and a slice of cheese that tasted as if it had spent most of its life in plastic. The prosecco was bitter and almost completely flat; even the coffee was bad. Disgusted with his meal and angered by the disappointment of his hopes, he walked dispiritedly down to a small park, bent on sitting in the sun to allow his mood to lighten. He sat on the first bench he saw, put his head back and turned his face to the sun. (*A Sea of Troubles,* ch. 20)

Brunetti is surprised as well by a suspect's house, which is vastly different from the normally fastidious exteriors of the Burano home owners.

The house on the right of Spadini's was bright red, the one
to the left as bright a blue. The Spadini house, however, was
a pale pink, bleached clean by years of rain and sun. Brunetti
noticed other signs: a curtain falling from the rod at one of
the windows, the right side of a shutter all but eaten through
by rot. The Buranesi were, if nothing else, a houseproud
people, and so it surprised him to see such patent signs of
neglect. (*Sea*, ch. 20)

LE VIGNOLE (6)

South of Burano lies the tiny island of Vignole, still relatively
untouched either by tourism or crime, thus enjoyed by the
residents of Venice. In good weather, Venetians take to their
private pleasure boats and row or motor out to the seafood
trattoria near the water. In *A Noble Radiance*, Brunetti,
distracted by the death of the young Lorenzoni heir, dismisses
a laughingly minor crime out on the island with the disdain
of a long-term policeman:

Back upstairs, Brunetti slipped the four sheets of paper inside
the folder and placed it in the drawer which he usually pulled
out to prop his feet on. He kicked the drawer shut and turned
his attention to a new folder which had been placed on his
desk while he was in Patta's office: the motors had been stolen
from four boats while their owners had dinner at the *trattoria* on the small island of Vignole.

The phone saved him from the contemplation of the full
triviality of this report. (*A Noble Radiance*, *ch. 24*)

LIDO (7)

Also south of Burano sits the long littoral of the Lido, cele-
brated by visitors for centuries for its beauty, reviled by many
for its crowds and 'vulgarity'. Not all of the places to stay
on the Lido cater to the wealthy foreigners who flock there
in summer and for the September Film Festival. The days

when Thomas Mann stayed and Gustav Aschenbach died at the Hotel Les Bains are less in evidence now with the addition of more modest *pensioni*. In *The Death of Faith*, the young nun who cared so generously for Brunetti's mother has left her religious order and sought escape on the Lido. She comes to Brunetti with a bizarre tale of crime and corruption in her order and the reasons for her hiding out in the *laguna*.

With no warning, she got to her feet. 'I think I'd like to leave now, Commissario.' Her eyes were less calm than her voice, so Brunetti made no attempt to stop her.

'Could you tell me the name of the pensione where you're staying?'

'La Pergola.'

'On the Lido?' (*The Death of Faith*, ch. 1)

In Brunetti's world, the Lido exists only as a remote location to investigate a crime or find a wounded witness. He expected neither when he last saw the ex-nun, until an unexplained 'accident' forces him out to the Ospedale Al Mare in search of help.

Brunetti could think of no response to make to this, so he said nothing until the boat pulled into one of the landings restricted for ambulances at the back of the Ospedale al Mare. They jumped from the boat, telling the pilot to wait until they had some idea of what was going on. A gaping door led to a white, cement-floored corridor. (*The Death of Faith*, ch. 8)

At the southern tip of the Lido, past Malomocco, lies the beach of Alberoni **(9)**, adding its own special twist to the littoral's reputation. In *A Venetian Reckoning*, a contact of Signorina Elettra's has come to Brunetti for help with a false arrest.

'As I said, it's about the conviction.' He looked up, and Brunetti smiled, nodding his head encouragingly. 'For indecent exposure.' Brunetti's smile didn't change; Rondini seemed encouraged by that.

'You see, Commissario, I was on the beach two summers ago, at the Alberoni.' Brunetti's smile didn't change, even at the name of the beach out at the end of the Lido so popular with gays that it had come to be known as 'Sin Beach'. *(A Venetian Reckoning*, ch. 18)

SAN SERVOLO *(8)*

San Servolo, west of the Lido is the island with the grimmest memories for Venetians. Originally a Benedictine monastery, it later held an infamous insane asylum until 1978. In *Wilful Behaviour*, one of Paola's university students wants to clear the name of her grandfather who has been accused of extortion during the war and sent to the asylum.

Paola, careful not to inquire about who the person might be, considered this before she asked, 'And where was he sent?'

'To San Servolo. He died there.'

Like everyone else in Venice, Paola knew that the island of San Servolo had once been the site of the madhouse, had served that purpose until the Basaglia Law closed the madhouses and either freed the patients or removed them to less horrendous locations. (*Wilful Behaviour*, ch. 1)

The girl, eventually going to Brunetti for advice, explains how a plea of insanity saved her grandfather from prison. The information produces another reflection from Brunetti on the desolation of the lagoon and its historically nefarious uses.

'And the judges believed it, too, so when they sentenced him, they sent him to San Servolo.'

It would have been better to have gone to prison, Brunetti found himself thinking, though this was an idea he decided to spare the girl. San Servolo had been closed decades ago, and it was perhaps best to forget the horrors of what had gone on there for so many years. What had happened, had happened, not only to the other inmates, but probably to her grandfather, and there was no changing it. A pardon, however, if such a thing were possible, might change the way people thought about him. If – he found a cynical voice saying – anyone bothered to think about such things any more or if anyone cared about what had happened during the war. (*Wilful Behaviour*, ch. 5)

PELLESTRINA (11)

Past Alberoni sits the landfill of Pellestrina, setting for Donna Leon's *A Sea of Troubles*. This novel, more than any other in the Brunetti series, traverses the *laguna* and engages the world of men who live off the sea – the fishermen and the dreaded *vongolari*, the clam gatherers, with their giant digging forks mounted on the prows of boats. To reach this furthest of Venice's inhabited islands, any boat passes numerous small atolls, and the water and light take on an increased clarity so far from the city of Venice. Goethe, in his *Italian Journey*, gives a glorious description of his long lagoon ride where the whole scene approached the condition of art:

As I glided over the lagoons in the brilliant sunshine and saw the gondoliers in the colourful costume, gracefully posed against the blue sky as they rowed with easy strokes across the light-green surface of the water, I felt I was looking at the latest and best painting of the Venetian school.

Over two hundred years later, Brunetti, like Goethe, journeys across the lagoon entranced by its beauty, but even more amazed at how incomprehensible the waters are, even to a native.

In the officers' room he found only one pilot, Rocca, and told him he needed to be taken out to Pellestrina. The pilot's face brightened at the news: it was a long run, and the day was glorious, a brisk wind coming from the west.

Brunetti stood on deck all the way out, gazing at the islands they passed: Santa Maria della Grazia, San Clemente, Santo Spirito, even tiny Poveglia, until he saw to their left the buildings of Malamocco. Though Brunetti had spent a great deal of his youth on boats and in the *laguna*, he had never fully mastered the art of piloting and so had never burned into his memory a map of the most direct routes between various points in the *laguna*. He knew that Pellestrina lay ahead of them, in the middle of this narrow spit of land, and he knew that the boat had to stay within the rows of slanting wooden pilings, but had they strayed into the expanse of water on their right, he would have found it embarrassingly difficult to get them safely back to Venice. (*A Sea of Trouble*, ch. 4)

No other Donna Leon novel opens with so long and detailed a description of place as *A Sea of Troubles*. The island's geography and its residents, food and manners are all used to demonstrate its remoteness from Venice. Even the taciturnity and reserve of the other lagoon populations pale next to the stern toughness of the Pellestrinotti. Brunetti's world experiences its greatest expansion in his introduction to these faraway 'neighbours'.

Pellestrina is a long, narrow peninsula of sand that has, over the course of the centuries, been turned into habitable ground. Running north and south from San Pietro in Volta (10) to Ca' Roman, Pellestrina is about ten kilometres long, but never more than a couple of hundred metres wide. To the east, it faces the Adriatic, a sea not known for the sweetness of its temper, but the west side rests in the Lagoon of Venice and is thus protected from wind, storm and wave. The earth is sandy and infertile, so the people of Pellestrina, though they sow, are able to reap little. This makes small difference to them; indeed, most of them would no doubt scoff at the very idea of earning a living, however rich, from the earth, for the people of Pellestrina have always taken theirs from the sea.

Many stories are told about the men of Pellestrina, the endurance and strength that have been forced upon them in their attempt to wrest a living from the sea. Old people in Venice remember a time when the men of Pellestrina were said to spend the nights, winter or summer, sleeping on the dirt floors of their cottages instead of in their beds so as to more easily push themselves out into the early morning and make the tide that would carry them into the Adriatic and thus to the fish. Like most stories that are told about how much tougher people were in the olden days, this is probably apocryphal. What is true, however, is the fact that most people who hear it, if they are Venetian, believe it, just as they would believe any tale that spoke of the toughness of the men of Pellestrina or of their indifference to pain or suffering, their own or that of others. (*Sea*, ch. 1)

Although the island's character changes when the summer crowds arrive, the two worlds, of the tourists and the fishermen who labour to feed them, remain eternally separate.

During the summer Pellestrina comes alive, as tourists arrive from Venice and its Lido or across from Chioggia **(12)** on the mainland to eat fresh seafood and drink the crisp white wine, just short of sparkling, that is served in the bars and restaurants. Instead of bread, they are served *bussolai*, hard oval pretzels whose name, perhaps, comes from the *bussola*, or compass, that has the same shape. Along with the *bussolai* there is fish, often so fresh it was still alive when the tourists set out to make the long and inconvenient trip to Pellestrina. As the tourists pulled themselves from their hotel beds, the gills of the *orate* still fought against the alien element, the air; as the tourists filed on to an early morning vaporetto at Rialto, the *sardelle* still thrashed in the nets; as they climbed down from the vaporetto and crossed Piazzale Santa Maria Elisabetta, looking for the bus that would take them to Malamocco and the Alberoni, the *cefalo* was just being hauled out of the sea. The tourists often leave the bus for a while at Malamocco or the Alberoni, have a coffee, then walk on the sandy beach for a while and look at the enormous jetties that stretch out into the waters of the Adriatic in an attempt to prevent the waters from sweeping into the *laguna*. (*Sea*, ch. 1)

For Brunetti the divide is more one of lapsed time than unfamiliarity. Pellestrina, like Murano, takes him back to the days of his childhood when *trattorie* were simple, local, and unadorned.

To the side of the bar was a doorway of a sort Brunetti had not seen in decades. Narrow, it was hung with a row of long strips of green and white plastic, each little more than a centimetre wide, ribbed on both sides. As he inserted his right hand to slip half of them aside, he heard the gentle clicking sound he recalled from his youth. Once these dividers had hung in the doorway of every bar and every *trattoria*, but during the last couple of decades, they'd all disappeared; he couldn't remember the last time he'd seen one. He held aside the still clattering strips until Vianello was through, then listened to them fall back into place.

The room they entered surprised him by its size, for it must have held thirty tables. The windows were set high in the walls, and plenty of light streamed in. Below them, fishermen's nets covered the walls, each embedded with shells, pieces of dried seaweed, and what looked like the petrified corpses of fish, crabs and lobsters. A low serving counter ran along one side of the room. In the back, a glass door, closed now, led to a pebble-covered parking lot. (*Sea*, ch. 4)

Once inside, memories revived, Brunetti and Vianello lapse into a kind of shared comfort in the absence of a menu, the confidence that they can count on freshness in the food before the tourist season begins. But some things have changed. And their discussion of Vianello's recent refusal to eat anything from the *laguna* casts a pall on the meal as Brunetti wonders how any Venetian could give up the food of his childhood.

'What can you recommend today?' Brunetti asked.

'The *antipasto di mare* is good. We've got cuttlefish milk or sardines if you'd like them, instead.'

'What else?' Vianello asked.

'There was still some asparagus in the market this morning, so there's a salad of asparagus and shrimp.'

Brunetti nodded at this; Vianello said he wouldn't have antipasto, so the waiter passed on to the *primi piatti*.

'*Spaghetti alle vongole, spaghetti alle cozze*, and *penne all' Amatriciana*,' he recited and then stopped. (. . .)

'We come out to Pellestrina and you don't eat fish,' Brunetti said, making it a statement rather than a question, though it was.

Vianello poured them each a glass of wine, picked up his, and sipped at it. 'Very good,' he said. 'It's like what my uncle used to bring back from Istria on his boat.'

'And the fish?' Brunetti asked, not letting it go.

'I don't eat it any more,' Vianello said. 'Not unless I know it comes from the Atlantic.' (*Sea*, ch. 4)

The distrust is not only of the safety of the waters, but also a Venetian disdain for the islanders themselves, or any people who live off the *laguna* – and the attitude extends all the way to the Questura, Brunetti discovers, speaking to Signorina Elettra:

He nodded. 'It looks like one of the men in the boat was murdered.' He stopped there, wondering if she already knew all of this.

'Pellestrina, eh?' she asked, with an intonation that turned the question into a statement.

'Yes. Nothing but trouble, aren't they?'

'Not as bad as the Chioggotti,' she said with a shudder that was neither delicate nor artificial.

Chioggia, a mainland city the guidebooks never tired of calling 'the faithful daughter of Venice', had indeed remained loyal to her throughout the reign of La Serenissima. It was only now that animosity existed, violent and constant, as the fishermen of the two cities fought over ever-diminishing catches in waters which increasingly suffered the impositions of the Magistrato alle Acque, as larger and larger portions of the *laguna* were closed to fishing.

The idea had occurred to Brunetti, as it would to any Venetian, that these deaths had something to do with this competition. In the past there had been fights, and shots had been fired in anger, but nothing like this had happened. Boats had been stolen and burned, men had been killed in collisions on the water, but no one had yet been murdered in cold blood.

'*Una brutta razza*,' Signorina Elettra said, with the scorn that people whose families had been Venetian since the Crusades reserve for non-Venetians, regardless of their origin. (*Sea*, ch. 4)

Despite Signorina Elettra's contempt for the brutal race of islanders, she is still Italian, and family trumps residence every time. After Brunetti and Vianello's failures to elicit any help or information from the witnesses to the boat fire and the recovery of the bodies, Brunetti discovers that the Signorina has a relative on Pellestrina, but she is quick to explain that her Venetian cousin made a shocking island marriage. This discovery will finally move one of the Brunetti novel readers' favourite characters away from her role as mistress of the Questura into a central place in *A Sea of Troubles*.

'Do you know anyone out there?' he asked suddenly.

'I have a cousin who has a house in the village,' she answered modestly, disguising any pleasure she might have felt in finally being asked this question.

'In Pellestrina?' he asked, with interest.

'Actually, she's my father's cousin. She shocked the family, ages ago, by marrying a fisherman and moving out there. Her eldest daughter married a fisherman, too.'

'And do you visit them?'

'Every summer,' she said. 'I usually spend a week there, sometimes two.' (*Sea*, ch. 4)

There is not a great deal to do on Pellestrina except relax, walk, bathe, and eat – all things Signorina Elettra enjoys. Her walks from the little town centre encompasses the majority of the island's area. She walks along the seaside and the beach to the northern point of the island, San Pietro in Volta **(11)**, before returning along the massive and impressive sea walls, the Murazzi. Venice, ever frightened by the threat of the rising sea, used her might and resources in the eighteenth century to construct four kilometres of Istrian stone blocks for protection.

She continued down the beach, away from the village, glad of the feel of the sun on her back, intent on nothing more than reaching San Pietro in Volta and having a coffee before turning back to Pellestrina. She lengthened her stride, aware at every step of how long she'd been sitting at a desk and how much her body rejoiced in this simple act of walking on the beach in the sun. (. . .)

Elettra paid for the water and the coffee, said how wonderful it was to be out here again, and left. She used the sea wall to walk the entire way back to Pellestrina, and by the time she got there she was thirsty again, so she went into the front part of the restaurant for a glass of prosecco. And who should serve her but Pucetti himself, who paid her no more attention than he would any other attractive woman a few years older than he. (*Sea*, ch. 14)

Elettra's presence on the island, her apparent idleness, continues while she hopes she will be able to break through the screen of polite silence that has greeted even the friendly Vianello. His customary ease and success with witnesses in every *sestiere* of Venice here is blocked by the islanders' mistrust of anyone outside their immediate circle. Even the current of gossip is dry.

The people to whom Vianello had spoken had not been uncooperative in any way: they had all answered whatever questions he put to them. But no one had volunteered any information beyond that contained in the simplest, most direct response. There had been no extraneous detail, no release of the tide of gossip in which all social life swims. They had been clever enough not to answer in bare mono-syllables and managed to suggest that they were doing every-thing they could to recall whatever might be of use to the police. And all the while, Vianello had known what they were doing, and it was likely that they knew he knew. (*Sea*, ch. 6)

Where policemen in uniform, even the most likeable, might fail, the bond of boat men who make their living on the water should prevail. But even the boat pilot discovers that, like Brunetti, he too is in an alien world where being Venetian means nothing. The tight-lipped islanders see even him as a 'foreigner' not to be talked to. They have as little regard for their neighbours from nearby islands, dismissing any consideration of concern for mere Muranesi.

The pilot answered both questions with the same shrug, then said, 'No one told me anything exact, but it was clear that no one liked him. Usually they pretend they do, at least they do when they're talking to foreigners like me. But not with Bottin. I figure it's something he did, but that's just a feeling. I don't have any idea what it could have been, but it was as if they didn't consider him one of them any more.'

'Because of the way he treated his wife?' Brunetti asked.

'No,' he said with a sudden shake of his head. 'She was from Murano, so she didn't count,' and with that, he dismissed her humanity as easily as the possibility. (*Sea*, ch. 11)

Brunetti encounters an even nastier attitude to the island dwellers from Burano. As he interrogates the only witness willing and eager to malign her neighbours, her vituperation comes as no surprise to him

'And you've lived here how long, Signora Boscarini?'

'All my life,' she answered, equally careful to speak Italian but not finding it at all easy. 'Sixty-three years.'

Emotions or experiences he couldn't imagine made her look at least ten years older than that, but Brunetti did nothing more than make another note. 'Your husband, Signora?' Brunetti asked, knowing that she would be complimented by the assumption that she must have one, insulted to be asked if she did.

'Dead. Thirty-four years ago. In a storm.' Brunetti made a note of the importance of this fact. He looked up again and decided not to ask about children.

'Have you had the same neighbours all this time, Signora?'

'Yes. Except for the Rugolettos three doors down,' she said, giving an angry toss of her chin to the left. 'They moved in twelve years ago, from Burano, when her grandfather died and left them the house. She's dirty, the wife,' she said in dismissive contempt and then, to make sure he understood why, added, 'Buranesi.' (*Sea*, ch. 18)

At every juncture in *A Sea of Troubles*, Brunetti is reminded again how remote from his familiar Venetian home are the islands, the people, the language. The distance may be short but the gap is enormous.

She ignored him and turned back to Signora Follini. 'And a package of candles and half a kilo of flour,' Brunetti thought she said, though her dialect was so strong he wasn't sure. Here he was, less than twenty kilometres from his own home, and he found it hard to understand the natives. (*Sea*, ch. 10)

Perhaps a suitable scene to end a book exploring Brunetti's Venice is when he sits next to Vianello on a quiet bench along the shore of Litorale di Pellestrina, looking across the *laguna* towards home. His familiar Venice has been revealed in numerous walks through all the *sestieri* of the city, just as his world has been challenged by renewed contact with the islands and their residents. How poignant that the two characters who have so intimately shared these journeys gaze off in the distance to a Venice they cannot see.

Neither of them much minded having to wait, and they were happy enough to sit on a wooden bench that looked across the waters in the general direction of Venice, though all they could see was the water of the *laguna*, a few boats moving across it, and the topless, endless sky. (*Sea*, ch. 11)